ST ALBAN

1650–1700

Clare,

In happy recollection of much helpful support our conversation —

John

ST ALBANS
1650–1700

A THOROUGHFARE TOWN AND ITS PEOPLE

EDITED BY

J.T. SMITH AND M.A. NORTH

FOR THE

ST ALBANS SEVENTEENTH CENTURY

RESEARCH GROUP

ST ALBANS AND HERTFORDSHIRE ARCHITECTURAL

AND ARCHAEOLOGICAL SOCIETY

HERTFORDSHIRE PUBLICATIONS

an imprint of

University of Hertfordshire Press

First published in Great Britain in 2003 by
Hertfordshire Publications
an imprint of the
University of Hertfordshire Press
Learning and Information Services
University of Hertfordshire
College Lane
Hatfield
Hertfordshire AL10 9AB

Hertfordshire Publications, an imprint of the University of Hertfordshire Press,
is published on behalf of the Hertfordshire Association of Local History

British Library Cataloguing-in-Publication Data.
A catalogue record for this book is available from the British Library.

ISBN 0 9542189 3 0

Design by Geoff Green, Cambridge CB4 5RA.
Cover design by John Robertshaw, Harpenden AL5 2JB
Printed in Great Britain by Antony Rowe Ltd. Chippenham SN14 6LH

Front cover: St Albans Market Place, 1805. From an aquatint by Cornelius Verley.
Photographed by David Kelsall.
Rear cover: A section from the strip map of the road from London to Holyhead;
plate 21 in *Britannia*, published by John Ogilby, 1675

W HOSO DESIRETH to discourse in a proper manner concerning Corporated Towns and Communities must take in a great variety of matter, and should be allowed a great deal of Time and Preparation. The subject is extensive and difficult. In England much hath been said by Writers to Puzzle and entangle, little to clear it.

THOMAS MADOX FIRMA BURGI 1726

CONTENTS

PART ONE: THE TOWN

The skeleton of the town; topography and administrative areas; the condition of the town; landownership around the town; St Albans and the Civil War

Interior improvements; houses in and around the market area; gentry houses; public buildings: the parish churches; chapels; the town hall; in the market place; inns: the legacy in 1650; a major inn and its appointments: the White Hart; side-entrance inns; forms of enlargement; where did the poor live?

The Burgesses or Freemen; the Mayor, Principal Burgesses and Aldermen; the Assistants, the Wardens of the Companies and the Bailiffs; other Officers; the Charters of 1664 and 1685; property; income and expenditure

The vestry; the churchwardens; presentment on religious grounds; upkeep of the church: the fabric; the bells; upkeep of the fittings; the keeping of accounts; the costs of establishment; churchwardens' duties; the poor law; the poor rate; support of the poor; one poor boy; rent payments; sickness; almshouses and charities

From Reformation to Restoration; after the Restoration; occasional conformity and social stability; persecution and toleration; nonconformist groups in 1669 and after; how many nonconformists? who were the dissenters? the established church

PART TWO: THE PEOPLE

LIST OF ILLUSTRATIONS

PREFACE

A BOOK DEALING with a small town over a short period of time requires justification. The project began in 1991 with the realisation that since 1909, when William Page's excellent study of St Albans appeared in the *Victoria County History of Hertfordshire*, subsequent historians had been largely content to recycle his work. Moreover, urban history was by then being pursued with new vigour and new objectives, as, for example, by Penelope Corfield in *The Impact of English Towns 1700–1800* and Peter Borsay in *The English Urban Renaissance*, and its problems were being tackled through important local studies of Chester, Shrewsbury and Uttoxeter. By then, too, small towns were attracting interest, so that the time was clearly ripe for a fresh look at St Albans. Accordingly, a research group was set up under the aegis of the St Albans Architectural and Archaeological Society.

The form the work took was governed by two conditions, the first being that if the result was to be more than a retouching and general improvement of Page's work, which covers the whole span of the town's history, and if there were to be any hope of producing a publication, it had to cover a limited period; and the second was that it was to be done by a group composed almost entirely of amateurs. A period of history suitable to these requirements is that covering the Commonwealth and extending to the accession of Anne, one that is covered by the three urban studies just mentioned in respect of social and economic change and which also embraces religious and political changes of great interest in the life of a town of strongly dissenting opinion.

A further consideration was the need, in the light of developments in demographic history, to ascertain as accurately as possible the size of the population. The work began with counts of vital statistics from the parish registers and the collection of data relating to individuals such as occupation and civic or parish office. It was transformed by the acquisition of a computer, the gift of the St Albans Architectural and Archaeological Society, which permitted efficient data linkage and proved unexpectedly advantageous for the whole enterprise.

Chapters of the resulting book have been written by several people but given the amount of collaboration and the extent to which every contributor has been dependent on others it would be invidious to identify the principal authors of chapters without acknowledging the labours of those who contributed significantly to the final result. A list is appended of all members of the Group who contributed to its work to whatever degree. The editors are identified as a concession to librarians who prefer a named individual for ease of cataloguing; the first-named produced a text from drafts by the respective authors, the second undertook the whole labour of revising and preparing it for submission to the Press and of making subsequent corrections.

It would be unjust not to acknowledge certain important contributions other than written ones. Dr Jane Kilvington provided houseroom for the computer, mastered it herself and organised members to input data, and Pat Howe subsequently provided similar access to her own computer. Dr D.J. Smith established the initial database; Norman Alvey provided expert assistance with the many software problems that arose; Heather Smith as Secretary organised the work at the outset, produced and distributed regular progress reports and fostered morale by holding annual summer parties. Special thanks are due to Pat Howe for making her thesis available to the Group.

The Group is indebted to many other people for help. Dr David Kelsall took all the requisite photographs. Professor Peter Clark and Professor Penelope Corfield commented on several chapters; Dr Dorian Gerhold, Professor David Hey, Mary Hodges and Professor Ronald Hutton advised on specific matters; and Dr Kate Thompson and the staff of HALS (formerly Hertfordshire Record Office) gave unstinted assistance in producing and photocopying documents. The officers and council of the St Albans Architectural and Archaeological Society supported the enterprise in every way possible for more than a decade. Particular thanks are due to Professor Nigel Goose and Arthur Jones who provided detailed comments on different drafts of this book.

CHAPTER AUTHORSHIP

1   Frank Kilvington and J.T. Smith
2   J.T. Smith with contributions from Lionel Baker and Norman Oldknow
3   Betty Masters
4   Gerard McSweeney and Mike North
5   Pat Howe
6   Norman Alvey (Population); Pat Howe (Family Reconstitution); J.T. Smith with contribution from Pat Howe (Occupational Structure)
7   J.T. Smith with contribution from Norman Oldknow
8   Frank Kilvington
9   Frank Kilvington

10 Frank Kilvington
11 J.T. Smith with contribution from Heather Smith
12 J.T. Smith

LIST OF MEMBERS OF THE GROUP (†=DECEASED)

† Eveline Alty
Norman Alvey
† Ernest Amsden
Margaret Amsden
Lionel Baker
Carol Boseley
Marion Brown
Carol Burke
Brenda Burr
John Cadisch
Rita Cadisch
Irene Cowan
John Cox
Ann Dean
David Dean
Jane Dismore
Martin Dismore
Joy Dodd
William Dodd
Clare Ellis
Pat Mundy

Susan Gilliam
† Katherine Goad
Chris Green
Paul Harding
Ailsa Herbert
Harry Hopker
Paule Hopker
Madeleine Hopkins
Pat Howe
Van Hryniewicz
Evelyn Isherwood
David Kilvington
Frank Kilvington
Jane Kilvington
Betty Masters
Gerard McSweeney
Brian Moody
Kathleen Moody
Kate Morris
Sam Mullins

Pat Nellist
Mike North
Norman Oldknow
Carol Parker
Meryl Parker
Lyle Perrins
† Alan Pickles
Gwen Hewett Ritchie
Andrew Robley
Michael Rochford
Janet Rose
Pat Shea
Heather Smith
J.T. Smith
Margaret Taylor
† Muriel Thresher
Joyce Wells
George Wilde
Frances Younson
† John Everett

PUBLICATION HAS BEEN MADE POSSIBLE BY A
GENEROUS GRANT FROM
THE MARC FITCH FOUNDATION

EDITORIAL NOTE

SPELLING

Except in quotations, modern spelling has been used, particularly in standardising the spelling of personal names. Even when people could themselves write, they would spell their names differently, even within the same sentence, and with the illiterate majority the clerk would make a guess at the spelling from the sound of the name. Since virtually all of the original records are hand-written, a flourish by the writer could easily change, or add, a letter to the word. A final 'e' was particularly liable to appear because of this and, although it was probably not pronounced, seems to have given rise to the modern 'old' English of 'fayre', 'shoppe', etc. The word 'ye' was a clerks' abbreviation of 'the' and was quite probably read as 'the', rather than in the modern quaint way.

MONEY

In the seventeenth century the pound sterling (£1) was divided into twenty shillings (20s) and each shilling into twelve pence (12d). In addition use was made of the halfpenny (normally pronounced like 'hay-pny') and the farthing ('farth-ing') which was one-quarter of a penny. An entry of, say, £1 6s (sometimes expressed as 26s) would be £1.30 in modern money.

Of course, the purchasing power of the money was totally different from today. Officially, the £1 of the later seventeenth century is equivalent to about £75 now but, with such different societies and economies, this is only a rough relationship. It seems that about 1s 6d was considered as a reasonable reward for a day's labouring work in our area; thus a labouring man who worked for five days would take home a sum of about 7s 6d (37.5p). His present-day counterpart would surely expect a wage of, at least, £200 for his week's work, more than 500 times as much (although deductions for income tax, etc. would not have been taken from his predecessor).

DATES

At this period the year was taken as starting on 25 March. Thus a date originally written as, say, 24 March 1651 would now be considered to be 24 March 1652. To avoid confusion, all dates in this book (unless contained in a quotation) have been expressed in the modern system starting on Jan 1. Several official years, such as mayor's accounts and poor law records, began some time after 1 January and thus spanned parts of two calendar years. Where this is the case, the notation 1674/5, 1679/80, etc. is used to express this overlap.

ACKNOWLEDGMENTS

Figs 1.1, 1.5, 1.6, 2.2, 2.7, 2.16, 2.17, 2.18, 6.2, 6.4, 6.5, 6.6, 7.2, 7.3, 7.4 are by A.T. Adams; Figs 1.2 and 7.5 are by Chris Green. Figs 1.3, 2.1-2.6, 2.8-2.10, 2.12–2.15 3.1, 5.1, 5.2, 8.1, 8.2a, b, 11.1 are from photographs by Dr David Kelsall. Figs 2.11, 6.7 are by E.A. Kent.

Fig.1.4 is reproduced by permission of the British Museum.

Figs 2.4, 2.13, 2.14, 5.1, 5.2, 8.2a are from material in the possession of St Albans Cathedral and are reproduced by permission of the Cathedral Archivist.

Figs 2.8, 11.1 are reproduced by permission from slides in the possession of St Albans Central Library.

Fig.3.1 is reproduced by permission from the St Albans mayors' accounts held at Hertfordshire Archives and Local Studies Library.

PART ONE: THE TOWN

I

THE TOWN AND ITS HISTORICAL SETTING

"ST ALBONES," declared William Smith in 1588, "is the fayrest and greatest [town] in the shire," an opinion endorsed by Daniel Defoe in 1724: "St. Albans is the Capital Town, tho' not the County Town of Hertford-shire."[1] What made it so? Partly it is because topography divides the county between the basins of the River Lea to east and the Colne to west, so that although the hills between them are hardly a serious obstacle they favoured north-south movement. More importantly the historical circumstance of a martyr's shrine situated on a major Roman road gave rise to one of the great-est English monasteries and procured for the town around it a lasting impor-tance neither the county town nor the commercially successful Hitchin to the north ever quite equalled. How St Albans maintained that position from the end of the Civil War to the accession of Queen Anne will be told below.

THE SKELETON OF THE TOWN

The origins of St Albans lie in the late tenth century when an abbot of the Benedictine monastery from which the town takes its name established a market and built three churches on roads approaching it (Fig. 1.1). The monastery flourished and with it the market, so that when the former was dis-solved in 1539 the inhabitants took over a small but prosperous town in whose government they had by then gained at least an informal share, and in 1553 a charter of Edward VI created a self-governing borough. In the seventeenth century the boundary, which is shown on a plan made in 1634 by Benjamin Hare[2], was marked in part by the Tonman ditch that ran parallel to the line of one of the principal streets, St Peter's Street. The important route running south-east to north-west to connect the capital with Chester and thence Ireland followed the steady rise of Sopwell Lane and the steeper Holywell Hill to skirt the market place and descend Church Street (now George Street) and Fish-pool Street; and from it the route to Bedford, Derby and beyond traversed the

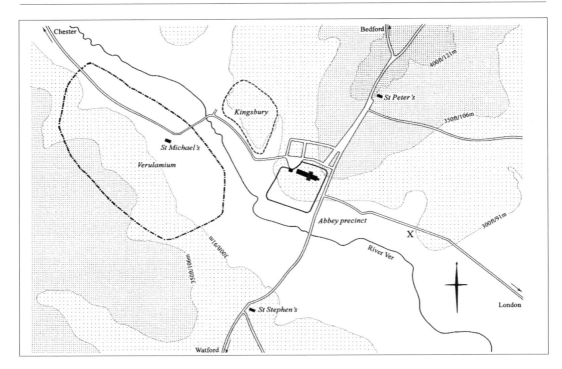

1.1 The topography of St Albans. The Hollar view (1.4) was taken from about the point marked X.

markets along the present Chequer Street and St Peter's Street (Fig. 1.2). Two cross-country roads, one leading to Watford and Reading and the other to Hertford and Colchester, provided an east-west route of more than local importance, though not at all comparable in volume of traffic to the Chester and Bedford roads. The only other streets were Dagnall Lane, which turned through a right-angle to link Fishpool Street and the upper end of the market place, and Spicer Street, linking Dagnall Lane and the large open space called Romeland, where the fairs were held. This road system and the large market place at its heart formed the setting for the town's prosperity and growth.

TOPOGRAPHY AND ADMINISTRATIVE AREAS

Administratively the town was divided between four parishes and the borough into four wards. Poor relief and highway maintenance were the principal responsibilities of the parish; tax collection was by wards, under constables appointed by the mayor and corporation. The centre of the town, that is to say the southern half of the ancient market place and the area bounded by Dagnall Lane and George Street, formed the Abbey parish. Two parishes, St Peter's and St Michael's, were typical of those in ancient towns in extending

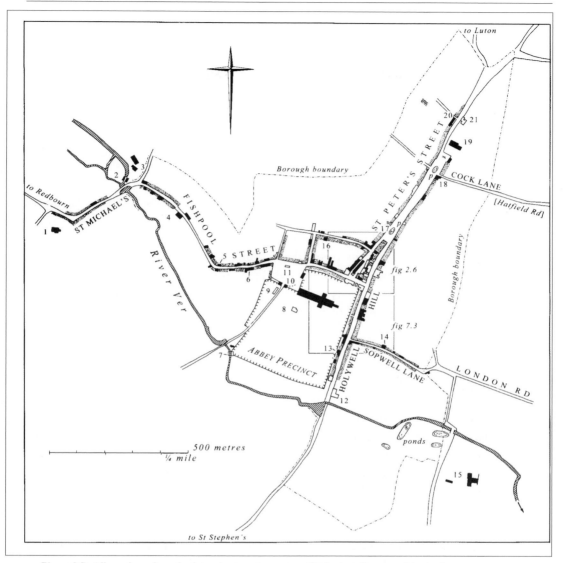

1.2 Plan of St Albans based on the late nineteenth-century Ordnance Survey, with roads, boundaries, and extent of settlement from John Oliver's map of 1698. Surviving or part surviving seventeenth century and earlier buildings are shown solid. Demolished buildings of this date are shown in outline. The settlement, shown schematically by Oliver, is stippled. For Market Place and inns see Figs 2.6 and 7.3 respectively.

Key to Fig. 1.2

1. St Michael's Church 2. St Michael's Mill 3. Kingsbury 4. John Gape's House [St Michael's Manor] 5. Lower Red Lion Inn 6. Crow Inn 7. Abbey Mill 8. Col Cox's House (formerly Prior of Tynemouth's Lodging) 9. King's Stables 10. Liberty Gaol 11. Romeland 12. Holywell House 13. Edward Crosby's House 14. Goat Inn 15. Sopwell House 16. Presbyterian Chapel 17. White Horse Inn 18. Cock Inn 19. St Peter's Church 20. Pemberton's Almshouses 21. Hall Place
p. pond

Table 1.1 Number of hearths paid for in 1663, excluding inns as special-purpose buildings

Ward	10.	5–9	4	3	2	1	Total
St Peter's	4	12	10	10	16	6	58
Fishpool	3	15	3	8	10	3	42
Holywell	1	8	6	7	18	6	46
Middle	2	17	23	28	19	1	90
Total	10	52	42	53	63	16	236

far beyond the urban area.[3] A third parish, St Stephen's, of which only a tiny part fell within the borough, was wholly rural.

The four wards of the borough were St Peter's, Fishpool, Holywell and Middle, each having its distinctive character. St Peter's ward coincided with that part of the parish within the borough and thus included the northern half of the market place. It is clear from the Hearth Tax of 1663 (Table 1.1) that the ward had a good spread of properties, dominated by four large houses rated at ten hearths or more. That two were in the northward continuation of St Peter's Street is known: they were Hall Place, a house of medieval origin adjoining the church on the north, and a house with a frontage of 36.5m (120ft)[4] belonging to Dr Thomas Arris, the leading medical man in the town and one of its MPs from 1661 to 1679. South of the church on Cock Lane (now Hatfield Road) stood the manor house of Newland Squillers, occupied by the Robotham family, with its status symbol of a dovecote opposite. The fourth house stood somewhere nearby and, with Hall Place, is linked to two names. One occupant towards the end of the century was James Rudstone, a gentleman with a London background, and the other, considerably earlier, was William Foxwist, Recorder of the borough from 1644 to 1661; but which man lived where is not known. This group of houses is the only evidence of social separation in St Albans which otherwise shows the mingling of people of varied wealth and status found in Chester, Edinburgh and other large towns.[5]

Fishpool ward, which included Romeland and the west side of Spicer Street as well as Fishpool Street, was likewise dominated by several large houses, but with a difference; here the three largest properties, those with over ten hearths, lay at the Romeland end of the ward near the town centre. They belonged to William Wiseman, a gentleman with a London background, Lydia Hope, a rich widow, and Edward Carter, rector of the Abbey parish from 1662 to 1687. But there were also a considerable number of houses with between five and nine hearths, notably one which belonged to the Gapes (now a hotel called St Michael's Manor, Fig. 8.1) and another, now called Manor Garden House, which belonged to the Doggetts; both families were tanners.

1.3 No. 70 Holywell Hill, possibly Edward Crosby's house. The principal part, of brick with three eighteenth century Venetian windows, was originally timber-framed and perhaps of the sixteenth century; the chimney stack replaced an earlier one in the late-seventeenth century. The fourth bay appears to incorporate a cross-wing.

Few small properties paid Hearth Tax in this ward in 1663, when the return is unaccompanied by a list of those exempt on grounds of poverty. A truer picture appears ten years later when 61 exemptions were listed.

Holywell ward, comprising Holywell Hill and Sopwell Lane, took its distinctive character from the almost continuous line of inns, some sixteen in all, extending down Holywell Hill from the Bell or Bluebell along the east side of Chequer Street (in Middle ward) to the Chequer on the lower side of Sopwell Lane (Fig. 7.3). They ranged in size from the Bull, with its twenty-three chambers and eight parlours, to small inns like the Dolphin and the Saracen's Head, rated respectively at six and seven hearths and their long yards extended to the borough boundary. The one really large house was Holywell House, the seat of the Jenyns family, standing in extensive grounds beside the river and separated from Sopwell Lane by a range of buildings.[6] On the west side of Holywell Hill inns were precluded by the nearness of the precinct wall of the abbey, except for a small inn whose name is uncertain opposite Sopwell Lane. Some distance

1.4 The oldest view of St Albans, by Wenceslaus Hollar, c.1660, from *An Orthographical Designe of Severall Viewes upon the Road in England and Wales*, British Museum Prints and Drawings 1924–5–7–1. © Copyright The Btitish Museum.

below it a second house, being sited down the quite steep hill slope above a basement, has a prominence disproportionate to its real size. Its importance is apparent from the version of the 1634 Hare map in the City Library and it may have been where Edward Crosby, a former royalist officer, lived (Fig. 1.3).

Middle ward, as its name implies, covered the centre of the town and contained the public buildings. Much the most important part was the triangular space forming the south half of the tenth-century market place. This had gradually been encroached on by two rows of buildings dividing it into French Row, Market Place and Chequer Street (Fig. 2.7). At the north end stood the Town Hall (now the W.H. Smith shop) and dominating its lower end was the fifteenth-century Clockhouse (now Clock Tower); nearby was the Eleanor Cross, by then called the Market Cross from its being the central support of a roof carried on posts[7] and becoming dilapidated in consequence; and on the south side of High Street stood the fourteenth century Waxhouse Gate, one of the few relics of the abbey precinct wall. Part of French Row, probably the east side, was called Cordwainers' Row and at the south end was the Women's Market[8] for dairy produce. To the east lay the Leather Market[9], a function still commemorated by the Boot public house, and north of that the Market House where corn was traded. North again was the Butchers' or Flesh Shambles, and the Fish Shambles was hereabouts. The Malt Market is now Chequer Street, the Hay Market and Cattle Market being to the north of it successively. At the corner of High Street and Holywell Hill stood the Tavern, a place exclusively for the sale of wine and probably, as the name of that locality, The Vintry, suggests, the successor to medieval wine vaults.[10]

The rest of Middle ward was also densely built over. French Row contained, on the west side, the top end of a line of inns extending almost uninterruptedly down Church Street; most of which had long, curving yards running to Dagnall Lane from which vehicles approaching along Fishpool Street could enter. The opposite side of Church Street, where again the abbey precinct restricted the length of plots, was occupied by small buildings each comprising, when they were built in the fifteenth century, only a shop, hall and chamber above with perhaps, by analogy, a rear lean-to.[11] This ward had nearly two-fifths of the properties included in the Hearth Tax return, including a third of all those rated at five to nine hearths and two large houses, one of which, in High Street, belonged to the prosperous mercer Thomas Cowley, the other, in Dagnall Lane, to the no less prosperous lawyer Joshua Lomax.

It remains to say something of the abbey precinct. At the Dissolution the great church had been sold to the corporation to become the most imposing parish church in England. Being a civic building it housed the town grammar school in the Lady Chapel and, at election times, the hustings in the nave, but its upkeep was a heavy financial burden. Beyond the west end the great gateway had become a prison serving the Liberty of St Albans which was the large area of the former Cashio hundred that corresponded to the possessions of the abbey in Hertfordshire and which had its own magistrates. In 1651 the first floor, which had been used for the borough sessions, became a house of correction for both liberty and borough, the sessions being transferred to the town hall. Of the other abbey buildings the Great Court, with stables on its west side and a house which became the headquarters of Colonel Alban Coxe, the Parliamentary cavalry commander for the area; the King's Barns and the Watergate also remained after the general demolition of the claustral buildings.

What St Albans looked like to the traveller sighting his destination from a distance is well conveyed in the earliest representation of it, Wenceslaus Hollar's woodcut of 1641 taken from the London road (Fig. 1.4). It has the characteristic appearance of a medieval or early modern town familiar from many such prospects of continental places, the skyline being dominated by the principal religious and secular buildings and particularly by the massive bulk of the Abbey church on its hilltop: a domination that can still be sensed today when approaching by rail from the south or by road from the west.

THE CONDITION OF THE TOWN

For all the praises heaped upon it St Albans was a rather dirty place, even squalid by modern standards, though probably not more so than many towns of its size. The streets were nowhere paved (Fig. 1.5) and in order to improve the approach to the Town Hall gravel was laid before the Counter door "to amend the way" in 1673/74.[12] To the same end Nicholas Sparling laid a "Causey"[13] in front of his house in the Leather Market; it was ordered to be

1.5 Market Place looking S, by Cornelius Varley, c.1810. On the extreme right is No. 1 St Peter's Street: the coach entrance is flanked by two coeval pedimented structures, the nearer perhaps a gatekeeper's lodge, the farther the archway leading to the stables. A little way beyond is Dagnall Lane, the Elizabethan town hall being on the near corner and the King's Head with its timber balcony on the far one. At the extreme left is the gable end of Clark's almshouses. The gabled house in the middle now bears the painted date 1637.

dug up in 1683/84 for extending too far into the highway. Drainage of the unpaved streets was by gutters and from time to time the mayor's court warned householders or the parish surveyors to clean them.[14]

The lack of paving allowed people to use the street in front of their houses as they wished, short of creating a serious public nuisance. A court leet book of 1663 reveals that the ward constables presented three classes of offence relating to the environment: building works, trading activities, and noisome deposits. Among the craftsmen cited by far the most numerous are carpenters and other woodworkers, sixteen in all, of whom four in St Peter's are presented for making sawpits in the king's highway and they and the rest for having stacks of timber there. The sawpits are easily explained: the houses were built on narrow plots lacking rear access and few except for inns had the wide gateway that would have allowed tree trunks to be carted into back yards for preparation; Edmund Howe, a lathrender, whose will mentions a gatehouse at one of his properties, was unusual in this respect. William Nicholls' inventory of 1666 illustrates the problem. He had "Sawed Stuffe and Cleft" in the yard and the garden, "Sawed Stuffe in the house both above Staires and belowe" and also in the street; but the only timber (in the form of logs) was in the street, next to the pit where it was to be sawn. Nor was the carpenter's trade the only one to feel this limitation, which could only be overcome by using an adjoining inn entrance to secure access to the rear premises next door. In 1665 Jeremy Fitch, baker, was fortunate in being granted passage for his servants, horses and carts through the Dolphin gatehouse for storing wheat and corn, and the use of a well and trough too. In the case of a carpenter, if the officers had carried out the law to the letter they would have driven him out of business; better to impose what was nominally a fine but in practice a rent; and, besides, a change of occupier might bring a different occupation. No doubt the same applies to all the woodworkers who were presented for laying timber in the highway, meaning that they worked up their raw material to greater or less degree in the street. Ten of them were in St Peter's ward and it may be relevant that at the south end of St Peter's Street was the Woodyard, where wood was stored for issue to needy residents in hard weather.

Two men in the metal trades were presented for conducting business in the king's highway. Edmund Dawton, a blacksmith in the Hay Market who was evidently also a cutler, had set up a grindstone. William Pembroke on the other hand, variously described as ironmonger and grocer, who was before the court "for layeinge of several vessels and tubbs before his doore … in the Leather markett", was only displaying his wares; nails of various sizes and door latches and locks were articles suitable to be shown to customers in this way. One or two building encroachments were occasioned by trade. Dawton, for example, had added a penthouse (a lean-to) to his house, which perhaps sheltered his grindstone, and William Lockey, a farrier, added another to shelter him as he worked; while William Tryant, tobacco-pipe maker, who set up a stall against his house, no doubt wanted a fixed counter on which to display his wares. Another nuisance was created by ladders: Richard Millard had one "standinge against his dwellinge house in the … highway", as, too, had William Stone in Holywell Street. Their occupations are not known but the necessity for access to upper floors is demonstrated by the case of Jeremy Fitch, whose permission to use the next-door Dolphin yard included space for a ladder to reach the wheat and corn stores. Any trade requiring movement of heavy or bulky goods from the street into an upstairs storeroom would need a ladder if there were no hoist.

Similar considerations affected the twenty-five dung-heaps that were complained of, nine being in St Peter's Street. Dung was a valuable agricultural commodity which, stored behind houses, might prove even more of a nuisance, both publicly and privately, than in the street. Even if the five days allowed such heaps were exceeded, removal by the bailiffs would have aroused hostility. Butchers were a different case; their trade wastes from

slaughtered beasts, after every usable part had been removed, were offensive
and dangerous to health. Two were presented at the court leet for "laying of
stinckinge goare" in their gore yards, an offence caused, presumably, by
depositing in an enclosed yard the wastes from beasts cut up in a slaughter
house. Tanners presented a less obvious nuisance because their trade was of
necessity carried on away from the centre of the town, on the side of Fishpool Street nearer the river, but the powerful smells given off by the cleaning
and soaking of the hides and skins were surely noticeable even in an age that
was not overly fastidious.

Fortunately the owner's liberty to utilise the public space in front of his
house could take more agreeable forms than these. The wish to keep all and
sundry from approaching close to the house caused some to enclose a space
with posts or railings, for which they paid a small fine at the court leet, and
others to plant trees in a search for privacy in a highly public place. One
person who seems to have done this was a butcher, named in a mayoral court
order of 1687 that the Wednesday cattle market be held "before Mr Norris's
rails and shambles"; and he appears again in February 1703 when the court
heard that a "wheeler" had recently bought eight elms that grew upon the
waste before Mr Norris's house, upon whose directions they had been cut
down. At the same time several persons were presented for cutting down and
taking away trees from the public waste, while twenty years later several elm
trees on Romeland were ordered to be cut down and sold.[15] These incidental
mentions show that the trees forming so agreeable an amenity of St Albans
today are not only a modern feature of the townscape, even though they were
less regularly set out in former times.[16]

LAND OWNERSHIP AROUND THE TOWN

The immediate environs of the town comprised a mixture of gentry estates
and yeoman farms (Fig. 1.6). The biggest estate by far was Gorhambury, where
Sir Harbottle Grimston, Master of the Rolls from 1660 to 1685, lived in the
Elizabethan mansion built by Sir Nicholas Bacon. He enlarged his original
holding of 1658 until it became a great swathe of land down the west side of
the town. The Grimstons were one of only two gentry families of national
standing; the rest were county or parish gentry, either post-Restoration pur-
chasers or minor landholders of somewhat longer standing. On the north side,
the Childwick estate changed hands in the 1660s from the long-established
Preston family to the wealthy and ambitious lawyer, Joshua Lomax. A short
distance beyond lies Rothamsted Manor, enlarged and encased in brick in
1647-53 by Sir John Wittewronge who was an important figure in the Eastern
Association. It descended to his son James, St Albans Recorder from 1699 to

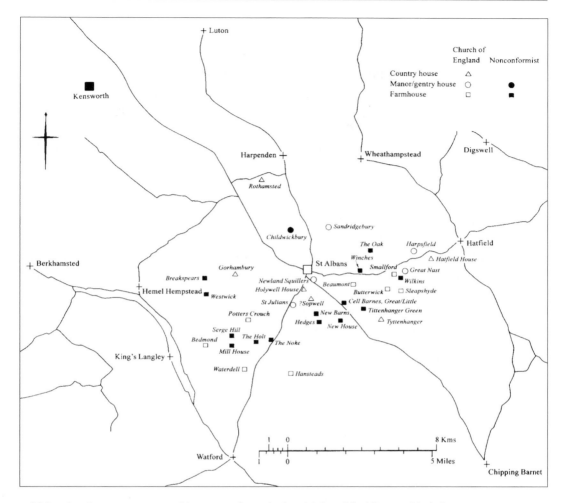

1.6 Map showing gentry seats and important farms in the vicinity of St Albans, with their religious affinities; also the strongly nonconformist village of Kensworth. Whether Sopwell remained in occupation throughout the period 1650–1700 is not clear.

1721. To the north-east the manor of Sandridge, belonging to the Jenyns family, was adjoined to the south by the manor of Newland Squillers owned by the Robotham family and to the east by the small estate of the Coxes, prominent on the Parliamentary side in the Civil War, at Bemonds or Beaumont. South of the town lay a string of manors and estates once owned by religious houses. The most distant was Tyttenhanger, the second major gentry seat, rebuilt in the 1650s by Sir Henry Pope Blount, author and traveller. Sopwell, a nunnery, was rebuilt as a country house after the Dissolution and by 1624 belonged to the parliamentarian Sadleirs; and a barn of this cell of St Albans abbey gave name to the farms Great and Little Cell Barnes where two branches of the widespread Ayleward family lived; while due south of the town was the small estate attached to the leper hospital of St Julians which had been no more than a farm prior to its purchase in 1663 by a rich London draper, John Ellis, who built a new house. The remaining landowners were mostly yeomen such as Thomas Robinson at New Barnes and William Ayleward at New House. These families participated to a varying extent in the affairs of the town without any becoming a dominant force.

Such was the setting for the turbulent events of the 1640s, a decade that moulded the lives and opinions of the town's inhabitants for much of the next half-century.

ST ALBANS AND THE CIVIL WAR

During the Civil War St Albans, on the fringe of the Eastern Association, not far distant from royalist strongholds and astride the junction of one of the 'Great Roads' of England with a major east-west road, had been strategically important for the parliamentary forces, for whom the town was a staging point for the movement of troops and a garrison when London was in any way threatened. The inhabitants of St Albans were close to events and not always in an agreeable way. Three times St Albans was an army headquarters: in 1643 for the Earl of Essex, when Charles I's army confronted the London militia at Turnham Green, Chiswick, and in 1647 and 1648 for General Thomas Fairfax; and a garrison was still present in 1649. Cryptic references in the mayors' accounts hint at continued close control of the town after the war. In 1653/4 William Graives was paid for "amending the turnpike at St Michael's" and another at St Peter's; and in 1655/6 he was paid for mending the "scrue" and for a plate for the turnpike at St Michael's, as well as for mending "the other turnpikes at several times". The words 'other turnpikes' no doubt refer to Holywell Hill, Sopwell Lane and probably the road to Hatfield. They had evidently been set up in the early 1640s and were presumably overseen or guarded until 1659/60 when such entries disappear.

However much the inhabitants may have disliked control of this kind – and it was no more than any town with walls and gates and a vigilant civic body had always endured – they had more serious concerns. The "great Burthen of free Quarter", by which payment for accommodating troops was promised but postponed, had caused widespread complaint and even though it ceased in 1650/1 the strong puritan and parliamentary sympathies evoked during the war could not disguise the cost of billeting. Its effect is implicit in a letter of that mayoral year asking the quartermaster-general at Barnet "to enlarge the Quarters of this Borough whereupon we had taken off from quartering here at that time four Troops of Horse" – that is, 400 men, their officers and horses –

whose presence must have been very strongly felt among at most 3,500 inhabitants. In the following mayoral year payment was made "for the Guard when the Trayne of Artillery went down to Scotland" on its way to defeat the Scots at Dunbar, and another for a guard in the market house "being of Colonel Pride's regiment" – the same body of men who, four years earlier under their regicide colonel had carried out 'Pride's Purge', excluding from parliament those members wishing to make an agreement with Charles I; while in 1654/5 the considerable sum of £4 16s 6d was spent in coals and candles for the soldiers of Colonel Sadleir's regiment "in their Courts of Guard", who were in the town, presumably, as a precaution during Penruddock's rising in March 1655. And once in 1655/6, soon after the military government that took over in the last years of the Protectorate was installed, the mayor and aldermen entertained one of its important personages, William Packer, deputy major-general for Buckinghamshire, Oxfordshire and Hertfordshire, who was no doubt surveying his new responsibilities and making his presence felt. Two more names of persons prominent in Commonwealth councils are mentioned in the mayors' accounts: in 1652/3 a lame soldier of "Colonel Barkstead's regiment" was conveyed away – this must be Sir John Barkestead the regicide, who, at about that time, was appointed governor of the Tower of London; and in 1659/60 payment was made for "sixteen nights firing with coals for the Court of Guard ... and for sending a soldier of Captain Claypoole's to London which was sick" – Claypoole being Oliver Cromwell's son-in-law.

Most tense of all these occasions were the few weeks prior to the restoration of the monarchy. On 24 December 1659, when the army in London, desiring to restore a free parliament, put itself under the control of the Speaker of the House of Commons. Major-general John Disbrowe (or Desborough), in hopes of counter action, hastened "to his regiment of horse att St Albons, but they would not march one foot; hee away to Lord Lambert ..." Shortly afterwards Monck, on his way from the north to London to restore Charles II, reached St Albans with his army. Three loads of straw were provided "for the soldiers to lie in" – in the abbey church, probably – "when the Lord General Monck's soldiers quartered this Borough", and coals and candles were provided in the usual way for the Court of Guard. Not all the 4,000 foot and 1,800 horse which entered London with Monck on 8 February 1660 could have been billetted within the confines of the borough but the numbers give some idea of the huge disruption they must have caused. To St Albans came, before then, Thomas Scott, yet another of the regicides, in the capacity of a commissioner (one of two) sent by parliament "to attend Monke on his march to London, and he to whom Monke at St Albans sollemnly swore ... that he would be faithfull to the Parlament."[17] The town must have been alive with rumour, speculation and, for a few, a knowledge of events hardly available to many outside London; and to committed republicans the future looked bleak.

But how many such people were there in St Albans? Few, it seems. The hostility evinced among many shades of opinion by Charles I's arbitrary government and the unity it produced in support of Parliament began to disappear quite soon after the royalist defeat in 1646, although local evidence of that change has not come to light. A few years later, however, the financial burdens and measures of social control imposed during the government of the major-generals took a heavier toll of republican zeal, as much in St Albans as in the country generally. To judge by the names recurring in the list of mayors there was a remarkable continuity between the years of military and civil turmoil and the first decade of the restored monarchy. Thomas Oxton first held the office in 1636, when he was doubtless one of the growing number of people discontented with Charles I's personal government; next in 1644, by which time his sympathies are clear; again in 1656, when they can hardly be guessed; and finally in 1667, by which time his earlier fire must certainly have died down. Similarly with Thomas Cowley, of whom it was alleged in 1661 that "… when forces were raisinge for ye Parliament putt on his sword sayinge I have not wore a sword theise 20ty years butt now I doe itt to encouradge ye people to ffight against ye Kinge." He was mayor in 1639, 1650 and 1661. The same transition was made by Ralph Pollard, mayor in 1647 and 1665, and, most strikingly, by William Marston, who held the office first in 1651, when support for the Cromwellian government reached a peak,[18] and again in that year of reaction 1662. Similarly with the aldermen: of thirteen created under Charles II's charter of 1664, seven had been mayor during the Civil War or Commonwealth. Matters were doubtless made easier for the corporation by the fact that its Chief Steward from 1660 was the major local landowner, Sir Harbottle Grimston, Master of the Rolls from 1660 to 1685 (Fig. 5.1) who, as the newly elected Speaker of the House of Commons, delivered an address to Charles II which was "fulsome and servile in the extreme."[19]

Not surprisingly, the king's return was welcomed more warmly in the established church, although even there signs of the development of moderate opinion appear, paralleling that in the mayoral families. Only at St Michael's was the Restoration literally so: the aged and failing Abraham Spencer, vicar 1617-43, returned to his vicarage in 1662 for the remaining year of his life. He ousted Nathaniel Partridge who had ministered there occasionally in addition to his duties at the abbey church since 1657; yet, since he is noted in the parish register as officiating at marriages three times in 1658-60 and Partridge conducted a burial in January 1663, parochial antagonism between their very different viewpoints cannot have been strong. The situation seems to have been similar at St Peter's. There William Rechford had been minister since 1647, a year when the presbyterian system had given a committee of prominent parishioners the chance to elect a suitably zealous preacher after the previous non-resident incumbent had been found unsatisfactory. But by 1658 Rechford's opinions lagged so far behind those of his most active parishioners, those who were the trustees of the living, that they requested him to depart, at the same time refusing to continue the augmentation of his stipend that he had hitherto enjoyed. He did not go, and a minute of 28 April 1659 notes: "Whereas Mr William Rechford … hath not quit the said place as was intended; it is ordered that the order of these Trustees of 26th October 1658, whereby the augmentation … was suspended, be taken off and discharged".[20] This implies a change of heart, or at any rate a change of profession, on Rechford's part, as well as lukewarmness and indecisiveness on the part of the trustees. By 1662 Rechford's son John was installed.

One of the godly ministers, though, proved a man of different stamp. Nathaniel Partridge (Fig. 5.1), who had been at the Abbey parish only a few years, remained stubbornly consistent in his views, conformable to the example of his distinguished predecessor, John Geree[21], the most eminent puritan St Albans ever knew. Ejected in 1662 and followed by a "considerable number" of his congregation[22], he continued to minister in London where he was reported in 1669 to preach to 150 people. Partridge's consistency runs counter to the change of heart which had come over a town that was not merely anti-royalist but strongly puritan only a decade before, and emphasises by contrast how little clash of opinion, whether political or religious, the Restoration provoked locally among men of substance. Lower down the social scale, among the poorer Baptist and Quaker adherents of whom we know hardly anything, feeling against the Caroline changes no doubt ran more strongly.

Against this background the following chapters will describe how the town developed during the next forty years, how its inhabitants earned a living or failed to do so, and how, in detail, its administration worked.

NOTES AND REFERENCES

1 Smith [1588]; Defoe 1724-26, Vol.1, p.389
2 Hare's map — reproduced, VCH, Vol.2, pp.472-3 — is known only from a copy made in 1789; Wilton 1900. For the Tonman ditch see Slater 1998, pp.167-8
3 Reynolds 1977, p.191
4 The frontage measurement occurs in a deed of 1657 in the City Library. For the architectural history of Hall Place see Herts. Archaeology (forthcoming).
5 Chester: Alldridge 1985; Edinburgh: RCAM Edinburgh
6 This range of buildings was purchased for demolition during the first half of the eighteenth century; Spencer archive, Northamptonshire Record Office.
7 "Six posts about the Cross" were renewed in 1681/2.
8 So called in 1702; Gibbs 1890, p.100

9   Position fixed by deeds of 1650-70, HRO D/Z18 T2. In 1556 it was near the Town
    Hall; Marian Survey, s.v. Henry Gape

10 The London Vintry was where wine merchants hired cellars; Schofield 1993, p.77.
    The alternative, 'a small vineyard' (Smith 1956, Vol.2, p.232, following Ekwall
    1954) has also been applied to St Albans but Schofield's interpretation of both
    word and buildings makes this unlikely. In addition to the Tavern two wine
    licences were granted to inns.

11 Comparable to Abbey Cottages, Tewkesbury; VCH Gloucs, pp.129–30

12 Town Hall and Counter were one building; see pp.19–21 and Fig. 3.2.

13 A 'pavement before a door', 1663, OED

14 As in 1588 and 1686; Gibbs 1890, pp.27, 87

15 Gibbs 1890, pp.100,112

16 Short rows of trees are depicted on both sides of St Peter's Street in the 1634 Hare
    map.

17 Rugg 1661, p.23

18 Gardiner 1894-1903, Vol.2, p.13

19 DNB

20 Urwick 1884, p.174; quotation from parish register, 26 Oct. 1658

21 DNB

22 Urwick 1884, p.170

2

SOCIAL HISTORY IN ARCHITECTURE

T HE REIGN OF CHARLES II saw changes in the appearance of many English towns resulting from the decline of traditional building techniques going back to the fourteenth century or earlier. By the 1690s a person aware of architectural matters, such as Celia Fiennes, distinguished between places with 'good new buildings' and those dominated by houses with exposed timber-framing and jetties (projecting upper storeys) even if individual buildings qualified as 'good old houses.'[1]

2.1 No. 1 St Peter's Street (the Mansion House); timber-framed, Elizabethan; refronted in brick c.1700.

2.2 Nos. 11, 13 Market Place (middle), probably of the 1650s.

NEW STYLES IN BUILDING

Such judgments resulted partly from the introduction[1] of brick, a material new in small towns[2] that produced the 'good new buildings'; but houses wholly of brick were fairly rare, and even the cheaper alternative of a smart new brick front to an old timber house, like No. 1 St Peter's Street, refronted c.1700 (Fig. 2.1), was not common. Timber-framing continued in use but to provide the new fashionable flush front, jetties were abandoned, as at No. 11 Market Place (Fig. 2.2).[3] Fashion coupled with the desire for improved and differently propor- tioned windows further altered the appearance of older houses. Plas- tered walls had an economic benefit in permitting the reuse of timbers sal- vaged from demolished structures or the use of not quite straight timbers in place of the carefully worked ones needed previously to produce an aesthetic effect: a contrast observable at the White Hart, where the principal part of the framing was never intended to be exposed (Fig. 2.3). Brick buildings were copied in other ways – new treatments of the roof eaves, classically-inspired detail, a greater symmetry – that gave these structurally traditional houses an up-to-date look. At the same time they were made more comfortable in various ways, the most obvious external sign being the building of imposing chimney- stacks for extra fireplaces.

A frequent form of improvement was to rebuild the ground-floor front flush with the jettied storey above: a proceeding implied by a lease dated 1656 to Thomas Watts, butcher, of a parcel of ground "whereon part of the house" stands in the Hay Market; and by another of 1678 to Mr William Pembroke of "the ground in the Leather Market on which his buttery stands"; and by the rent paid by William Mitchell, butcher, "for the encroachment of his house … in St Peter's Street. One or two owners had greater building ambition. William Rechford in 1656 had a lease of the ground in front of his "new built house … whereon the porch stands". He paid a rent of 6d for it whereas Thomas Guldham, paying 2s 6d, had perhaps added a larger enclosed porch. William Oxton paid only for a smaller encroachment of two posts although these

2.3 The White Hart. The north end (left) was faced in lath and plaster to conceal the sixteenth century jettied timber-framing visible in the adjoining part. Beyond the covered gateway is late-seventeenth century flush framing originally plastered over and exposed by 'restoration'.

probably supported a square first-floor room projecting above the doorway of his house. Small annual rents sometimes specify other forms of encroachment; thus between 1687 and 1700 Nicholas Spurling paid 6d p.a. for, first, his yard, then his yard and "palisadoe", and finally "the encroachment of his house", and Dr John King paid 6d p.a. for "the plot of ground before his dwelling house whereon his rails stand" in Spicer Street.[4] Fencing in ground at the front distanced householders from passers-by or people attending the market and was not discouraged by the corporation because it improved the appearance of the town.

These changes in building practice produced houses with continuous stretches of wall unknown earlier and lacking a jetty to provide contrasts of light and shade and an ornamental finish. At a time when richness of ornament and decoration was prized builders responded to the new large surfaces by breaking them up in several ways. In this respect St Albans is of wider cultural interest for its taste in plaster decoration; not the vigorous East Anglian pargetting exemplified by bold scrollwork at Hertford, Ashwell and Berkhamsted[5] but

2.4 No.17 High Street, fifteenth century, refaced in rusticated plaster in 1665.

the more sober classical imitation of masonry called rustication found at No. 17 High Street (Fig. 2.4). This old jettied house was improved and the wall surfaces rusticated in 1665, at much the same time as the Crow in Fishpool Street was embellished in the same way. A gentry example of this kind of ornament can still be seen on the brick gate-piers at Hall Place, St Peter's Street.[6]

As those gate-piers show, brick lends itself to bold treatment. Striking examples occur in the oldest surviving brick house in St Albans, now Nos. 52/54 Holywell Hill, a building of the late 1650s formerly an inn whose name is unknown. In the wing facing the courtyard, as formerly on the street front, a heavy moulded brick band marks the level of the first floor and the windows have raised architraves (Fig. 2.5) derived from the finest mansion in the vicinity, Tyttenhanger House, begun around 1655.[7] In the 1690s that fashion was superseded by the pilasters and polychrome brickwork of No. 1 St Peter's Street where the jambs and heads of openings and the eaves cornice are worked in orange-coloured rubbed brick and the walling between is of blue headers. Common bricks patterned with alternating red stretchers and blue headers provided a less expensive alternative.

One building material, roofing tile, is so familiar in St Albans as to be taken for granted. Clay tiles were employed already in the Middle Ages and by the mid-seventeenth century were used on every building of any consequence. Not that thatch was unknown; James Field's inventory of 1685 includes "700 of Thatchen laths" and a thatcher's probate inventory exists; and, although no surviving building is known to have been thatched, a late nineteenth century drawing of the tiny 'Woodman's Cottage' (not identifiable on the large-scale Ordnance Survey town plan of 1886) shows it thatched.[8] The abandonment of thatch must be the main reason why St Albans never suffered such a disastrous

2.5 Nos. 52–54 Holywell Hill: rear wing with brick architraves, moulded band and rusticated quoins; Cromwellian.

fire as ravaged many towns in the seventeenth and eighteenth centuries[9], because timber-framed houses are not in themselves highly combustible.

Digging clay to make tiles and bricks produced quantities of flint. In the Middle Ages it was the local substitute for good stone, as in the abbey gateway, whilst the wall in front of Hall Place still shows stretches of the flint and stone chequerwork so highly esteemed in the fifteenth century. By the Restoration its principal uses were for footings and garden walls, although for the latter brick was the prestige material. About 1660-70 the wall at Hall Place was largely renewed in brick and handsomely finished with a moulded capping and gate-piers with big ball finials; and whereas in 1673/4 a man of the social standing of Serjeant Farrington paid an encroachment rent for the rails in front of his house in Spicer Street, by 1681/2 he paid for a brick wall. Even for the lining of cellars brick, with its greater ease of laying and superior finish, was customary, leaving flints for inferior uses.

Lowest in the scale of building materials was clay which, when mixed with chopped straw and cow dung, was used for walls and buildings – in Hertford-shire, only minor buildings, unlike Devon. The only mention of it is in the survey of the site of the Abbey[10] made in 1548 in which mention is made of "a

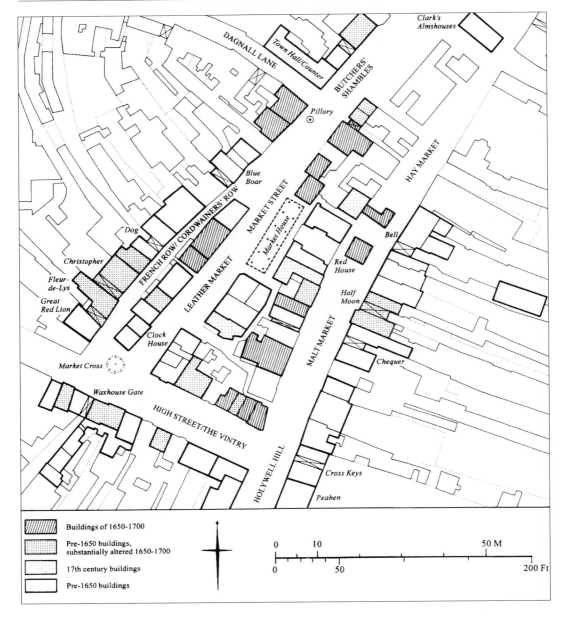

2.6 Plan of town centre showing the legacy of buildings in 1650 and those new-built or considerably altered between then and 1700.

mudde wall on the south parte of the New Ordynance Orchard" and another "about the Laundry Garden", but if it was used for minor abbey purposes it must certainly have been used fairly extensively outside.

An attempt has been made to show both the legacy of pre-1650 building and the amount of new building in the town centre between 1650 and 1700 (Fig. 2.6). Much has been lost by demolition or re-styling so that the result is inevitably impressionistic, yet the maps may convey an idea of the changes in the town's buildings that occurred during our period, even if its appearance did not strike Celia Fiennes as remarkable. Two points arise from it. The street fronts on the west, east and south sides of the market area were fully occupied in 1650 by buildings that needed only improvement, much of which can no longer be documented. In contrast, new buildings are concentrated in the streets formed within the original triangular end of the market place, and it is unlikely that they replaced any substantial predecessors.

INTERIOR IMPROVEMENTS

One general innovation was the use of roof spaces, superseding the older practice of leaving the top storey open to the apex. An attic floor increased the number of rooms in a given volume of building and, coupled with the concealment of structural timbers by plasterwork, increased the warmth and comfort of the rooms below. Most pre-1650 houses underwent such improvement, often simultaneously with the provision of upstairs fireplaces. In many medieval buildings the roof space was obstructed by structural posts that precluded attics; some, and all later buildings, had simpler roof constructions which allowed the insertion of a floor at eaves level for attics lit by dormer windows, with a ceiling high up the roof slopes. By the middle of the seventeenth century most new houses were either of two storeys with attics, as No. 14 High Street, or of two-and-a-half storeys – that is, the attics had low walls, as in Nos. 2, 4 High Street (Fig. 2.7).

Fireplaces contributed to the improvement in comfort. Prior to the Civil War a vernacular building generally had only ground-floor fireplaces some 2–3m. wide discharging into a tapering flue made of timber and plaster.[11] When, later, a fireplace was desired in an upstairs room it was impossible structurally to add a second flue and a completely new brick chimney-stack was needed; then fireplaces could be provided on all floors, attics included. Illustrations convey how extensive such work was, despite the demolition of so many buildings, because the new stacks were of distinctive shapes and capped by a heavy corbelled top. That and sometimes their corner position indicate a late-seventeenth century date as, for example, chimney stacks added to the Bull (Fig. 2.8).[12]

2.7 Old drawings as historical evidence. This one by J.B. Buckler, dated 1836, shows what the north side of High Street looked like c.1700 except for late eighteenth-nineteenth century shop fronts. All the buildings are timber-framed and were later rendered to conceal the framing. From right to left: Nos. 2, 4, 2½ storeys, 3 bays (windows) wide, that to right belonging to Chequer Street premises; late seventeenth century, dated by roof trusses (shown in old photograph) and windows. No. 6, 2 bays; older than adjoining buildings because windows and eaves are lower – perhaps fifteenth century, windows and dormers being late seventeenth century alterations. No. 8, 2 bays, NB tall windows hence lofty 1st-floor rooms, early eighteenth century; glazing added to older open shop front. Nos. 10–16 , all gabled, stand on narrow medieval plots, unheated as built; Nos. 10, 12, 14 of fifteenth century origin, 10 refronted early eighteenth century; 12, late seventeenth century alterations.; 14, fireplaces, staircase added late seventeenth century No. 16, probably much as 14. Corner block, 2 storeys, jettied to south and west, carved corner post, early fifteenth century (10, 12, 14 personal observation; rest long demolished).

In the principal rooms a fireplace of the 1660s and 70s might have moulded stone jambs and a lintel carved in low relief, as in three chambers at the Christopher inn. The new fireplaces, though smaller than their predecessors, were large enough for the splayed sides to be painted or, in the better houses, covered with Dutch tiles; and to protect the brickwork at the rear from a banked-up heap of hot ash an iron fireback like the "old Back" at Childwick Bury noticed in an inventory of 1690 was both useful and decorative. Cheaper ones made of baked glazed clay were probably once common.[13] Fires, too, were made differently, with the increasing use of coal. As early as 1661 Andrew Whelpley's house had, in the chamber over the shop, "in the Chemney a paire

Old Building, top of Albert, St Albans. Sketched Jan? 1892

2.8 The Bull inn from east (Holmes Wynter drawing).

of Cole Irons" which were probably the same as the "Barrs to burne Coale wth." in the chamber over the hall of Samuel Turner's house by the Abbey mill (1671). Both entries imply that new brick chimneys were being built to meet the demand for heated upstairs rooms. By the 1690s fireplaces were being built to contain iron grates intended to burn only coal, although it was some time before such new fittings became familiar; those appraising the goods of Edward Smith, gent, in 1686 listed "one Coale iron wth. Brass heade 2 things to putt in the Chimney to putt fire shovell and tongs in".

The concealment of timberwork included the plastering of ceiling timbers which, in a reversal of taste, are now frequently stripped bare. Seventeenth century plaster ceilings often had a simple combed border but in the 1650s and 60s some had geometrical patterns formed by broad bands of ornament in fairly bold relief, as in the most important room of the former inn, now Nos. 52/54 Holywell Hill. This ceiling is unusual in incorporating profile busts of Roman emperors which are a humbler version of those at, for example, Salisbury Hall, Shenley, and reflect the beginings of classical taste in architecture at a social level below that where it was previously found. Later ceilings were finished more plainly with a plaster cove, then the wood or plaster cornice with simple classical mouldings such as exists at the former Swan inn.

Internal decoration is totally at the mercy of fashion. At the White Hart alterations revealed a large Elizabethan wall-painting depicting Venus and

Adonis which had been hidden about 1680–90 behind the kind of panelling then fashionable; chance alone preserved the sole evidence of how the town's best inns were fitted out at their most flourishing periods. As late as the 1930s the last panelling carved with geometrical figures in relief, comparable to the Holywell Hill ceiling, was stripped from the principal first-floor room in No. 1 St Peter's Street, which had been refitted in the Cromwellian period with fireplaces to match and had survived intact. Even more vulnerable were the embossed leather hangings favoured in the mid-century for gentry houses, such as those in James Rudston's "Matted chamber over the greate Parlor" which in 1674 had "Hangings … of Gilt leather and red Serge" like those surviving at Rothamsted Manor.

HOUSES IN AND AROUND THE MARKET AREA

From developments common to town buildings generally we turn to particular houses.

Not surprisingly, the trading heart of the town, the area bounded by High Street, Chequer Street and French Row, underwent considerable rebuilding between 1650 and 1700. A dozen or so houses of the period are known, one of which, No. 11 Market Place (Fig. 2.2), reveals by its three storeys with attics and cellars the pressure on land in this part of the town. Built in the 1650s or 60s, it is timber-framed with a flush front broken by shallow bay windows that hark back to Jacobean fashion, yet the overall appearance and especially its height must have been new and impressive. The plan comprises two principal rooms facing the street in each storey with fireplaces discharging into a common chimney-stack, and behind the stack is a staircase flanked by two service rooms. The present shop front under a lean-to roof probably replaces an unglazed opening closed by the traditional large shutter called a flap and, standing as it does in advance of the main structure, represents the kind of encroachment in Middle Row for which Edmund Howe and John Sparling were in arrears of payment in 1697/8.

On the opposite side of Market Place Nos. 33/34, a two-storeyed building of the 1660s, was built for a butcher. At the front, facing the Butchers' Shambles, an unheated shop and a hall/kitchen were entered from a passage between them; above are two chambers and garretts and behind, a service room, staircase and a rear wing. The wing, of striking external appearance, has an unusually tall ground-floor and an upper room of unusually bold projection (Fig. 2.9). The lower room, devoid of all detail, has no known parallels but its use is clear. In an adjoining slaughterhouse beasts were killed and skinned, with the unusable residue put into a "stincking gore yard". In this lofty, cool room, whose height was increased by a sunken floor, the carcasses

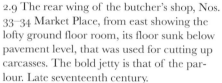

2.9 The rear wing of the butcher's shop, Nos. 33–34 Market Place, from east showing the lofty ground floor room, its floor sunk below pavement level, that was used for cutting up carcasses. The bold jetty is that of the parlour. Late seventeenth century.

2.10 21 Market Place; timber-framed, late seventeenth century, refronted in brick early nineteenth century.

were hung for cutting up (as happened until recently), with the two high north-facing windows framed in plaster ornament[14] admitting enough light but minimal warmth. In the shop offal was prepared and joints of meat cut up for sale over a flap at the shop front or, on market days, in a stall outside. The family ate in the adjoining room or enjoyed in the panelled parlour above the carcasses a commanding view up St Peter's Street.

These two houses improve on earlier ones in being two rooms in depth. Nearby, No. 21 (Fig. 2.10), originally timber-framed with a bold end-of-the-century eaves-cornice, has on each floor two rooms at front and back with, between them, a staircase and a space of corresponding depth occupied by closets,[15] thus producing a compact centralised plan which is a marked improvement on No. 11. Before its renewal in brick the front appears to have been of four bays, entrance being into the smaller north room which was a combined entrance hall and room retaining the quasi-public character of earlier halls. It may well have been built for a professional man.

Nearly all the old buildings between French Row and Market Place are (or were) two rooms in depth, of two-and-a-half storeys and built after about

2.11 The west side of Chequer Street c.1900. The 3-storey brick front of No. 15 (left) is late seventeenth century; No. 13, of 2+1/2 storeys and with lower proportions, is probably late sixteenth century. The next three timber-framed houses, all rendered, have eighteenth or nineteenth century windows; No. 23, the Duke of St Albans public house, has a brick front of c.1700.

1640.[16] No. 13 bears the unsubstantiated but not impossible (and not old) painted date of 1637 (Fig.1.5); No. 3 has a few mid-seventeenth century roof details and staircase balusters; No. 11 is probably of the 1650s; and a house on the site of No. 9 had timber-framing of late seventeenth century type.[17] They suggest the piecemeal replacement over some forty years of a first generation of encroachment, replacing smaller buildings or permanent market stalls.

Among the plastered buildings in the central area a long-demolished brick house at No. 15 Chequer Street, dated by its glazed blue headers to the 1680s or 90s, stood out as much by its height of three storeys and semi-attics as its material (Fig. 2.11). Its plan must have resembled that of a house dated 1675 in Hitchin which has two ground-floor rooms, a shop at the front, a hall-kitchen behind and the two heated by a central chimney stack flanked by a staircase; and just such a house was built next to the Chequer inn in 1720.[18] All reflect the growing demand for ample floor space on a small central site.

GENTRY HOUSES

One other house, now misnamed St Michael's Manor, Fishpool Street (Fig. 8.1) deserves mention for its association with the Gapes, a family of tanners. After the Restoration John Gape, already twice mayor and the probable builder, wanted a house appropriate to his acquired status. That consideration and the family business may explain its unusual siting.[19] Most unusually, the quite impressive principal elevation facing the street is not the entrance front, which stands at right-angles to it, and the point of this may have been to remove several rooms from proximity to the tannery while providing an office in the entrance front from which work and movement could be supervised. The house is small, though, compared with many of its kind and its rooms lacked the closets which distinguish true gentry from vernacular houses at this period.

PUBLIC BUILDINGS: THE PARISH CHURCHES

The Abbey church, by far the largest building in St Albans, had provided during the Civil Wars a barracks for parliamentary soldiers and a prison for their royalist prisoners and at the Restoration was still scarred by wartime uses and the officially inspired or casual defacement of images during the previous decade. Only with the reinstatement of the ecclesiastical hierarchy in 1660 did refurbishment of the interior begin to adapt it to Charles II's religious settlement and permit its repair as far as local funds allowed.[20] A new wooden font and altar rails were the first requirements, together with the emblem of restored supremacy, a painted Royal Arms placed over the west tower arch to face the nave – a position suggesting that that part of the church was still in religious use or expected to be so for a generation after 1660. Systematic adaptation to the requirements of the civic body and a fairly small parish had to wait on the urgent work of repair. By February 1681 that need was sufficiently apparent for a brief to be issued, the money collected being used to repair the wooden vault of the presbytery. It was insufficient, and although money was still coming in in 1684, further contributions were perhaps discouraged by the accession of James II, as the immediate recognition of the church's requirements and a grant of money by William and Mary suggest. That permitted the recasting of the interior as a preaching church, abandoning most of the nave for services and making the crossing tower the centre of what was functionally a cruciform plan with four equal arms. Dominating it at the south-east corner of the crossing was a high pulpit with elaborately carved panels and tester – a roof acting as a sounding-board – and to reinforce the visual and acoustic effects a wooden saucer dome cut off the upper part of the tower (Fig. 2.12). To complete the transformation from processional church of a monastery to preaching auditory of a corporate, town pews well furnished with fabrics and cushions were built for the civic officers in 1692/3, a gesture which must have had some resonance for people mindful of James II's attacks a few years earlier on corporations and the Church of England.

The other parish churches, St Peter's and St Michael's, are less instructive. Overshadowed by the abbey, their interiors were little recorded by artists or photographers and the former lost nearly all its historical interest through, first, partial collapse and later an extensive reconstruction; a loss to some small extent counterbalanced by churchwardens' accounts which reveal the pattern

2.12 The Abbey church, the crossing looking east.

of expenditure on fabric and fittings (below, pp.78–84). Thus in 1650/1 some £39 – much the largest amount except for a special assessment in 1670/1 – was spent to put right wartime damage and neglect. How either church was adapted to post-Restoration religious needs is not known.

CHAPELS

Important though dissenters were in St Albans, no Presbyterian chapel was put up until 1698. Like all such buildings it was an auditorium for preachers, designed to enable as many people as possible to hear the Bible and the doctrines drawn from it expounded. Consequently it had galleries and two tiers of three windows on the two sides, and because no architectural style had specifically Protestant connotations, even supposing any kind of monumental treatment had been felt appropriate, it inevitably had a somewhat domestic appearance (Fig. 2.13). The building,12.5m x 9.5m internally, was entered by two wide doorways (for men and women) placed near the ends of the front and opening near the foot of corner staircases which rose to deep galleries. On the wall opposite the entrances were the pulpit and communion pew. This was the arrangement in 1894 and it had probably never been altered. In 1886 the town plan shows it as having seats for 200 persons and the congregation in 1690 was said to number 300.[21]

A small Quaker meeting house had been erected in 1672 when land was acquired for the purpose in what is now Spencer Street, and in 1676 the "building lately erected" was transferred to trustees. Nothing is known about its appearance.

The old Unitarian Chapel, Lower Dagnell street. St Albans.
Sketched Sep 24. 1898.

2.13 The Presbyterian (later Unitarian) chapel, built 1698.

PUBLIC BUILDINGS: THE TOWN HALL

After St Albans acquired a charter in 1553 the corporation replaced the abbots' seat of government, the Moot Hall, by a building suited to new requirements and free of any taint of past subjection. The new town hall was completed by about 1570 as a two-storeyed, jettied range with a short wing at each end and met the corporation's needs for 130 years before extensive renovation in the late 1690s (Fig. 2.14). From the mayors' accounts showing in detail what was done it is possible to discover how the building functioned, the task being made easier by the distinction drawn between the Town Hall (meaning the principal chamber) with its named end rooms and the Counterhouse, embracing all the rest of the building including the exterior.[22]

The principal function of the Town Hall, a long, lofty first-floor room, was to provide a dignified setting for meetings of the mayor and burgesses and the borough court (Fig. 2.15). At each end was a square room, to the west the council chamber and to the east the jury room, both being entered from the town hall. No mention is made of a fireplace or braziers in any of the rooms. Access to the town hall from the street was by the tallest of three doorways (Fig 2.14) into an entrance hall, off which a staircase at the rear rose to a first-floor gallery. In 1697/8 £12 10s 11d was spent in repairs and improvements to the town hall and £77 18s on the counterhouse.

2.14 The town hall as drawn by Oldfield c.1800.

A beginning was made by recladding the roof, using "ten square and 40 foot of tiling" bedded on, or pointed with, moss,[23] work which may have been connected with the repair and renewal of ceilings which took place next. Quantities of laths and "lining" were probably used to conceal the mouldings on the posts and beams which embellished the old building but, surprisingly, no mention is made of panelling, only of oak boards. Windows, too, were improved by casing the oak frame of the "new window at the upper end" in deal and fitting it and the "great window" lighting the body of the hall with an iron casement complete with spring.

References to windows and furnishings in the accounts give some idea of how the town hall was used. "The Table in the town hall" where the magistrates sat stood next to the upper window, the one nearest the council chamber: in 1664/5 a glazier mended a pane of glass "agt the Table in the town hall".[24] Two benches set up in the hall in 1653/4 may have been for those around the table, upon which was "a faire large greene Carpet of Broad-cloth contayneing fower yards London measure" that was dyed and repaired in 1664/5. Chairs are not mentioned but twelve new cushions provided some

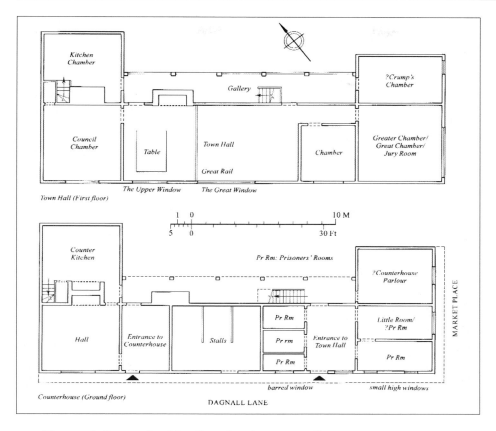

2.15. The town hall, ground and first floor plans (reconstructed).

comfort for the mayor and his brethren in 1681/2. Those attending the court were separated from the table by the "great rail of 15ft", the bar put up in 1681/2 at which pleas were heard; and "9 heads for the rails" were presumably finials for newel-posts in that and other rails. The informal, customary use of spaces in the town hall was being replaced by clear demarcation.

In the inner or council chamber was kept the most important piece of furniture, the Great Trunk, in which reposed the town charters and other documents; it is no doubt the same as the "great chest with three locks" mentioned in 1587.[25]

The Counterhouse served principally, until 1679/80, to accommodate the house of correction of the borough, to which persons found guilty of petty offences at quarter sessions were committed. It also comprised accommodation for the counterkeeper – hall, great parlour, "Crump's parlour',[26] kitchen and kitchen chamber – and, beneath the town hall, a stable for the counterkeeper's and others' horses. The kitchen served the counterkeeper's household (including the prisoners) and mayoral feasts, the last being suggested by the purchase in 1698/9, in London, of no less than six spits. Between the kitchen and the street was the great parlour; upstairs was the kitchen chamber. At the opposite end of the building the house of correction included a room with a large barred window and another which had only two high ventilation openings towards Dagnall Lane and was blind on the Market Place side. This must have been a dark and poorly ventilated cell with, perhaps, a better-lit day-room adjoining to north. Upstairs were the great parlour and Crump's parlour.

The programme was completed by the building in 1696/7 of "a buttery in the yard" which probably accounts for the slightly greater length of the kitchen wing; and in 1699/1700, of a new shed "round the Counter house" on the three sides facing the yard and open to it.[27] It may have been for exercise or work in bad weather. By then the exposed timbers of the town hall, which will have resembled those still visible over the gateway of the White Hart, were old-fashioned, and some of the large expenditure of 1697–9 on the Counter-house went into lath and plaster to hide the old decorative stud-work.

PUBLIC BUILDINGS IN THE MARKET PLACE

When St Albans received its first charter there were, as far as is known, no buildings erected specifically for market purposes. A generation later the town, like many others throughout England, felt obliged to provide shelter for the staple trade, whether wool or, in this case, corn, so in 1587–9 money was collected for the building of a market house. By April 1591, when Mr Richard Lockey gave half a hundred boards towards its lofting over and as an encouragement to others, the basic structure was complete; nevertheless, the building was still unfinished in 1596.[28] The difficulty in completing this rather basic structure hints at the burden that the building of the town hall must have imposed.

The market house, in the middle of the market place, is depicted in 1634 as an open-sided, gabled structure of eight bays on posts, with no visible "lofts". Payments in 1650/1 for "tiling the staircase" and in 1681/2 for "oaken feather-eridge (feather-edge) board" show that the staircase to the lofts was external and enclosed, and the amending of the corn shops in 1651/2 and the mending of the bailiffs' shops in 1691/2 suggest that the upper storey held a considerable quantity of corn. To reconcile the drawing with the accounts a stair can be envisaged rising to a doorway in the north gable and so into a corridor between corn shops on either side. Beneath the staircase a well enclosed by boarded walls and accessible by a locked door was for the use of those attending the market. In 1675/6, after the town fire hooks were mended, they were placed in the market house with a lock "to lock them to the Market House post" upon which public notices were set. Like the town hall, the market house was a multi-purpose building in which, in 1681/2 the stocks and "the bench belonging to the stocks" were set up. Nevertheless, by 1700 the need was felt for a new market house.[29]

The fourteenth-century Eleanor Cross served as a market cross and by 1650 those trading there were sheltered by a structure similar in size and probably date to one of 1571 at Retford.[30] A payment in 1681/2 "for setting down of 6 posts about the Cross and work in hewing them and in plank to stop the old mortisses", and a further one "for carrying away 5 posts or old pieces of timber from the Cross to Roomeland" imply an open-sided polygonal structure, a simpler version of the well-known one at Dunster in Somerset.

Once the town had received a charter and built the Town Hall, the original importance of the Clock Tower as the symbol of a struggle for civic liberties[31] was lost. Thereafter its usefulness to the corporation was limited to the clock and the bell and the rent from the tenement in it which comprised a shop with the living room and chamber above. In the sixteenth century a jettied two-storey house of one-room plan – shop and chamber above – was built against it facing south to High Street, and in the mid- or late-seventeenth century another building under a lean-to roof was added to east. The loss of these rents and the cost of demolition were no doubt why a decision of January 1700 to demolish the Clock Tower[32] was left in abeyance.

INNS: THE LEGACY IN 1650

Of the thirty-odd inns recorded in the late seventeenth century a few preserve sufficient detail to illustrate the principles of their planning, whilst probate inventories reveal how they functioned. The critical element was control of access to the various parts of the building. Compactness was therefore a virtue but one not easy to attain as long as the shutters of unglazed or partially glazed windows had to be closed against the wind on one side and opened for light on the other, thereby precluding buildings more than one room deep and producing the typical medieval courtyard plan.[33] By about 1600 improved glazing made inns two rooms deep feasible and led to a new kind of plan in which the problem of control was solved neatly by confining entrance to a single doorway from a covered gateway at the side of the plot.

The oldest inn, formerly the Tabard but the Antelope by 1650, had been built in the fourteenth century and still had, in the first-floor gallery facing the courtyard, the original traceried windows. This suggests what documents confirm, that by then it was an old-fashioned inn in decline.[34] Other medieval inns – the Christopher, the Fleur-de-Lys, the George and the White Hart – underwent more or less complete rebuilding in the sixteenth or early seventeenth century, even, in the case of the first two, to the extent of adopting the

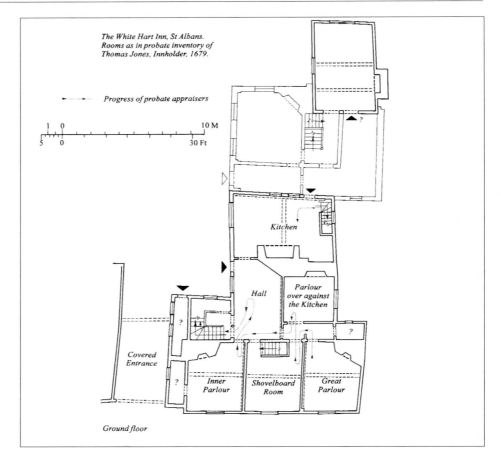

The White Hart Inn, St Albans.
Rooms as in probate inventory of
Thomas Jones, Innholder, 1679.

Progress of probate appraisers

10 M

30 Ft

Kitchen

Parlour
over against
the Kitchen

Hall

Covered
Entrance

Inner
Parlour

Shovelboard
Room

Great
Parlour

Ground floor

2.16 The White Hart. Plans of the ground (left) and first floors (right) showing how the probate appraisers went through the building. The room order permits a reconstruction of the late seventeenth century plan.

side-entrance plan.[35] New inns of the same type include the Swan and the Dolphin, although where the site permitted, as with the Crane, the courtyard type might be perpetuated.[36]

A MAJOR INN AND ITS APPOINTMENTS: THE WHITE HART

Enough seventeenth century structure remains of the White Hart to relate it to the rooms listed in the probate inventory of Thomas Jones, innholder, dated May 1679, who is the most likely person to have made the extensive alterations still visible. Jones came to an inn comprising a two-storeyed street range extending over and beyond the gateway and, behind it, the shell of a large medieval open hall that had been divided into two storeys and given a central chimney stack in Elizabeth's reign; he improved it by altering the plan of the

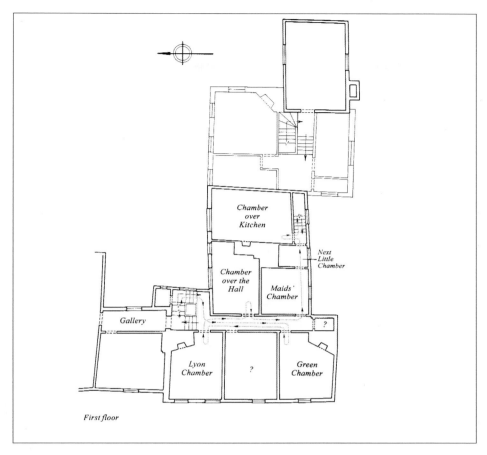

hall block and rebuilding completely the part in front of it. (Fig. 2.3). By following the sequence of rooms named in the inventory by the appraisers it is possible to follow their footsteps and see how the inn operated (Fig. 2.16).

In Jones' time the hall no longer provided for the reception and entertainment of most guests; it contained a long table, a settle, "odd Stooles and Chaires" and little else, not even a fireplace, so that it was a utilitarian room for hurried or poor travellers. For gentry guests proceeding to their rooms it was merely a passage, its dining function having been largely transferred to parlours or chambers. These had become self-contained rooms in which up to eight people slept and the best of them – the Swan, Bear, Star and Sun – were on the far side of the gateway. One was the panelled ground floor room mentioned earlier and another was the well-appointed Bear chamber; it had three standing bedsteads and two truckle beds (that could be pushed under the standing or high bedsteads) and its occupants also ate there, for otherwise the three tables, five red leather chairs, six stools and a form would have been unneccessary. Some other well-furnished rooms which had a fireplace and

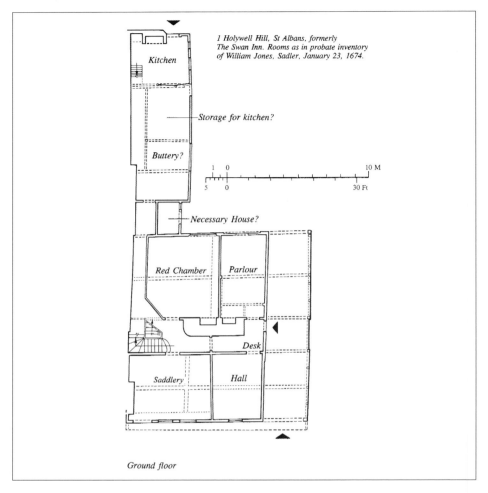

Ground floor

2.17 The former Swan inn, No. 1 Holywell Hill; ground (left) and first-floor (right) plans (reconstructed).

only one bedstead were suitable for dining or meetings and as bedchambers for richer travellers; indeed, there is so little difference between chambers and parlours that what are often thought of as separate kinds of room were interchangeable. Thus the Swan chamber contained a standing bedstead, a "trundle" (truckle) bed, a long table and frame, six chairs and eight joint stools, while the Great Parlour had the same first three items, "one other table", two chairs and three forms. Even the "Shovleboard Room" had two standing bedsteads and a press bed for when the inn was full. The Sun chamber in particular was better furnished than any parlour and with its three "Redd Chaires", a "Great wooden Chaire", a "Great wrote Chaire", three "wrote Stooles" and six "joynt Stooles" was suitable for a party conscious of status and precedence. Its "two Great Pictures" – the words suggest

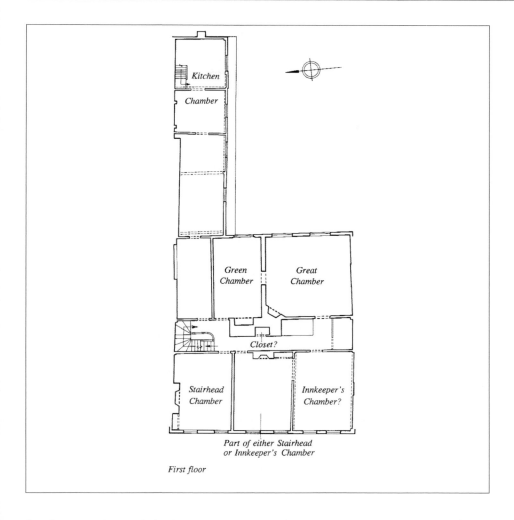

Kitchen

Chamber

Green
Chamber

Great
Chamber

Closet?

Stairhead
Chamber

Innkeeper's
Chamber?

Part of either Stairhead
or Innkeeper's Chamber

First floor

landscapes, then relatively uncommon – helped to create an agreeable setting for the mayor and burgesses at their corporate eating and drinking, or for the entertainment of a grandee on his passage through town.

The only rooms in the street range unaccounted for are the middle one on the first floor and those in the top storey: the semi-attics; presumably they were occupied by the innkeeper, whose belongings would not be listed. Male servants, both indoor and outdoor, probably slept in the yard buildings, the ostler over the stables and others in part of one of the several barns and sheds that were burnt down in 1803. Nothing there is listed in the inventory except for "four hoggs and All odd things and a Nagg", which may imply that all the stable equipment and contents belonged to the ostler. That was perhaps the case at a Maidenhead inn where Thomas Ellwood was asked for payment for his "horse's standing", not by the innkeeper but the ostler.[37]

SIDE-ENTRANCE INNS

Side-entrance inns have compact and efficient plans, that of the Swan (No. 1 Holywell Hill), built around 1600, being the most informative (Fig. 2.17) because it can be related to a probate inventory of 1674. The key to understanding is again the hall, sparsely furnished with two tables, two forms and, significantly, one desk at which, close to the entrance, the innkeeper awaited custom and oversaw service. Next to the hall and entered from the street was the shop/workshop containing the "Sadles Bridles whipps and other wares" made by the innholder, William Jones, saddler. On the other side of the passage next to the entrance was the parlour, furnished to receive gentry travellers with three leather chairs and another chair, six "Joynt" stools, a pair of small (?) tables, a looking-glass and five pictures. Beyond was the Red Chamber, William Jones's own; the significant pieces of furniture are "Two Cabinetts" for keeping valuables, money and papers. All these rooms, together with the cellar stairs and the passage to kitchen and buttery, were under the innkeeper's eye as he sat at his desk. The same was true at the White Hart.

Upstairs the unheated "Stair head Chamber" at the front was a storeroom for inn furniture, including a "lattis", which is a 'window of latticework (usually painted red) …formerly a common mark of an alehouse or an inn'.[38] In the opposite corner was the Great Chamber, equipped with two curtained bedsteads and one other bed, table (and carpet for it), four leather chairs and a looking-glass; also an amenity not often found, "One Close Stoole box and pan."

FORMS OF ENLARGEMENT

Although most building work at inns consisted of improvement, some went in enlargement. The prime example is the Saracen's Head, a small inn built c.1560-70 with no more than a hall to left of the gateway, a narrow room, probably a bar, to right and three first-floor chambers opening off a gallery. About a hundred years later the inn was doubled in size to provide a wide new staircase leading first to a landing from which opened a large back room – the Great Room of contemporary plays or the Great Parlour of probate inventories – and then up to a corridor leading to the Great Chamber and five unheated chambers.[39] These changes must have required more stables, hay lofts and other yard buildings, the whole amounting to a considerable investment.

The Dolphin, built in the 1570s and two rooms deep, like the Swan, could only be enlarged by adding a detached range in the yard like the one surviving at the White Hart. This, as built around 1620-30, provided four rooms, two on the ground floor sharing back-to-back fireplaces, two upstairs unheated. Around 1660 the timber chimney-stack was replaced by brick and first-floor fireplaces were added, probably by Nicholas Goulding, innholder, who died in 1674. Goulding's probate inventory includes rooms named the Crown, the Phoenix and an unnamed chamber in the "new Lodgings".

A third way of providing more rooms was to build upwards. At the Christopher in the 1660s or 70s a large chamber in the south wing was fitted out with panelling and a carved fireplace lintel[40] and above it was added a similarly well-appointed chamber. The Christopher then had two of the best inn rooms in the town, one being specially desirable for its lofty position, giving a prospect of the town as well as light and air away from the dirt and smells of the streets below. But it was not the only inn to be improved in this way. Very appropriately, another such room towered over the largest inn in St Albans, the Bull (Fig. 2.8), which was described by Thomas Baskerville in 1678 as the greatest inn he had ever seen;[41] its nine parlours and twenty-three chambers in 1687 made it big by the standards of all but the largest towns.

A prospect and fresh air were as much prized by townspeople as by inn guests. A three-storey house in High Street was surmounted by a belvedere, a glazed turret commanding a wide view over the whole town and a roof-top retreat to which the owner would retire on a fine evening (Fig. 6.7).[42] First-floor balconies, as well as serving the same purpose of enabling people to see also, and more importantly, enabled them to be seen. Thomas Ellwood, evading confinement in Oxford, was caught when "some of the [Lords] lieutenants … were standing in the balcony of a great inn or tavern,"[43] happened to see him. Balconies at the Fleur-de-Lys and former King's Head (No. 23 Market Place; Fig. 1.5) have disappeared,[44] leaving the one at the so-called Mansion House, (no.1 St Peter's Street; Fig.2.1) as the only survivor. All overlooked very public places.

WHERE DID THE POOR LIVE?

Hardly any clues remain to show the kind of houses occupied by the poor. Many of those on the margins of poverty, who in bad times might require poor relief, probably lived in the yards of houses in the heart of the town. An old photograph (Fig. 6.7) hints at conditions that must have existed for more than two hundred years. Those who lived in independent dwellings were unlikely to be much better off. The slightness of seventeenth century cottages is apparent from a biblical simile: "Behold the Lord maketh the earth empty …The earth …shall be removed like a cottage".[45] Only a single illustration of the kind of small, poorly-built house that may once have been common is known, a nineteenth-century drawing of the 'Woodman's Cottage'.[46] Possibly it had walls of mud, as found in the abbey outbuildings 300 years earlier, or at best mud-and-stud, that is, mud stiffened by posts, as used in Lincolnshire.[47] It cannot be identified on the immensely detailed Ordnance Survey town plan of 1886, perhaps because it was by then regarded as an impermanent structure likely to be removed at short notice. Although that particular cottage is unlikely to have been very old, some of the 171 householders listed as exempt from hearth tax in 1673 may have lived in houses no larger or better built, as descriptions of one or two houses at Myddle (Shropshire) show.[48]

NOTES AND REFERENCES

1   Contrast her remarks about Shrewsbury and Northampton; Fiennes 1957: 226,118 respectively.

2   Mercer 1975, p.129–31

3   Actually divided between Nos. 11 and 29A

4   The lease and the rents appear in mayors'accounts.

5   For houses at Hertford, Berkhamsted and Ashwell houses: Smith 1992, pp.159–60; for 17 High Street, Smith 1993, p.154.

6   Hitchin had a timber-framed house in the same taste; Smith 1992, p.90, reproducing drawing in Oldfield Vol. 4, p.151.

7   Smith 1992, pp.67–70 and front cover

8   Woodman's Cottage, Winter 1897-98, etching no. 7 dated 1883

9   Jones 1968

10 'Survey of the Scite of the Abbey of St Albans 2 Edw VI Feb 1 by Robert Chester and Fraunces Southwell', *The Reliquary* 14, 1873–74, pp.21–2

11 Smith 1992, pp.185-7

12 Smith 1992, pp.187-8. Illustrations of such stacks at the Potters Arms and the 'Old Building, top of Albert Street'(the Bull): Winter 1897–98, pp.30, 5 respectively.

13 Smith 1978, pp.127–8

14 Similar plaster detail of 1665 occurs in No. 17 High Street. Holmes Winter's sketch no.6 dated Mar 18th 1889 shows nothing like the existing original window and is clearly inaccurate.

15 A closet is a small room opening off a larger one and used for varied purposes, e.g., a book closet.

16 No. 1 next to the Clock Tower is an exception. Jettied on both sides and built without a chimney stack, it may be a late-sixteenth century warehouse with lock-up shop, comparable to one in York and smaller ones in Hertfordshire: Smith 1992, p.145, where the reference to No. 12 George Street is wrong.

17 Engraving in City Museum. Cf. No. 51 St Andrew's Street, Hertford, and No. 3 High Street, Stevenage; Smith 1992, p.164.

18 No. 4 Market Place, Hitchin, Smith 1992, p.162; St Albans house, Smith 1994–6, pp.129–34

19 The oldest part is said to be of 1586, the embossed date in the ceiling of the Oak

Lounge;VCH, Vol.2, p.402 RCHME 1911, p.192. However, the plasterwork fits the late seventeenth century ceiling structure and panelling whereas the date does not appear to be genuine and nothing else in the building is Elizabethan.

20 This paragraph is based on the much fuller account in Roberts 1993, pp.168–77

21 Based on Ruston 1979, O.S. 1:500 plan 1886 and Holmes Wynter drawing dated Sept 24 1898

22 In this chapter 'town hall' refers to the whole building, 'Town Hall' to the room.

23 'Tiling is measured by the square of 100 superficial feet', Gwilt 1842, rev. edn 1888, para.2301; for the use of moss, Innocent 1916, repr.1999, pp.180–1.

24 For such tables, Tittler 1991, pp.116–17

25 Gibbs 1890, p.19

26 Crump does not appear in other records; he may have been an assistant to the counterkeeper.

27 As was its replacement of 1791, outlined on the 1831 plan of the Town Hall.

28 Gibbs 1890, pp.39, 51

29 Gibbs 1890, p.96

30 Marcombe 1993, p.39

31 VCH, Vol.2, pp.401–2

32 Gibbs 1890, p.96

33 The only study of medieval inns as buildings is Pantin 1961.

34 The Antelope is known from a drawing by J.B. Buckler in 1824, reproduced in *Gentleman's Magazine,* September 1845, p.261 and Smith 1992, p.150; also a wash drawing by Cornelius Varley of c. 1810 in St Albans City Museum.

35 It is here assumed that the Christopher and Fleur-de-Lys changed plan form because no medieval example of a side-entrance inn appears to be recorded elsewhere in the town.

36 The Crane has been well published, though not completely, under its later name of the Crown and Anchor; Weaver and Poole 1961.

37 Ellwood 1714, p.75

38 OED, 'lattice', 1b

39 Described more fully, with plans, in Herts. Archaeology (forthcoming).

40 Similar lintels occur at Delrow, Bushey, of 1669; Smith 1993, p.45

41 Baskerville in Hist MSS Comm. Rept

42 The late seventeenth century Cupola House, Bury St Edmunds, takes its name from the 'tower and lanthorn' noted approvingly by Celia Fiennes in 1693; Morris 1949, p151–2. A square turret room on the roof of the headmaster's house of the original Shrewsbury School resembles the one that existed at the Bull.

43 Ellwood 1714, p.102

44 Little is said about balconies in architectural literature and their purpose is ignored. For the Fleur-de-Lys, Oldfield Vol. 8, f.477; for the King's Arms, Hebditch 1988, title page

45 Isaiah 24,20

46 See note 8 above

47 Cousins 2000, pp.5–9

48 Gough [1701], pp.107, 137, 234–5, 248; and Smith 1985, pp.33-4

3

THE BOROUGH

Following the dissolution of the great Benedictine abbey in 1539 the town of St Albans, so long dominated by powerful abbots, came into the possession of, or in legal terms was held of, the crown. On 12 May 1553 Edward VI granted a charter of incorporation to St Albans and this was confirmed by Mary, Elizabeth and James I. Charles I extended his charter (27 December 1632[1]) to include certain apparently customary practices. From 1553 until 1664 the legal title of the corporation was "The Mayor and Burgesses of the Borough of St Albans". With the charter the rights of jurisdiction and the profits of the market formerly enjoyed by the abbots passed to the corporation, which paid a rent of £10 p.a., known as the fee farm rent, to the crown. Under Charles II's charter of 27 July 1664 the corporation's title became "The Mayor, Aldermen and Burgesses of the Borough of St Albans".

The charter of Edward created the office of chief or principal burgess, a title equivalent to that of alderman subsequently adopted under Charles II's charter. The principal burgesses, a small group of prominent citizens from among whose members the mayor was always chosen, numbered ten plus the mayor from 1553 to 1664 and thereafter twelve aldermen plus the mayor. For a brief period under the charter of James II of 16 March 1685 the number of aldermen was increased to eighteen and included a number of non-resident gentry but the two men among the latter who were elected mayor each appointed one of the 'civic' aldermen as his deputy with full powers to act. On James II's charter being annulled in 1688 the charter of Charles II became operative once more and remained so until the Municipal Corporations Act of 1835.

THE BURGESSES OR FREEMEN

The burgesses were the freemen of the borough. In the sixteenth and seventeenth centuries admission to the freedom was sought chiefly for reasons of trade or business since only a freeman could practise as a master craftsman, employ journeymen or apprentices, keep a shop within the borough and be exempt from tolls. In addition, under Edward VI's charter, the freedom conferred the right to vote for the borough's two members of parliament. To be free was also an essential requirement for the holding of most civic offices, certainly all the higher ones, and such officers as were not already free took the oath of a freeman at the same time as the oath of office.

As in the City of London and elsewhere, there were three ways of becoming free. The first was by patrimony, that is as the son of a freeman. In many towns any son of a freeman born after his father's admission could claim his freedom by patrimony. In St Albans a freeman resident within the borough could choose one such son only to be made free and if the father did not exercise his right during his lifetime, then after his death his eldest such son could claim admission.[2] A man admitted by patrimony would not necessarily practise the same trade as his father. Thomas Jones, draper, for example, the son of Thomas Jones, innholder, claimed the freedom after his father's death in 1686. From at least as early as 1620, and possibly earlier, until 1689, all those admitted by patrimony paid 3s 4d towards the charges and repair of the Abbey church.

The second way of becoming free was by apprenticeship. A young man who had been apprenticed to a freeman for seven years could apply to become free himself provided that the indentures between him and his master had been enrolled in a register kept by the chamberlain of the borough. This register unfortunately has not survived for our period earlier than 1697.

The third method, available to those who could not claim admission by patrimony or apprenticeship, was by purchase or 'redemption' as it was usually called, paying a fee of £5. Such admissions required the approval of the mayor and principal burgesses or aldermen. Sometimes the fee was paid outright at the time of admission, increasingly so towards the end of the century, but more often the new freeman paid only part of the fee, say £1 or £2, and covenanted by bond to pay the balance in quarterly instalments.[3] The redemptioners' fees were a significant item in the corporation's yearly revenues. Fees were sometimes waived, perhaps if the high steward or one of the MP's for the borough sought to have one of his servants or dependants made free[4], or if a man taking up a civic office such as recorder or attorney of the court of record was not already free.[5]

Upon admission a new freeman was enrolled in one of the companies or guilds. The number of freemen was presumably too small to support the existence of separate craft guilds. Instead, at the beginning of our period there were four companies, the Innholders, Mercers, Shoemakers and Victuallers, each of which served as an umbrella guild for the freemen practising a number of specified trades. The Innholders Company, for example, included the innholders, tanners, tallowchandlers, curriers, pewterers, musicians and ropers. In 1667, or very shortly before, the companies were reduced to two, the

Innholders and the Mercers, with a consequent re-ordering of the crafts and trades associated with each.[6]

Except on fair days or as a journeyman or bona fide servant of a freeman, a non-freeman was not allowed to practice a trade or manual occupation within the borough. If he did so the court would order him to cease and he was liable to a fine of 2s for every day of such illegal trade. In such cases some sought to be admitted by redemption. Mary Merrit, milliner, the only woman whose admission has been traced, was ordered on 24 January 1694 to leave the town by Lady Day next but on 28 March paid £5 outright for her freedom. An interesting case is that of Anthony Boys, bookbinder, who on 27 January 1692 was "tolerated to trade in the town for a year's space" having paid £2 down and undertaken to become free and pay £3 more if he remained in the town at the end of the year. On 26 July 1693 Boys paid the additional £3 and was made free.

The gaps in the surviving records make it impossible to establish the number of those admitted to the freedom. About 300 admissions have been traced between 1650 and 1700 but this figure is inevitably a serious underestimate and a total of at least 500 would seem more reasonable. The size of the body of freemen at any one time is also difficult to estimate. A draft petition of c.1685 among the Gorhambury papers concerning elections alleged that the number of voters at elections was not less than 600 freemen and "housekeepers".[7] A list of voters at the election of 19 February 1690 totals 492 but appears to include some names of men not known to be free at that date.[8]

THE MAYOR, PRINCIPAL BURGESSES OR ALDERMEN

The constitution of the town was oligarchic in character, the civic hierarchy being headed by the small and powerful group of principal burgesses or aldermen already referred to. These men, drawn from a small number of leading civic families which, as is shown elsewhere, were closely linked by an intricate web of family, marriage, trading and commercial ties, enjoyed the sole right of election to any vacancy within their own ranks and the right of appointment to or approval of most lesser offices within the borough. Subject to good behaviour, competence and residence within the borough they could, and usually did, hold office for life. Tenures of office were long, especially in the earlier part of our period. A few principal burgesses or aldermen died or resigned before attaining the chair but the great majority went on to serve the mayoralty. Thirty-one men held office as mayor between September 1650 and September 1700. Including mayoralties also held by some of them before 1650 or after 1700, three of the thirty-one, Robert Ivory, Thomas Oxton and William Humphrey, served four times, nine others three times and eight twice. Nineteen of the thirty-one held office as principal burgess and/or alderman for more than twenty years and of these, five, Thomas Cowley I, Robert Ivory, Thomas Oxton, John Gape and William Marston II, for more than forty years. It was not unusual for more than one member of a family to be in office as principal burgess or alderman at the same time: Thomas Oxton and William Oxton, William Marston I and II (father and son), William New and his son John, John and his brother Robert and later the same John and his son, another John. Thomas Cowley I and II were also in office together. On St Matthew's Day 1660 they were the two nominees for mayor, Thomas the younger being elected for the first time to the chair and his father succeeding him in his third mayoralty the next year. In the seventeenth century, however, oligarchic local government did not carry the unfavourable connotation which it has today. Indeed, as Robert Tittler has pointed out, writing of a period immediately prior to our own, both local interests and the crown found oligarchy entirely appropriate.[9] The holding of high civic office was also demanding of time and was often financially burdensome and those who sought it must have been influenced by mixed motives in which the exercise of power, a sense of civic duty and family tradition all played a part.

The election of the mayor took place each year on St Matthew's Day, 21 September. The principal burgesses/aldermen, the twenty-four assistants (see p.49) and all the householders "or so many of them as they can find at their respective dwelling-houses"[10] were summoned by the serjeants at mace to attend at the Town Hall and there to vote by acclamation for one of two candidates nominated by the principal burgesses or aldermen from among their own ranks. Provision was made for the counting of heads should the result of the election by acclamation prove indecisive but it seems that in the second half of the seventeenth century the election was much of a formality, the first named of the two candidates being almost invariably elected and the other being named first and elected the following year. No instance has been found of refusal of office, the penalties for which were considerable. Following the election the mayor elect and the rest of the assembly escorted the old mayor home to his own house. The new mayor was installed in office on Michaelmas Day, 29 September, taking the required oaths at the Town Hall and afterwards being escorted to his house by the old mayor and company present. These two days were the most important in the civic calendar and the bells of the Abbey church were rung in celebration.

During his year of office the mayor was a justice of the peace for the borough and a justice of gaol delivery of the borough gaol, and also a justice of the peace for the liberty of St Albans, an extensive area around the town containing twenty-three parishes and almost co-extensive with the hundred of Cashio. From 1632, under the charter of Charles I, the immediate past mayor also held office as a justice of the peace for the borough, taking precedence during this time over the other aldermen. The mayor was also clerk of the market and had responsibility for the assize of bread, wine, ale and other victuals, setting the price at which bread and other foodstuffs were to be sold and supervising the accuracy of weights and measures. He was held responsible for a large part of the corporation's finances, presenting an annual account for audit by two of the principal burgesses or aldermen. He held one of the three keys to the town chest in the council chamber containing documents and the common seal, the others being kept by the immediate past mayor and the common clerk. He had at least formal responsibility for corporate property such as the civic plate, the mace, certain books and documents and the scales, weights and measures and other goods kept at the town hall. Inventories of all these were drawn up annually and appended to his account.

The mayor travelled outside the borough on the town's business: regularly, accompanied by his serjeant at mace, to the Summer and Lent assizes at Hertford, occasionally to visit a property at Romford which had been conveyed to the corporation by Thomas Gawen in 1634 upon trusts for the poor, and on many occasions to London, often accompanied by the common clerk and one or more of the principal burgesses or aldermen. The costs of his horse hire or coach hire and sometimes other expenses on these journeys, appear in his annual account.

The mayor was, however, only first among equals. He was expected to consult with his brethren about all important borough business and required their consent to being absent from the town for more than three days. Together they held a court known as the monthly court of the mayor and principal burgesses (later aldermen) for the public business of borough affairs. At this were present, under penalties for non-attendance, the constables, the wardens of the companies, the several viewers, the flesh and fish tasters and the searchers and sealers of leather, all of whom made report to the court as necessary. It was at this court that freemen were admitted, new officers appointed and others submitted their accounts, and non-freemen were reported for trading within the borough. Strangers, sought out by house-to-house enquiry, were presented by the constables. In 1686, for example, Edward Benson was fined 40s for harbouring an old man aged about eighty and a woman.[11] The court seems to have made or at any rate initiated orders of a kind usually made by the justices of the peace for the removal, either to a place outside the borough or from one St Albans parish to another, of persons who might become a charge on the parish rates. Thus Thomas Thorp, his wife and three children were ordered to be removed to Rushden in Northamptonshire[12] and Elizabeth Dolloway from the Abbey parish back to St Peter's[13], while Joseph Darvell and his sister were to obtain a certificate from St Michael's not to become a charge to St Albans

[Abbey parish], which it seems they were unable to do as they were later ordered to be removed.[14] It was in the court of the mayor and aldermen also that leases of corporation property were sealed and a variety of orders made concerning the town bell and clock, the pillory, the corporate finances and many other matters.

THE ASSISTANTS, THE WARDENS OF THE COMPANIES AND THE BAILIFFS

Next in importance to the principal burgesses or aldermen were the twenty-four assistants. Charles I's charter of 17 December 1632 is the first to mention them but in doing so was giving formal recognition to an office which had long been in existence, almost certainly from soon after the incorporation of the borough in 1553.[15] It was the duty of the assistants to aid the mayor and principal burgesses or aldermen in the management of the borough and like them they could hold office for life. Four of their number with two of the aldermen attended the mayor to church on Sundays and festival days, accompanying him "in civill and comely rank and good order" from his dwelling house to the Abbey church and back again.

During the period 1650-1700 there was a problem in keeping the number of assistants at full strength. After 1657 vacancies were not filled and by 1677 there were only six in office. On 11 July eighteen new assistants were appointed[16] although no hint is given in the records of the particular pressures which brought this reform about, and thereafter the full quota of twenty-four assistants was generally maintained. Tenure of the office of assistant varied greatly. Some men served only one, two or three years but Richard Ruth and Richard Millard, discharged from office as "old and feeble" on 30 August 1682, had completed 54 and 31 years respectively. Of the new intake of 1677 John Cowley served 35 years, Thomas Grubb 30, Thomas King 27 and Joseph Marshall 25 years. The decline in numbers between 1657 and 1677 makes it difficult to assess how far the office of assistant normally served as an avenue of advancement towards principal burgess or alderman. Of eighty-nine assistants in office between 1650 and 1699 only four were elected principal burgess and eleven aldermen but these figures were inevitably affected by the shortage and towards the end of our period, as at the beginning, some of the mayors do seem to have served a spell as assistant. Nevertheless, it would seem that many of the assistants came from families which were not of the same social standing as those which supplied the mayoralty.

The wardens of the companies were intended to be drawn from among the assistants. There were two wardens of each company, elected at Christmas and holding office for one year, so that there were eight wardens in all before 1667 and four after the companies were reduced from four to two. One cause for concern in the decline of the number of assistants was that the office of warden tended to fall into other hands. The responsibilities of the wardens included the enrolment of new freemen in the appropriate company's books, the joint holding of a quarterly court for the business of the companies, the receipt of the freemen's enrolment fees and quarterage dues and the rendering of an account to the mayor and aldermen upon leaving office. Sadly, no record of these activities survives.

Two other officers, the bailiffs, who held office jointly from Michaelmas to Michaelmas were drawn in rotation from among the assistants. Under the charter of incorporation the borough had been granted a market twice a week to be held on Wednesdays and Saturdays, three fairs at Lady Day (25 March), St Alban's Day (22 June) and Michaelmas Day (29 September), each of which lasted for forty-eight hours, and the view of frankpledge or court leet to be held twice a year. A fourth fair at Candlemas (2 February) was granted by the charter of Charles II. The bailiffs were the 'farmers' of all the profits of the markets, fairs and leet, that is they leased these profits from the corporation and retained them, paying an annual rent fixed by agreement. The office pre-dated the Dissolution, for the abbot had long appointed a bailiff to collect the market dues and in the early sixteenth century he let this office at farm for a term of years.[17] Under the corporation, however, the office was to be enjoyed for one year only, and indeed on 27 June 1649, following complaints that favouritism was leading to certain assistants holding the office of bailiff too frequently to the detriment of others, it was ordered that no assistant should be re-elected bailiff within ten years.[18]

The bailiffs entered into a covenant with the mayor and principal burgesses or aldermen and gave surety for due performance of their responsibilities, which were in effect the management and proper conduct of the markets and fairs, including the ringing of the market bell and keeping the market place clean.[19] The corporation, however, retained in its own hands the leasing of corn shops in the Market House and stalls in the Butchers' Shambles.

The rent paid by the bailiffs for the bailiwick fluctuated within the period 1650-1700 between £40 and £80 but was always the biggest single item in the corporation's revenues. For the corporation the certainty and simplicity of an annual rent compared with the labour of collecting what might prove to be variable profits was an advantage but as a result no details of the workings or the profits of the market and fairs, which were so important for the economy of the town, are to be found in the mayor's accounts. From time to time the bailiffs' expectations of profit failed to materialise. The bailiffs of 1681/2 were abated £10 of the rent due because of losses that year, and at the very end of the century, on 6 December 1699, they were authorised to prosecute persons bringing corn, grain and other goods to the borough's public fairs and markets without paying toll and other just dues "whereby the Bailiffs that rent the toll are wronged and defrauded".[20] One of the corn shops in the Market House, known as the toll shop, was leased to the bailiffs in office who paid for it a further 10s p.a. Unfortunately the bailiffs, like the wardens of the companies, have left no surviving accounts or other records — a grievous loss. A greater understanding of their office and its workings would have done much to illuminate the economic life of St Albans and its market.

The names of the bailiffs between 1650 and 1700 have all been traced.[21] All were assistants even in that period when the number of assistants was declining rapidly. Indeed the desire to circulate an office of profit within an ever-smaller number of men may have been a major reason why vacancies in the office of assistant were not filled, although the lack of new appointments must have been condoned by the mayor and aldermen. In consequence, despite the ordinance of 1649, a few individuals served as bailiff many times. Most notable was Solomon Smyth, dyer, who was a bailiff continuously from 1660/1 until his death in 1674. For the last seven of these years his co-bailiff was John Ruth. These two men both died within the year of office 1673/4 and, in accordance with a provision of 1587 that a deceased bailiff's executor or administrator could continue for the rest of the term, the two widows are found accounting for the rents of the bailiwick and the toll shop. Even more surprising perhaps is the case of James and Maria Tristram. On 6 June 1694 it was agreed at the request of the borough's high steward, the Earl of Marlborough, that James Tristram should become one of the bailiffs at Michaelmas 1695. James died before this date and the bailiffs for 1695/6 were William James and James Tristram's widow, Maria.[22]

OTHER OFFICERS

Charles I's charter of 1632 is the first to mention the high steward of the borough but by that date the office was already long established.[23] Between 1650 and 1700 it was held by three men who were not only eminent in legal, political or court circles but who had strong local connections: William second Earl of Salisbury, of Hatfield House, Sir Harbottle Grimston owner of the Gorhambury estate, and John Baron Churchill of Aymouth (later Earl and then Duke of Marlborough), who had married Sarah the daughter of Richard Jenyns of Sandridge, and who often resided at Holywell House in St Albans. The civic records yield little information as to relations between the corporation and their high steward whose function was doubtless to forward any concerns of the borough and act as a friend at court. He was paid an annual fee of a 20s piece of gold which cost the corporation £1 3s 6d and later £1 4s each time, and until 1677/8 he usually presented the corporation annually with a buck which was used at the feast known as the Venison Dinner.[24]

By 1650 the principal legal officer was the recorder who under Charles I's charter had taken over functions previously exercised by the steward. The latter office, distinct from that of the high steward, had been created by Edward VI's charter of 1553 but was discontinued after 1644 on the dismissal of the then holder. The recorder presided over the borough's civil court of record. He was also a justice of the peace and a justice of gaol delivery for the borough, and was charged with assisting the mayor with his best advice and counsel. From time to time he might appear on the corporation's behalf in a suit brought in the king's courts at Westminster, and he played a part in the ceremonials of the election and installation of the mayor, deputising if required for the outgoing mayor. The recorders in office between 1650 and 1700 were William Foxwist, esquire, barrister, appointed in 1644; John Simpson of the Inner Temple, esquire, barrister and son of John Simpson, mayor in 1648/9, who succeeded Foxwist in 1661; Anthony Farrington who was appointed by Simpson with the consent of the mayor and aldermen as his deputy in 1680 and then succeeded him on his death eighteen months later, and finally in 1699 James Wittewronge of Rothamsted and Lincoln's Inn, esquire, who resigned in 1721. Simpson and Farrington both became serjeants-at-law, then the highest rank of a common law barrister. The election of the recorder, and also that of the three or four attorneys permitted to appear in the court of record, was in the hands of the mayor and aldermen, although that of the recorder after 1664 was subject to royal approval.

The officer most vitally concerned with the day-to-day conduct of the corporation's business was undoubtedly the town clerk or, as he was more often called in the seventeenth century, the common clerk. The first common clerk, named as such in Charles I's charter of 1632, was Conon Rawlyn who had previously been the chamberlain. Charles' charter makes no mention of the latter office which had been created by the original charter of incorporation. After 1632 the common clerk carried out any duties pertaining to the chamberlainship which were concerned with freedom and apprenticeship and also seems to have acted as coroner, another office established by the charter of Charles I. Conon Rawlyn resigned on 6 September 1648 and his successor, Thomas Richards, was chosen common clerk by the mayor and principal burgesses and admitted a freeman, paying £1 down and covenanting to pay the remainder by 2s 6d quarterly. While continuing in office as common clerk, he was elected one of the assistants on 2 September 1653 and served twice as a bailiff, in 1657/8 and 1674/5. On his death in 1678 he was succeeded by his son, another Thomas, who became an assistant in 1692. On 31 March 1697 Edmund Ayleward was appointed common clerk in the place of Thomas

Richards, "lately absconded and removed from the said office", who had retained some of the corporation rents and records in his own hands (see p.69).[25] Ayleward, who had been a freeman and an attorney of the court of record since 1687, served as town clerk until his death in 1732 when his office was described as that of common clerk, chamberlain and coroner.[26]

The common clerk was responsible for keeping the minutes of the monthly court, writing and casting up the mayor's account, and collecting rents and freedom moneys. He travelled on corporation business even more extensively than the mayor, sometimes accompanying the latter but sometimes independently. He drew up indictments, leases, bonds, bills of sale, a survey of rents, tax assessments, passports (passes) for poor people passing through the town, the certificate required under the Test Act, 1673, that the mayor had taken the sacrament of the Lord's Supper in the Church of England, the indenture of election of the borough's MPs and a variety of warrants, including in 1673/4 a warrant "to compell Widd Aylin ye Midwife to goe to Edw: Chambers his wife's Labour" for which he was paid 6d.

Only a very few men received an annual wage or salary.[27] Between 1650 and 1700 Martin Elament, John Halford, Thomas Hiccox, George Brown, Thomas Hiccox again and Zachary Mountford successively received £2 and after c.1670 £4 p.a. for ringing the town bell and looking after the town clock, both of which were housed in the Clockhouse. From 1677/8 onwards Robert Gregory was paid 10s p.a. for looking after the fire engines and up to 1677/8 the keeper of the house of correction was paid £1 10s p.a. Until 1678 the post of keeper of the house of correction was held by the person holding the office of counter-keeper and gaoler of the borough gaol situated on the ground floor of the Town Hall, which suggests that until 1678 the house of correction may have been sited in this building.[28]

A counter was a term which generally comprised a court and its offices together with the gaol attached to the court and on Benjamin Hare's map of the borough in 1634 "The Counter" is to be found written along the Dagnall Street frontage of the Town Hall. Indeed, in the records the name of Counterhouse is often used of the building in general and Town Hall for the lofty, first-floor room where the courts and other assemblies were held (Fig. 2.15). The counter-keeper's duties seem to have been those of superintendent of the building as well as gaoler. He was quite often reimbursed small sums spent on providing bread and beer for workmen working at the Counterhouse and occasionally was repaid his expenses in conveying a prisoner to London or Aylesbury. The counter-keepers between 1650 and 1700, most of whom were inn-keepers or alehouse keepers, were successively John Woolhead, Samuel Sureties, John Ireland, George Feild, William Blowes, George Feild again and Richard Martin. They paid rent to the corporation, ranging from £6 p.a. to

£12 p.a., in respect of the profits of office as gaoler. The counter-keeper was paid a sum in the region of £2 p.a. for providing a dinner when the mayor sat as clerk of the market, and on 11 September 1700 it was ordered that the then counter-keeper be paid £5 annually for the use of pewter, linen, knives, forks, and brass kettles and pots for dressing and ordering the mayor's feast held on St Matthew's Day, the guests at which were to be limited to the number of 200.[29]

During the last two decades of the century the counter-keeper seems usually, if not invariably, to have held also the post of one of the two serjeants at mace who had duties of attendance upon the mayor. They were also officers of both the court of record and the monthly court of the mayor and aldermen, serving summons, arrests, attachments, warrants and precepts issuing out of these courts, summoning juries in the court of record, and collecting and keeping accounts of amercements (fines). They were appointed by the mayor and seem generally to have been re-appointed and served for a number of years, as was the case also with the two searchers and sealers of leather who examined leather on sale to see that it was sufficiently tanned and dried. Many minor offices, however, were served in rotation on a yearly basis by the inhabitants. These included four constables, one for each ward, four viewers of the streets and highways who sought out and reported nuisances and encroachments, two viewers of the market cross who saw that victuals sold at the cross were wholesome and that higglers or pedlars did not forestall the market, and two flesh and fish tasters who reported vendors of unwholesome meat or fish.

THE CHARTERS OF 1664 AND 1685

A new governing charter was granted by Charles II on 27 July 1664, replacing Charles I's charter of 1632. The charter, which created twelve aldermen in place of ten principal burgesses, seems to have had little effect upon the composition of the governing body, the then mayor, Robert New, being continued in office and all the ten principal burgesses being named among the first aldermen, together with two newcomers, William Rance and William Wiseman, both of whom according to the Hearth Tax returns, were men of considerable wealth. Rance took the oaths and subscribed the declaration on 7 September 1664 but Wiseman's doing so was never dated and signed and he is never listed among the aldermen in the Court Book. He did not formally resign, however, until 17 April 1666. Rance served as mayor in 1666/7 but was discharged from aldermanic office in December 1675 for having long absented himself from the corporation meetings and having gone to live in Redbourn. In accordance with provisions common to many borough charters granted in the early 1660s, Charles II's charter to St Albans specified that members should take the oaths of allegiance and supremacy as, in fact, they were already required to do under the Corporation Act, and that the election of the high steward, recorder and common clerk be subject to royal approval.[30]

In 1684 St Albans was one of many cities and boroughs which were forced to surrender their charters and obtain new ones. Many such towns, including St Albans, had supported Parliament during the Civil War and now counted among their inhabitants a strong nonconformist presence. The Exclusion Crisis of the years 1679-81 involved moves in Parliament to remove the right of Charles II's brother James, a Catholic, to succeed to the throne, reinforcing the view that religious dissent and political sedition went hand in hand. In consequence it became an object of both the Crown and the Tories or court party during the closing years of Charles II's reign to gain control of the boroughs. Since the constitution and liberties of the boroughs derived from charters granted by royal authority a means of achieving this was the revocation of those charters and their substitution by others ensuring stricter control. In the case of St Albans, however, it has to be said that none of the borough's MPs during this time, Sir Thomas Pope Blount of Tyttenhanger, a Whig, and Alderman John Gape, most probably a moderate Anglican, who were elected in March 1679, and Samuel Grimston, son of Sir Harbottle Grimston, another Whig, who replaced Gape in October of the same year, evinced any sign of conviction politics, their involvement in the business of the House of Commons ranging from mild participation to total inaction.[31]

In St Albans the surrender of the charter was signed by John Selioke, the mayor, and ten aldermen on 25 October 1684.[32] Even after a new charter was granted by James II on 16 March 1685 there must have been an underlying sense of unease and uncertainty. The Court Book contains the signatures of 125 men who between then and December 1686 subscribed to the declaration against the Solemn League and Covenant (the agreement in 1643 between Parliament and the Scots intended to secure the wide-ranging reformation of religion including the abolition of bishops), the new high steward, the mayor, recorder, town clerk and many of the aldermen being among the first to sign. Also between 1685 and 1687 a good many men seem to have sought the reassurance of being re-admitted to the freedom of the borough, presumably lest the surrender of the charter might have disenfranchised them.

The new charter brought substantial, if short-lived, changes in the membership of the aldermanic body. On 29 September 1684, the beginning of the mayoral year, this had comprised the new mayor, John Selioke, and the following twelve aldermen: John Gape, John New I, Thomas Cowley II, Ralph Pollard II, Thomas Hayward, John Doggett, Thomas Eccleston, William Marston II, John New II, Thomas Crosfield, Stephen Adams and Edward Seabrook. John Doggett resigned on 15 October and John New I died about this time (his probate inventory was dated 30 October). The new charter was to increase the size of the governing body to the mayor plus eighteen aldermen all of whom were removable at the king's pleasure.

Under the new charter John Selioke, who had been an alderman only since 1681 and was in his first mayoralty, was continued in office as mayor. Selioke must be considered the prime mover among the aldermen in the events of this period, probably from a mixture of personal political and religious sympathies and of a desire to preserve good relations with the national authorities. His opinions can be judged from the address sent by the corporation to James II, congratulating him on his accession to the throne "notwithstanding the spiteful contrivances of those that designed an interruption to your just and undoubted succession".[33] That is the language of zealotry and a clear sign of high tory views in keeping with the behaviour alleged by his opponents following the 1685 election, when he was accused of having threatened the town's inn-keepers and alehouse keepers with losing their licences and having dragoons quartered upon them at a ruinous rate, and of having rigged the admission of freemen.[34] He was probably also the instigator of the exceptionally lavish expenditure at James II's accession when festivities, including payments to musicians and wine for the townspeople to drink the king's health, cost £38 16s.

The new charter appointed eleven new aldermen, who were non-resident gentry and sympathetic to the crown's policies. They included Henry Guy, esquire, of Tring, a high churchman who had been a boon companion to Charles II and was secretary to the treasury, handling money for the secret services. Guy delayed taking his oath as alderman for some six months after the grant of the charter until he was elected mayor on 21 September 1685, whereupon he took the oaths of both freeman and alderman.[35] He was succeeded as mayor in 1686 by Sir Francis Leigh, also of Tring. Both Guy and Leigh appointed deputy mayors with full powers to act, respectively Thomas Eccleston, an alderman since 1673, and, once again, John Selioke. The eleven non-resident aldermen seem not to have intervened in municipal administration, nor had they any need to since their views were evident and the deputy mayors necessarily compliant. They may, though, have pressed for the implementation of measures against dissenters[36]; that, indeed, was probably the real point of their being foisted upon the townspeople.

Of the ten former aldermen who had signed the surrender with Selioke only seven were retained in office by the new charter. The three who were ousted, presumably on grounds of dissenting or Whig tendencies, were Thomas Hayward, John New II and Thomas Crosfeild, all former mayors. Crosfeild was elected an alderman again on 27 June 1687, by which time James II had been forced to adopt a policy of toleration and the Declaration of Indulgence had been passed (14 April 1687); and in September 1687 Leigh's successor was once more a 'civic' alderman, Edward Seabrook. Thomas Hayward and John New II, however, had to wait for the annulment of James's charter in October 1688: their restoration as aldermen was celebrated at a charge of 12s and at the next mayoral election in September 1689 Hayward became mayor for the second time.

Although the assistants, whose appointment lay with the mayor and aldermen, were not named in either the new or the old charter, three of the twenty-four holding office at the time of surrender, William Beech, John Edmonds and John Sheppard, were replaced by Christopher Loft, Zachary Reeve and James Bradbury.[37] The former assistants and their successors all appeared in court on 20 March 1685 and "prayed to have their freedom renewed". A John Edmonds, presumably the man who lost office in 1685, was elected assistant again on 21 August 1689.[38]

The then recorder, Anthony Farrington, and the common clerk, Thomas Richards II, were continued in office by James's charter, but John, Baron Churchill of Aymouth (later Duke of Marlborough) replaced Sir Harbottle Grimston as the borough's high steward. John Churchill's brother, George, was one of two Tory MPs elected for St Albans in 1685 when he was described as "a person never before seen or known by the townsmen".[39] The other was Thomas Docwra of Putteridge who was equally unknown.

In the few weeks before William of Orange's expedition landed at Torbay early in November 1688, James II made a number of tardy concessions to win the support of his subjects. These included the annulment, by order in council of 17 October, of all the municipal charters granted since 1679. In St Albans, therefore, Charles II's charter of 1664 became operative once more and the aldermanic body henceforth consisted, as before, of the mayor and twelve aldermen. New commissions of the peace for the borough and the liberty were obtained at a cost of £22 6s 4d. The sum of £8 6s 3d was spent in celebration of the proclamation of William and Mary in February 1689 but the auditors disallowed £3 3s 7d of this. At the parliamentary election that year, George Churchill retained his seat but was joined by Samuel (now Sir Samuel) Grimston in place of Thomas Docwra (Tory). Churchill and Grimston were re-elected in February 1690 in a three-cornered contest where the third candidate, the dissenter Joshua Lomax (Whig), secured a respectable share of the vote.[40] Grimston had remained in private life during James II's reign, being much disliked, it was said, by the king (despite his inactivity during the Exclusion Crisis). Certainly he was one of a number of men specifically exempted from the indemnity offered by the exiled king to his former subjects in 1692 if they would return to their allegiance.[41] Another was John, Baron Churchill, who had deserted James for William III in 1688. Grimston and George Churchill, Whig and Tory, remained MPs for St Albans until after

1700, a situation which typifies the somewhat ambivalent attitude towards national politics in the town in the second half of the seventeenth century.

PROPERTY

The three principal buildings owned by the corporation were the Town Hall and Counterhouse, the Market House and the Clockhouse (later to be called the Clock Tower). The history and architecture of the pre-1830 Town Hall and Counterhouse is discussed elsewhere (see pp.30–34). The most important room in the building, the council chamber on the upper floor, which was always referred to as the Town Hall, would have been the venue for the election of the mayor, for public meetings of the mayor and aldermen (private discussions may have been held in the parlour), for sittings of the court of record and the sessions of the peace and gaol delivery for both the borough and the liberty. The town chest, housing among other things the common seal made of silver, was probably kept here. As already stated, the counter-keeper, who was also the gaoler of the borough gaol located on the ground floor of the building, paid an annual rent to the corporation in respect of his office, of £10 p.a. at the beginning of our period, £6 p.a. in the 1670s and 1680s, and £12 p.a. in the last decade of the century.

The seventeenth-century Market House occupied the site of the Corn Exchange of 1857 where a succession of market houses seem to have stood. Begun in 1588, it is depicted on Benjamin Hare's map of 1634 as a long, narrow building running north to south and it remained in existence until replaced about 1728 by a new market house.[42] The building seems to have been used exclusively for corn and grain and contained, above an open ground floor, ten corn shops. This is clear from three surviving leases of the 1670s and 1680s.[43] By the terms of these leases each tenant was responsible for the maintenance not only of his shop, including the roof, floor, walls and any penthouses hanging on the side, but also of the posts of the lower storey within the circuit of the shop. Access to these shops was gained by a staircase, furnished with a door, lock and key, for which each tenant bore a proportional cost of any repairs. Beneath the staircase was a well, enclosed by a fence of boards with a door which could be locked. The lessees of the well, who paid a rent of 4d p.a., undertook to maintain the well and fence and to carry away any spilt water lest it be a nuisance to people coming to the market and pitching their sacks of corn on the ground floor of the Market House.[44] The covenants for repair in the leases meant that the corporation itself spent very little on the upkeep of the Market House. The rents for the corn shops ranged from 5s to 16s p.a. One, known as the toll shop, was leased by the bailiffs in office who in the 1680s and 1690s also held two other of the shops. The other lessees, who in the early part of our period included several of the principal burgesses, were often men not otherwise known to have associations with the corn trade. Towards the end of the century most of the lessees were seriously in arrears with their rent.

The Clockhouse, built on a void piece of ground to the east of French Row between 1403 and 1412, housed both the town clock and the town bell which was rung each morning and evening. From 1427 until 1553 the Clockhouse had been the responsibility of a large body of feoffees — trustees in whom the building was invested — whose functions passed on the incorporation of the borough to the mayor and burgesses. Both the feoffees and the corporation granted a succession of leases of the premises under which the lessees covenanted to ring the bell and look after the clock. But by the second half of the seventeenth century, as already shown, the corporation was paying wages each year to a man employed to carry out these tasks and neither the lessee nor the occupier, if this were a different person as was often the case, any longer had any responsibility therefor. A rent of £5 p.a. was paid for the premises which included a shop on the south side and other outbuildings. The corporation was responsible for repairs to the bell and clock and to the stonework and leads of the building.[45] Minor repairs to the clock, to the bell and its clapper, the bell wheel or the ropes figure in the mayors' accounts for many years. In 1684/5 the old clock was taken down and Joseph Almond was paid £7 2s for making a new clock and a few minor works. Joseph Carter was paid 16s 3d for the clock frame. New hanging the bell in 1690/1 cost £3 10s, the work being done by John Coles, and in the next year the dial at the clockhouse was painted and gilded by an unnamed craftsman at a cost of 16s. Maintenance of the town bell was important. It was rung not only both morning and evening and in emergencies, such as fire, but also to mark national events. Occasions of national rejoicing, such as a naval victory over the Dutch in 1653, the restoration of Charles II in 1660, the coronation of James II and the defeat of Monmouth's rebellion in 1685 or the proclamation of peace with France in 1697, almost always called for some corporate expenditure even if only for the ringing of bells or the lighting of bonfires.

The corporation also owned a small number of houses and tenements which it leased for terms of years for fixed annual rents.[46] Four properties in the heart of the town were generally leased to or occupied by butchers. The most substantial, which had formerly been two tenements, was situated at the southern end of St Peter's Street not far from the Butchers' Shambles and was held throughout the period 1650–1700 by Thomas Watts, butcher, or his widow Elizabeth, at a rent of £2 2s 8d p.a.[47] A stable or old house adjoining this property and a slaughter yard extending south from Dagnall Street to the barn of the Christopher were both leased by members of the Kinder family. The slaughter yard was described in 1671 as being "newly paled in" with a pale 6ft high.[48] The fourth property, opposite the town hall, was leased successively by Henry Gape, William Beastney and Robert Robinson, all butchers.[49] In addition, there was a house in Fishpool Street[50], a house on Holywell Hill and another, later divided into two, in Sopwell Lane.[51] The corporation also received rents for the well and well house in St Peter's Street (1s p.a) and more importantly for the stalls in the Butchers' Shambles. There were five permanent stalls, described as being "over against" or opposite the Counter or Town Hall for which the lessee paid £2 p.a. rising later to £3 p.a. When a new lease of these five stalls was granted in 1686 to George Feild, who for many years was the counter-keeper, for a term of thirty-one years it was a condition of the lease that he should at his own expense erect a new and substantial pillory at the end of the stalls and keep it and the stalls in repair during the term.[52] The corporation also let rights to place removable stalls in the Shambles. A number of butchers paid rents of 10s or 5s p.a. for 'stall roomths', which were sites where a stall of specified dimensions might be erected on market days on condition that it be dismantled and removed from the street on the evening of the same day.[53]

Because the commonalty was deemed to own the streets and open spaces of the town encroachments upon them had to be acknowledged by the payment of small rents from 4d to 1s a year. Nearly all such rents proved difficult to collect and were often in arrears. Fortunately, in the absence of any surviving contemporary rentals, the receipt of rents was recorded annually in the mayors' accounts which also listed rents in arrears, so that for periods when these accounts have survived a succession of tenants can often be traced. Indeed, the mayors' accounts, which are discussed more fully below, can often supply information where other sources have not survived.

The corporation also held a few properties upon charitable trusts. The property known as the Vine and the three cottages or almshouses adjoining in Spicer Street had been conveyed to the corporation by the will of Richard Raynshaw of 1569.[54] A tenement on the north side of the Clockhouse and another on the north side of Dagnall Street had been demised by Thomas Lathbury by his will of 1579 to the use of the poor.[55] The property next to the Clockhouse was at one time known as the Rose and Crown but in our period was often referred to as "John Kilbie's house" from the name of its occupier for much of the time.

INCOME AND EXPENDITURE

Much of the information on the activities of the corporation has been gleaned from the mayor's account which happily is more than a financial record (Fig. 3.1)

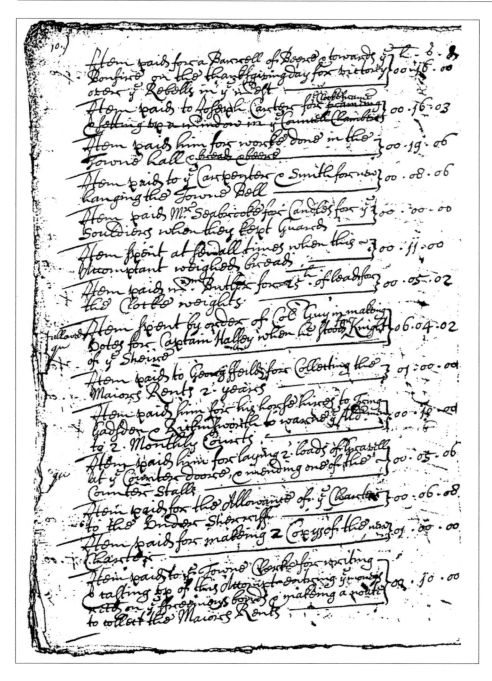

3.1 A page from John Selioke's mayoral accounts. Much the largest amount, £6 4s 2d, was
'spent by order of Col. Guy in making votes for Captain Halsey, when he stood for Knight of
the Shire'.

In the degree of detail, particularly on expenditure, it throws additional light on local activities and contributes to the picture of how life was lived in St Albans at the time; it also links with events taking place on the wider national stage of Stuart England.

As a financial record, however, two cautions must be observed. First, the purpose for which it was compiled must be remembered. It was never intended as a statement of the corporate finances but was a receipts and payments account of all moneys received or disbursed by the mayor, compiled with the purpose of establishing whether at the end of his term of office he had moneys in hand or was out of pocket. If the former, the balance was usually paid over to his successor who included it on the receipts side of his own account[56]; if the latter, he might well have to wait several years before being reimbursed, the eventual repayment being included among the disbursements of one or other of his successors. Clearly, this could mask the corporation's true financial position and the account, for example, of a mayor whose expenditure had exceeded the normal municipal revenue might nevertheless show a surplus at the end of the year if he himself had received a greater surplus from his predecessor. Moreover, no differentiation was made as to the nature of either the receipts or the payments. The former could include in one year a large sum raised by mortgaging the corporate property equally with the annual rent for a butcher's stall and the latter the repayment of the principal of a loan along with the interest due thereon.

Second, certain items may have been wholly excluded from the account. It is known from the Court Book that in 1655 two fire engines were purchased the cost of which was defrayed by a special rate levied to raise £40. Neither the produce of the rate nor the cost of the engines is recorded in the mayor's account. Loans raised by the corporation present another problem, the receipt of the money being sometimes but not invariably recorded and repayment of the principal sometimes entered but sometimes only the payment of the intere St Nevertheless, bearing in mind these reservations, an analysis of the mayors' accounts remains instructive financially.

The account ran from Michaelmas (29 September) to Michaelmas. Individual receipts and payments recorded in the accounts are scarcely ever dated and in the absence of other evidence can be attributed only to the year of the account. Thirty-one accounts,[57] plus one partial, rough account[58] are extant between 1650/1 and 1699/1700, many of them for years when the records of the mayor and aldermen's court are meagre. The losses, unfortunately, include the years following both the Restoration and the grant of James II's charter of 1685 as well as the account for 1689/90, the first full year after William and Mary's accession.

The accounts show that rents of one kind or another constituted the principal element in the corporation's regular revenues. A rate may have been levied occasionally for an ad hoc purpose, as in the case of the fire engines mentioned above, but the principal and regular rates levied upon the inhabitants of the town, namely the poor, church and highway rates, were raised and administered in the several parishes. The annual income and expenditure of these, as is shown in the chapter on Parish Administration, quite often exceeded that of the borough itself. As mentioned before, the most important rent received was that paid by the two bailiffs in office for their lease or farm of the profits of the market, fairs and leet.

The other rents, comprising that paid by the counter-keeper and gaoler for his office, the rents for the corn shops, the butchers' stalls and stall roomths, the premises leased for terms of years and for encroachments, together amounted annually to between £23 and £32. The property rental did not provide a source of income capable of much growth since once a lease was granted the rent was fixed for the duration of the term and, even on the renewal of a lease, the corporation did not always increase the rent. There was also a problem with arrears. As already mentioned, the small encroachment rents proved very difficult to collect and were often many years in arrears. Of greater financial significance were occasional arrears of the larger rents. These were rarely for more than a few years at a time but exceptionally could be considerable. The remaining source of regular revenue was income from fees paid by those admitted to the freedom by purchase or redemption which fluctuated widely from an exceptional maximum of £44 in 1679/80 to an exceptional minimum of £4 in 1687/8 but averaged about £19. Rents of various kinds, freedom purchase and apprentice enrolment fees were basic sources of income common to many towns.

Other income was generally small. It included amercements (fines) set by the mayor sitting as clerk of the market (given in total only), a few fines imposed at sessions, an occasional distress or the value of a strayed animal. Many fines and the revenue from tolls were part of the farm of the bailiffs and were not received by the corporation. In 1664/5 £1 8s was received of John Longe "for the Elme which stood on Roome Land" and in 1674/5 17s 6d from Robert Robotham, esquire, "for part of the Pesthouse on Barnett [Bernards] Heath when it was pulled downe". Unusually in 1682/3 the large sum of £20 11s was received for lead taken off the Cross (intended for use at the Abbey Church?). The money was paid by Alderman John Gape.

Expenditure was much more diverse but many disbursements can be seen to fall within certain broad categories. One comprises payments to craftsmen and labourers. In addition to much work about the town hall and occasionally other buildings, the stocks, the pillory, the cucking stool, the firehooks, ladders and buckets all required money spent on them from time to time. The fire engines had to be kept in repair and tested by playing. Andrew Darvoll was paid 8s in both 1658/9 and 1659/60 for erecting a polling place in the Abbey church for the parliamentary elections and in 1697/8 "old Bradwyn" was given 1s "for mending the Pavement in the Vestry that was broake up att the Election". A new pew lined with green baize was made for the aldermen's wives in 1678/9, Richard Fearnsley made a new pound for £8 in 1683/4, and in 1696/7 John Hawgood was paid £3 "for makeing and setting up the Jibbott to hang Thomas Nash for murdring his mother". In 1681/2 a hand post, later identified as the hand post which points to the London road, was erected on Holywell Hill and a number of substantial "Freedom Posts" were erected and painted, probably at points on the borough boundary to mark the limits of the freedom.

Entries in the mayor's account showing expenditure on coach hire and horse hire for the mayor, the town clerk and others travelling on corporation business, particularly to London, provide a graphic indication, especially in the absence of other local records, of the response to political events at the local level. For instance, the mayor's account appears to provide the sole evidence of the corporation's dealings with the Committee for Regulating of Corporations in 1652/3. The question of how corporations could hold their charters under the authority of a commonwealth was under consideration at this time[59] and, at the behest of the committee, the mayor, Ralph Gladman, accompanied by alderman William New and the common clerk Thomas Richards, went up to London by coach, taking the charter with them. Expenditure on their lodging and diet, on coach hire and boat hire and on fees paid to several of the committee's officials, is noted in the account. Horses were hired and taken to London for the mayor and alderman to ride home while Thomas Richards remained in London a little longer "about getting the charter back again" and then returned with it in the coach.

From 1685 a minor official known as the bellman or bellman and wardsman, who was presumably a sort of watchman, seems to have been entitled to a new coat each year, and from 1689 12s was spent each year on staves for the constables. The mayor himself received three allowances which are entered on the disbursements side of his account. One, a small allowance of £1 10s, which did not vary at all throughout 1650-1700, was for his expenses at the court dinners. The second, of £2 p.a., was for distribution among the poor, including maimed soldiers and poor strangers passing through the town, and is recorded as being allowed in all the surviving accounts of the same period. Both these allowances were already in existence in 1638 when the mayor's third and very much larger allowance for his charges and expenses during his mayoralty was instituted.[60] Originally set at £32 p.a. this was reduced to £30 in the mid-1640s. It seems that a considerable part of the allowance came to be regarded as a contribution towards the cost of the mayor's annual dinner since there were several years when the mayor was allowed only £10 "because he kept no Feast". In consequence of the allowance no details are recorded in the accounts of expenditure on the feast. From 1677/8 to 1683/4 the allowance was raised to £40 but following the financial crisis which resulted from the cost of obtaining a new charter in 1685 it was reduced to £20. In three successive years from 1690/1 it was raised to £25 p.a., £35 p.a. and £40 p.a., at which rate it remained for the rest of the century.

There was some expenditure every year on wining and dining at one or other of the principal inns of the town. Four dinners were held on the occasion of sittings of the borough quarter sessions. Mrs Pollard (of the Christopher) was paid £12 for the four dinners in 1655/6, £3 4s was spent on wine, 4s 8d on "Tobaccoe and beere which was expended after the said dynners" and 5s 7d on "beere and Sugar which the Justices dranke for their morneing draughts before the said dinners". Until 1679 a "Venison Feast" or dinner was held once a year. The venison, which was made into venison pasties, was generally provided by the borough's high steward, whose keeper was rewarded with a fee. In 1653/4, 18 pounds of butter and 17 pounds of suet were supplied for making the pasties. In 1678/9, the last time the feast is recorded, the cost was nearly £17. The corporation also repaired to an inn to pay respects to distinguished visitors to the town, to celebrate some occasion of national rejoicing such as the proclamation of a new sovereign, or to mark a domestic event such as the election of a new alderman. The sums laid out on occasions of this kind were generally fairly small and carefully recorded in the mayor's account as "spent by consent of the Company", that is by consent of the mayor's fellow principal burgesses or aldermen.

Small sums were dispensed on a regular or frequently recurring basis, for example, to the ringers of the Abbey bells on the days of election and installation of the mayor, to the rector for preaching a sermon on the same days, in taxes or quitrents in respect of corporation properties, to six poor men who were given the task of collecting the measures when the mayor sat as clerk of the market or to messengers bringing proclamations, writs or bundles of acts of parliament from London.

There were inevitably other occasions when the corporation incurred exceptional and heavy charges. Sometimes these were for practical necessities. In 1675/6 two new fire engines, a "first" engine and a hand engine, were purchased in London for £25 plus part-exchange of an old engine. A sum of £3 8s was spent "at the buyeinge of the Two Towne Engines & tryeinge of them and playeinge of them 3 severall times", and £12 15s on erecting an engine house in St Peter's Street. Altogether £44 16s was spent in this matter. But many instances of occasional and sometimes heavy expenditure can be seen to be linked to political events at the time.

One of the first things which the corporation did following the establishment of the Commonwealth was to redeem the fee farm rent of £10 p.a. which had been payable to the crown ever since the charter of incorporation of 1553. The amount paid for it in 1650, which presumably represented several years' purchase, is not recorded, only certain minor expenses in connection therewith. Most, possibly all, of the then principal burgesses lent money for this purpose but the receipt and amount of their loans is not recorded. Some repayments or partial repayments were made to them in 1650/1 and the following year. It was in 1650/1 that the corporation borrowed £30 of Abraham Cowley, mercer, not himself a principal burgess but son of mayor Thomas Cowley I, upon the security of the corporate plate, a debt which was taken over in 1651/2 by the mayor of that year, William Marston I. Whether this loan was also raised to meet the charge of purchasing the fee farm rent is not known. However, at the Restoration this purchase of the rent proved not to be acceptable to the crown. The mayor of 1659/60, John New I, and others of the corporation twice travelled to Whitehall to surrender the 1650 grant, their total expenses, including 2s 6d given to servants at the Cock in Aldersgate Street, amounting to £13 14s, and the rent of £10 p.a. became payable once more. It was finally redeemed in 1683/4 by which time it had ceased to be payable to the crown.

During the Civil War and Commonwealth St Albans, on the line of march to and from London, had often been a rendezvous for troops whose quartering was a considerable burden. In the last years of Charles II's reign and in James II's, military activity again appears strongly in the mayors' accounts, beginning about the time of the Rye House plot when a guard was lodged in the Quakers' Meeting House, the barricaded door of which was broken down. The account for 1684/5 shows £1 3s paid to the quartermaster to remove two companies to Redbourn and Hemel Hempstead when Lord Ferrers' regiment lay in the town, and in 1688/9 he was given 10s 'when the Irish souldiers came hither for easing the Towne'. Small sums were paid from time to time, particularly in the 1680s and 1690s, for coals, kindling and candles provided for a guard of soldiers in the town or to convey sick or lame soldiers or occasionally arms and baggage out of the town; and in 1687/8 a guard was in the house of correction. In most of the years from 1687/8 to 1699/1700 the common clerk was paid 10s for making warrants to impress waggons and carriages for the use of regiments and companies passing through. In 1691/2 and the next account, following the disbanding of the army in Ireland, and in the accounts from 1696/7 onwards, following the conclusion of peace with France, the mayor received an additional allowance of £2 towards his charges in relieving "multitudes" of poor soldiers and distressed persons passing through St Albans. Many of these, it seems, were Irish soldiers returning from the continent.

Under the Commonwealth, in 1651/2, the corporation acquired a new silver mace. Both William Marston I, the mayor, and Thomas Cowley I, the immediate past mayor, went to London about this, each receiving 8s for his horse hire and expenses. The cost of the mace, which was the subject of a part exchange, is not known, £3 5s being paid "more for the new Mace than the old Mace the plate and the 10 li which this Accomptant rec'd of the Company". The sum of £10, which represented £1 each received from ten principal burgesses, was repaid in the following year. William Graives, the smith, was paid 6d for making a place fit for the setting up of the mace in the Abbey church. But at the Restoration a new mace bearing the symbols of royalty had speedily to be obtained. It seems probable that the Commonwealth mace was altered rather than traded in as the account for 1659/60 records £21 4s paid for change of the mace and 2s paid to one Stephen Pricklove, who was a coachman, for carrying the mace up to London and bringing it down again. The mayor, John New I, went up to London himself about the matter and received 10s for his horse hire and horse meat (i.e. fodder). The mace, bearing the royal arms and the initials CR as well as the words "Anno Domini John New: Maior" is the mace still used by the corporation.[61]

In those years when the mayor's disbursements exceeded his receipts he was generally expected to bear the loss himself until such time as he could be repaid. In the late 1630s and 1640s the corporation had become indebted to several mayors of the period who, despite the institution of the mayoral allowance in 1638, were out of pocket at the end of their term and who were to be repaid only by instalments over a number of years. By 1657/8 all the debts to former mayors were cleared as well as a mortgage of the corporation plate for £30. But the Restoration brought new expenses. Both receipts and payments in the mayor's account for most of the 1650s had been less than £100. In 1659/60 expenses, largely owing to alterations made to the mace, reached nearly £122, offset by income of only £107 (excluding the surplus received from the preceding mayor). The accounts for 1660/1 to 1672/3 inclusive are all missing save one (1664/5) but the only surviving minutes of the court of mayor and aldermen during the period, for 1663/4, show that on 28 October 1663 it was ordered that Thomas Cowley II, mayor in 1660/1, should be paid £5 11s 8d in full satisfaction of money due to him upon his account and that his father, Thomas Cowley I, mayor in 1661/2, should be paid 25s and the remainder due to him, unspecified but obviously considerable, at £10 per quarter.[62]

By 1673/4, when the accounts resume, the crucial rent for the bailiwick had risen to £80 p.a. and the financial situation had improved. Two loans of £10 and £50 owed to Thomas Oxton, alderman and four times mayor, were paid off in 1674/5 and 1676/7, repayment of the principal being listed in each case among the mayor's disbursements. The highest expenditure at this period occurred in 1675/6, the year in which the new fire engines were acquired. A drop in the bailiffs' rent in 1678 to £60 p.a. brought temporary difficulties but the receipts for the three surviving accounts of 1679/80, 1681/2 and 1682/3 at an average of nearly £135 comfortably outstripped expenditure at an average of nearly £111 and Thomas Crosfeild, the mayor of 1682/3, benefiting from several years in surplus, was able to hand over nearly £56 to his successor.

In the next two years, however, the corporation was to suffer a serious financial crisis occasioned in part by its own actions but in part by measures forced upon it by the crown. By 1673/4 the right to the St Albans fee farm rent of £10 had been sold by the crown and acquired by John Gape, son of Alderman John Gape, to whom it was paid in this and succeeding accounts. In 1684 the corporation bought the rent at twenty years purchase of Mr. Gape for £200. Why the corporation decided on this course is unknown. It sent the mayor's disbursements, which in the previous two years had been held at just over £111 and £108, rocketing to an unprecedented £311 10s and forced the corporation to raise several loans totalling £145. The loans were provided by the trustees of the charities of Thomas and Margaret Hall (the Claypitts account), Robert Skelton, Ann Goldsmyth and the governors of St Albans school.[63]

It was at this unfortunate juncture that the borough was forced by Charles II to surrender its charter. The agitation experienced during the months from the surrender in October 1684 until 16 March 1685 can be glimpsed behind the factual entries of the costs occurred in the mayor's account. Coach hire to and from London for the mayor, recorder, two of the aldermen and the common clerk when they went to deliver up the surrender and charter to Charles II and to petition for a new one; their expenses in the capital; a payment for assistance in drawing up the petition; and the enormous sum of £148 13s 6d dispensed among various of the high officers of state and their doorkeepers, clerks and "inferior officers". The lord keeper and the clerk of the Crown and their clerks and inferior officers were paid £21 12s for renewing the commission of the peace for the borough and for getting the mayor and recorder into the commission of the peace for the county. The result was that the mayor's disbursements in 1684/5 rose to £352 13s 5d. There was no way in which this level of expenditure could be financed out of ordinary revenues. This time the corporation borrowed £200 of John Gape junior at 6 per cent interest. The younger John Gape was not himself a member of the borough's governing body but along with the common clerk and two others had witnessed the signing of the surrender of the charter by the mayor and ten aldermen, including his father. As security for the loan the corporate estate including the toll, Clockhouse, Market House and Counterhouse, was mortgaged to him in August 1685.[64] Even so, the mayor's receipts totalled only £322 5s 4d. Unfortunately neither of the accounts for the next two years is extant to show the immediate aftermath of the crisis caused by the exceptional financial demands of 1683/4 and 1684/5, but later accounts indicate that in the late 1680s there was a serious attempt to curb ordinary expenditure, the reduction in the mayor's allowance already mentioned being a case in point. Major disbursements by the mayor in office in these years were generally partial repayments of debts owed by the corporation. By 1692/3 a great part of the moneys borrowed from charity trustees for the purchase of the fee farm rent as well as the mortgage debt to John Gape junior had been repaid. It was largely because of the repayment of debts that each of the five mayors from 1687/8 to 1691/2 ended his term out of pocket. Most were reimbursed within a few years but the final instalment of moneys due to Thomas Hayward (Howard), mayor for the second time in 1689/90, was ordered to be paid to his executor as late as 23 November 1698.[65]

It seems also that following the financial crisis of the mid-1680s a short-lived attempt was made to farm the rental, that is, to sell the right of collection for a fixed sum, the buyer to make what profit he could . A lease dated 14 July 1686 of all the corporate property save the Counterhouse was made to Thomas Richards II for eleven years from Michaelmas 1686 provided that he remained in office as town clerk. He was to pay £27 p.a. and to allow the existing leases to continue. This transaction is not mentioned in the Court Book and the rough minutes note briefly only the decisions to make a lease of the corporate rents and to seal it.[66] Curiously, the surviving accounts for 1687/8 and 1688/9 reveal nothing of this. No rent from Richards is entered and individual lessees are recorded as paying their individual rents as usual. On 21 August 1689 the town clerk noted in the rough minutes "I am to bring in my lease and assign the other leases over next court".[67] Thomas Richards II proved to be a dishonest common clerk whose later financial misdemeanours led to his dismissal from office. In 1694/5 the only rent received was the £5 for the Clockhouse and the mayor, William Marston II, annotated his account, "All the rest of the rents due to ye Corporation in my time was Colleycted and rec'd by Tho. Richards and by him never yet accompted for So the Totall of the Receipts are but 86.00s.00d". Fortunately expenditure this year exceeded this sum by less than £1. This note may have been written at the time of the audit which was delayed until as late as 17 December 1700. What happened in 1695/6 is not known as the account has not survived but, as already noted (see p.52), on 31 March 1697 the Court Book records the appointment of Edmund Ayleward as common clerk in the place of Thomas Richards "lately absconded and removed from the said office".

A rise in expenditure to £148 16s 7d in 1697/8 and to £152 12s 2d in the

following year was largely occasioned by the very substantial works of renovation being carried out at the Town Hall and the corporation once again borrowed money, this time £68 from the Claypitts charity. In 1699/1700 the
expenses dropped to £120 8s 6d and were nearly equalled by receipts but the
bailiffs were having some difficulty in collecting the toll and paid only £70 of
their rent of £80. Some of their tenants, notably those holding leases of the
corn shops, were in arrears for the rent, and the financial state of the corporation on the threshold of the new century seemed no more certain than it had
been during the previous fifty years.

In the second half of the seventeenth century the freemen and householders of the town participated in borough administration at all levels but power
remained in the hands of the small, self-perpetuating group of principal
burgesses or aldermen, drawn from a small number of prominent families,
who nominated the mayor from among themselves, controlled admission to
lesser office and to the freedom, held office themselves for many years and
often served the mayoralty two, three or even four times. Recruitment to this
group from among the twenty-four assistants, although by no means unknown,
was certainly not a regular avenue of promotion and would seem to have
depended largely on social status. However, the burdens of aldermanic office
were considerable: attendance at meetings and courts; journeyings to London
and elsewhere on corporation business; dealings with central government;
additional duties as justice of the peace for the mayor and immediate past
mayor. Moreover, an alderman was often called upon to dip into his own
pocket either to provide a loan in support of municipal revenue or to bear any
loss upon his mayoral account until such time as he could be reimbursed.
There is little evidence that these men did not carry out their duties conscien-
tiously, and those who failed to do so — whether by failure to attend meetings,
like Alderman William Rance, or by improper use of their power, like Alderman Edward Seabrooke, who was convicted of illegally making freemen
during his mayoralty of 1701/02 and refusing to hand over the civic plate —
were dismissed.[68]

The routine conduct of civic administration, including the holding of
courts, the collection of rents and the maintenance of corporate property, was
unaffected by the political upheavals of 1650-1700. But the underlying tensions
occasioned by national events are evident from the mayors' accounts. Owing
to the paucity of records there is little of this kind of information for the
Restoration period but such anxieties are clearly apparent in the aftermath of
the surrender of the borough charter in 1684, a time when political and religious loyalties were tested. A few aldermen, notably Thomas Eccleston and
John Selioke, were zealous in the Tory cause. Three others of dissenting or
Whig sympathies, including Thomas Hayward, were ousted from office

although later restored. The majority probably bowed to the prevailing wind, something which must have happened on a number of occasions in the course of the half century. Men who held high office under the Interregnum, for instance, continued to do so after the Restoration. The normal pattern for the choice of mayor whereby the unsuccessful candidate of the two put forward could be certain of being nominated first and chosen in the following year, and the normal cycle whereby an alderman might expect to be re-elected to the chair about every ten years or so, was broken only at the elections of 1685 and 1686 when the candidates for mayor were non-resident aldermen named in James II's charter. Nevertheless, towards the close of the century a change in the personnel of the aldermanic body was becoming apparent. Families such as the Oxtons, the Cowleys and the News who had served through two or more generations were beginning to disappear from the scene and the mayors of 1690-1700 include seven new names, the majority of whom appear to have had Tory sympathies.

NOTES AND REFERENCES

1   The dates given in Gibbs 1890 for the Edward VI and Charles I charters are incorrect.
2   Constitutions 1633, art. 47; 1667, art. 48. In the case of a principal burgess/alder-man, the son need not have been born after the father's admission to freedom (ibid., art. 16, 17). The Constitutions set out many rules and procedures governing municipal administration and were to be read aloud in the common hall of the borough at least twice a year (ibid., art. 32, 34). There were only minor variations between the two sets, plus a very few additional articles in 1667.
3   Of 31 recorded admissions in the 1650s £5 was paid outright by only two men, William Rance and William Rugge, both future mayors. Of 42 admissions in the 1690s the full fee was paid in 18 cases.
4   For example City 290,12 Sept.1694, 26 Aug.1696; City 299,14 Sept., 12 Oct.1698, 7 Aug.1700
5   For example, City 290, 22 Aug., 20 Sept. 1693; City 299, 11 May 1698
6   There were still four companies in 1663/4 (City 293). The change was not brought about by the charter of 1664 which makes no mention of the companies, but more probably under the new constitutions. The trades linked with each company are listed in the Constitutions, 1633, article 30 and 1667, article 32.
7   Howe 1988, appendix II, transcribing HCRO Gorhambury MSS 557
8   HCRO MSS 9243
9   Tittler 1991, p.99
10 Constitutions 1667, article 1. The corresponding article in 1633 has "all the house-holders or the most part of them"
11 City 290, 28 Dec 1685, 13 Jan 1686
12 City 290, 28 Oct 1691
13 City 290, 27 May 1691
14 City 299, 26 Jan, 30 Mar 1698

15 A petition presented at the monthly court on 4 Sept 1587 (City 312) alleged that the office dated from the time of incorporation.

16 City 313

17 VCH Vol.2, pp.478, 481

18 City 313

19 Particulars of such a covenant agreed 4 Sept 1587 were entered in the Court Book (City 312). The agreement between the corporation and bailiffs must be presumed to have continued on much the same lines.

20 City 313

21 From the mayors' accounts supplemented by the Abbey parish poor rate book (City 311)

22 City 290, 6 June 1694; City 313, 29 Sept 1695

23 Gibbs 1890, pp.295–7

24 William Foxwist, the recorder, gave the venison in 1654/5 and Thomas Pope Blount, MP, in 1678/9 (Mayors' accounts).

25 City 313

26 In the register of apprenticeship enrolments 1697-1732 (City 287) the indentures are subscribed as enrolled "by me, Edmund Ayleward chamberlain".

27 Any such salaries are recorded in the Mayors' accounts.

28 He was sometimes formally designated "counterkeeper and under gaoler", i.e. under gaoler in that he acted for the mayor and burgesses to whom a gaol had been granted by the charter of 1553. The mayor's account of 1650/1 includes disbursements by the mayor for work at the house of correction and making new beds. In 1678/9 the entry of the wages for the keeper of the house of correction is marked "not to be allowed" and is not found again. The date coincides with that of an elaborate scheme, embodied in an agreement of 27 Aug 1680, for a house of correction and workhouse for the three parishes which seems to have come to nought owing to the new master having run away with the money raised to buy materials and tools. (City 115)

29 City 299

30 Miller 1985, p.66

31 Henning 1983, Vol.1, pp.669-70; Vol.2, pp.371–2, 448

32 A copy of the instrument of surrender was entered in the Court Book (City 313).

33 Luttrell 1857, 4 March 1685. Professor Ronald Hutton kindly commented on the implication of the words.

34 Howe 1988, App. II

35 DNB; City 290

36 Howe 1988, pp.36–7

37 City 313

38 City 290

39 Henning 1983, Vol.2, p.68

40 HALS MS 9243

41 Steele 1910, Vol.1, p.490

42 Gibbs 1890, pp.115-6

43 City 757-9

44 City 736

45 Clockhouse deeds, City 656–669. City 669, 14 June 1676, is the only lease extant within the period 1650–1700.

46 The rents are recorded in the mayors' accounts. Such leases as survive are cited in the following notes.

47 City 703, 706

48 City 755

49 City 739, 742

50 City 696, 699

51 City 763

52 City 710

53 City 706-9

54 VCH Vol.2, p.512. From 1673/4 to 1682/3 a short account relating to this property is appended to the mayor's general account. For a lease of 1691, City 756

55 VCH Vol.2, p.512. From 1677/8 onwards an account of the Lathbury charity is appended to the mayor's general account.

56 There were exceptions. Of a surplus of £10 0s 6d on the account for 1664/5 £10 was given to Edward Carter, rector of the Abbey church, with which to pay his first fruits, and of £20 1s 5d on the account for 1679/80 £20 was advanced towards the costs of the brief for the repair of the Abbey church. The repayment of this last sum, out of collections on the brief, appears among the mayor's receipts in 1682/3.

57 City 174–183 (1650/1–1659/60), City 184 (1664/5), City 185–191 (1673/4–1679/80), City 192–195 (1681/2–1684/5), City 196–197 (1687/8–1688/9), City 198 (1690/1), City 200 (1692/3), City 201 (1694/5), City 202–205 (1696/7–1699/1700)

58 City 199 (1691/2)

59 Henderson 1912, p.130. The statement that the charter was revoked in 1652 (Corbett 1997, p.62) is false.

60 Gibbs 1890, p.71

61 In the seventeenth century the mace is described as silver and not silver gilt as now.

62 City 293

63 Mayor's account 194

64 Mayor's account 195; City 290, 26 August 1685

65 City 290

66 City 960; City 290, 19 May, 14 July 1686

67 City 290

68 City 313; Gibbs 1890, pp.99–103

4

THE PARISH AND THE POOR

THE FORMAL CONSTITUTION of the borough and the powers exercised by its officers are not the whole story of town government. After the mayor and burgesses and their various officers, the parish officials played a great part in the smooth running of the town. Their roles and the extent to which they fulfilled their obligations can be illustrated from St Peter's and St Alban's (or Abbey) parishes. Unless otherwise stated, the principal source has been the Churchwardens' Accounts of St Peter's, distinguished as 'Borough' and 'Country'.[1] Those of St Michael's and St Stephen's were not examined in detail.

THE VESTRY

Parish affairs were formally the responsibility of the vestry, 'the parishioners in vestry assembled', although its members, as such, were not parish officers. To the medieval responsibilities of the parish, Tudor and subsequent legislation added a greater liability for the conduct of civil affairs that were to be administered by the vestry. In practice, it was restricted to the property-owners or occupiers of rented property who paid church and poor law rates and, although female occupiers of such dwellings in St Peter's parish are known, none signed the vestry minutes. Of the 148 parishioners who signed (or marked) the vestry minutes in our period, twenty-one do not appear on any of the lists of those assessed for rates of some sort although some of them are known to be men owning or renting property. The rents can be calculated from various assessments and, from the names of those signing the vestry minutes, it is apparent that payment of an annual rent of as little as £1 a year was a sufficient claim to vestry membership.

Officers were appointed annually in Easter week with the exception, between 1670 and 1693, of the surveyors, who were appointed in December, usually on the twenty-sixth of the month. Extraordinary meetings, sometimes two in a year, amounted to thirty-eight over the fifty-year span. The number of signatures on each occasion varied from four to twenty (with a median figure of nine) and, since these were from a ratepaying population of about 150, it appears that the parish was in the hands of a small proportion of the whole. Whether St Peter's was a 'select vestry' (i.e. membership by co-option) or an 'open' one, which all ratepayers could attend (but which, in St Peter's, few did), is uncertain, since the basis of its recruitment is unknown. An entry for 26 August 1670 illustrates the point. At a previous vestry meeting the churchwardens were ordered to take workmen to examine the structural defects of the church 'and give publique notice and report to the parishioners' on the repairs needed and the probable cost, which they did on two Sundays, reporting that 'no small sume of money was requisite'; and in order that no-one liable to pay should have cause to complain of lack of notice of a meeting where they could vote on what should be done they announced on those Sundays that a vestry would be held 'this day by nine of the clock in the forenoon desireing the parishioners and all the holders of land … to meet here' to decide on the repairs and the rate to be levied.

This is the only recorded vestry which a considerable number of the parishioners might be expected to attend although, by inference, there were other such vestries. The record of this meeting states that "We the parishioners … whose names are subscribed being the major part of the parishioners convened …" but yet it was signed by only eight members, the vicar (John Rechford), two churchwardens (Philip Tarboxe and Thomas Marston), the lord of the manor (Robert Robotham) and four prominent citizens (Dr Arris, James Rudston, Edward Seabrooke and John Smith). Presumably the words 'major part' were intended in a social rather than a numerical sense, so that the fewness of the signatories does not necessarily mean that they alone were present.

The vestry took on a wide range of responsibilities. Apart from ordering the levying of rates it appointed the parochial officers, that is to say the churchwardens, overseers of the poor, surveyors (of roads), sidesmen and auditors of accounts. Since these officers had to submit their audited accounts to be 'allowed' or for some items to be queried, the vestry in effect controlled all aspects of parish life, constituting a form of local government.

Appointments were recorded each year and the care with which due legal form was followed can be seen in the vestry proceedings of 4 November 1660. On that occasion it was stated that the three persons elected at Easter to be overseers of the poor had not been nominated within a month by the two Justices of the Peace as the statute of 43 Elizabeth required. The meeting went on to indemnify the overseers against any "Actions Suites and damages … in respect of their distrayning any parishoners" for not paying the poor rate assessment, and also promised to reimburse them for money paid out, provided they did their best to collect the rate. Presumably the vestry foresaw some ratepayers invoking the letter of the law to avoid paying. The tone of the record reflects the economic difficulties of the last years of the Commonwealth as well as doubts about recent administrative lapses and the consequent uncertain legality of the proceedings under a new regime.

THE CHURCHWARDENS

The diverse matters for which the vestry was responsible were attended to by several executive officers, chief of whom were the churchwardens. Churchwardens prior to the Reformation were primarily concerned with ecclesiastical matters, notably the maintenance of the nave and provision of whatever was required for the conduct of all religious ceremonies. They were commonly chosen from a rota of places of residence[2] but the basis of choice in St Peter's is uncertain because little is known about where parishioners lived. Of ninety-two churchwardens' names recorded in the period 1650-1700, only four have not been found in the rating assessments examined. So, although the office never carried a property qualification,[3] in practice, all were of sufficient means to pay at least a low rate.

Formally, the churchwardens had to ensure that parishioners attended church and brought their children for baptism, present them before the archdeacon for offences within the jurisdiction of the church courts and report any failure of duty on the part of the incumbent.[4] On the last point none of the parishes found anything amiss. Presentments in the archdeaconry court from the St Albans churches between 1671 and 1697 survive.[5] Good relations in St Michael's parish are attested by the report of 1679:

> Our minister is orthodox and of sober life and conversation and doth catechise when the children can come and expounds upon the church catechism all the year one part of the day. Our church is well filled though most parishioners have a long way to it and for all we know some may go to other churches nearer. Schools: we have none except some poor women that teach only a few ABCDarians.

Not surprisingly, the burdens of office occasionally led men to refuse to be churchwarden,[6] but there is little suggestion of that in St Peter's parish unless it be the occurrence, several times, of one name in two successive years. Perhaps it proved difficult to persuade a nominee to accept or was a way of helping the new office-holder. There is no indication of a vicar's warden, the only distinction being between the 'Town' and 'Country' churchwardens, sometimes two of each. Their duties fall into four groups relating to ecclesiastical observance and church attendance, upkeep of the church, poor relief and record-keeping.[7] In a period spanning the puritan dominance of the late 1650s, the church settlement of 1662 and the varying fortunes of Dissenters under the changing policies of Charles II and James II, the first group is the most interesting in a town notorious for its nonconformity.

PRESENTMENT ON RELIGIOUS GROUNDS

They follow a *pro forma* under various headings, many of which, being merely endorsed *omnia bene*, are uninformative, and despite the number of Dissenters, few are for non-attendance. Nor do many reports of misdemeanours, penances and the like appear in the registers of St Peter's, unlike those of many parishes elsewhere in the country.

The comparatively infrequent record of failure to attend church probably masks the absence of some Dissenters and the statement about attendance at St Michael's quoted above suggests a lack of enthusiasm for pursuing the matter. Some presentments were accompanied by sworn statements, like one in 1683 declaring that John Clarke was sick in London and "unable to go abroad without danger"; and in the same year John Cole, rector, certifies that Anne Smith, suffering from lameness, "lives neare three miles from church and also I am creditably informed that whilst she was able she was a constant observer of all Church orders and never frequented conventicles …". It was the frequenting of conventicles that upset the established church, and presentment on these grounds was sometimes followed by excommunication. The few such instances recorded appear to have been directed at prominent nonconformists like Joshua Lomax who in 1683, was described as a person "being disaffected to the doctrine and discipline of the Church of England and a depraver and evil speaker of the rites and ceremonies thereof", after which abuse came the real failing: "[you] have also made yourself an utter stranger to your parish church" — this, of a landed gentleman.

Failure to present for non-attendance underlies the sole record of a St Peter's parish officer failing in his duty. On 18 January 1684 William Nicholls, churchwarden, admitted that his return to the archdeacon's court "of those persons that do not frequent their parish church and had not received the Holy Sacrament" the previous Easter, had omitted Thomas Flindell and John Nicholls, and for this he made an abject apology.

Now Flindell and John Nicholls were highly regarded among Dissenters, who frequently called on them to appraise the goods of deceased persons, and their omission is so blatant as to imply strong sympathy for their religious opinions on William Nicholls's part. For such people the strongest penalty, that of excommunication, had no force, nor can it have had much for William Nicholls who himself was excommunicated in the following October for "continuity in not presenting disorders'. That was all the vicar and vestry could do short of dismissing him, and the fact that they chose not to go that far must be due either to his usefulness in office or, possibly, to unwillingness to stir up resentment among parishioners, not a few of whom must have shared his views; indeed, he served again in 1685.

UPKEEP OF THE CHURCH: THE FABRIC

Maintenance of the nave formed an important part of the vestry's responsibilities and the amounts of the church rate spent show the care the churchwardens took over this part of their duties, yet the accounts are often insufficiently precise to provide a picture of the repairs undertaken. As can be seen from Table 4.1, the proportion such outgoings formed of the total expenditure varied considerably from year to year, prompting the following comment by the auditors of the 1670 accounts:

> … we cannot allow that many of the particulars accounted for should be paied out of the church rents but desire that for the time to come a rate may be made for the extraordinaries and that the church rents be expended only for repairing the church and paying the quitrents and taxes imposed upon the lands and tenants of the church.

This does not seem to have made any difference, in subsequent accounts, to the extra payments, examples of which will be given later.

The work undertaken at St Peter's appears to have been confined to essential maintenance as defects appeared and is often described merely as 'work about' the church, steeple or wall. More informative are the materials detailed in the accounts. Purchases of sand, hair (8d a bushel), and, occasionally, dung indicate the need for re-plastering, the hair plaster being probably for internal use. Two loads of flints (1s 8d) are intended for the walls of either the churchyard or the church itself. The former was certainly of chequerwork (blocks of stone alternating with squares of flint) and the latter probably, prior to a ruthless Victorian restoration, so that the bricks purchased at 1s 3d for fifty may well have replaced decayed masonry blocks of soft Totternhoe stone; and both needed mortar for which lime was bought at 7d a bushel. The frequency of such purchases suggests that the outer skin of the walls was in need of serious repair. Boards for the carpenter often feature in the list of payments, being needed, probably, to replace decayed ones forming an inner cladding of the roof to which the outer one of lead was fastened and which the plumber was frequently called upon to repair. Some of the roof trouble may well have begun during the Civil War, when lead was needed for musket balls and old, thick plates were replaced by thinner ones. Laths bought periodically are likely to have been for the repair of ceilings put in some time after the Reformation and affected by damp caused by roof defects.

Constant "repairs to the North Yle" foreshadowed a greater need which came to a head in July 1670, when the churchwardens selected workmen to examine the church. They reported that "it was very ruinous … and that no small sume of money was requisite", whereupon it was ordered that a rate of

Table 4.1 Amounts spent on repairs (St Peter's) for selected years

Year	Repairs, etc			% of disbursements
	£	s	d	
1650/51	*39	6	6	85
1651/52	9	2	4	27
1652/53	5	1	5	20
	5	0	7	20 (for church house)
	29	11	8	99 (special assessment for almshouses)
1653/54	15	18	6	49
1654/55	9	5	6	29 (inc. £8 15s 1d for glass)
1656/57	8	14	8	37
	3	9	3	15 (for north aisle)
	3	3	1	15 (for vicarage house)
1657/58	1	12	4	20
1658/59	3	19	0	11
1659/60	12	4	3	20
1660/61	4	1	11	16
1665/66	5	1	5	32
1670/71	87	15	1	93 (special assessment for church repairs)
1675/76	2	14	4	15
1681/82	6	10	2	25
1685/86	12	10	7	33
1690/91	10	6	6	30
1695 & 1696	24	10	4	26
1700/01	6	17	4	22

* This figure includes a sum of £28 3s 10d to George Barnes, plumber,
with no indication as to where the work was done.

3d in the pound (based on rents) be levied and paid to the churchwardens within fourteen days of demand. Failure to pay, either by neglect or refusal, would cause the churchwardens "lawfully … to leavy the said sumes … by distress and sale of the goods of such person". In spite of the need for the money and the threat of penalties considerable difficulty was encountered in collecting it, for in the assessment of 1670/1 following the levy nearly all the ratepayers in the 'Town' assessment were recorded as in arrears and, to make up the shortfall, the churchwardens borrowed £35 from John Clark, mercer. Presumably, the rates were eventually collected and he was repaid, although the matter is not mentioned. These problems notwithstanding, in 1671 St Peter's was able to report to the archdeacon that 'whereas our parish church was formerly as much out of repair, now repaired and many things that were out now put into good order'.

Sizeable building works had always to be financed either by a special rate or borrowing. In 1651 three almshouses were ordered to be "newe built with chimneys" at a cost of £20 11s 8d and to meet the cost a special assessment was made and a rate levied. If these were the three Clark almshouses of 1605 the wording suggests that wooden chimney stacks were being replaced by brick, perhaps, in this instance, to reduce the danger of fire. A quite exceptional instance was the building, approved by the Vestry in 1661/2, of 'two Church Houses'. It is not clear why the parish needed houses costing almost £75 each, for at that price they were more than the almshouses appropriate to the deserving poor. However that may be, they cost Edmond How, as churchwarden, £149 6s 7d, in addition to the ordinary disbursements and as a result he was out of pocket by £100 7s 3d. It appears, though, by a later vestry minute (19 December 1662) that How and the other churchwardens had borrowed £100 from John Clarke to meet the debt, and only then did the vestry make arrangements to repay the money.

St Stephen's parish records lack the detailed payments underlying the confident report to the archdeaconry court in 1676, saying that the church was 'in very good repair [and] we have repaired all our almshouses'. On the other hand, the Abbey church in the same year, only five years before an appeal went out for funds, was "very much out of repair and the parish not able to repair it … as for furniture and ornaments all in good order"; not that this was news to the archdeacon, who was also the rector of the church.

UPKEEP OF THE CHURCH: THE BELLS

St Peter's church had a ring of several bells. Maintenance was expensive, every yearly account having disbursements for their upkeep (Table 4.2), and in 1699 the third, fourth, seventh and tenor bells were cast or recast.[8]

In considerable part these costs arose from the duty of the established church to celebrate official occasions of all kinds by extensive ringing, with consequent wear on the bells and especially on the bell ropes. A typical series of entries are those in the account for 1675 (Table 4.3). 'Shuting' (shooting) a rope was mending by splicing.

UPKEEP OF THE FITTINGS

As might be expected with a preaching ministry, the pulpit featured on several occasions. The pulpit cloth required mending over the years and was evidently of costly materials; "Damaske for lining the pulpit cushion and doeing it" cost £1 4s. Later, a vestry agreed that "whereas Mr Kentish hath been pleased to bestow a Pulpit Cloth and Cushion … [he] may have the disposall of the Old Cushion". A mat (8d) and an hour-glass (7d) were also provided for the pulpit. The communion cloth was mended in 1693 (2s) but by 1700 it was necessary to

**Table 4.2 Expenditure on the
Bells for selected years (St Peter's)**

	£	s	d
1650/51	1	15	1
1651/52	2	19	2
1654/55		15	10
1656/57	1	15	11
1657/58		13	10
1658/59	1	4	8
1659/60	3	1	1
1660/61		17	2
1665/66	1	8	10
1675/76	2	19	0
1681/82	1	0	2
1684/85	2	13	6
1690/91	1	18	10
1695/96		18	10
1700/01	3	3	6

Table 4.3 Amounts spent on bell maintenance, 1674–5

	s	d
Shuting a bell rope		2
A rope for the Great Bell	5	8
Mending a Bell wheele	4	6
A trorle for a Bell		4
Mending two Bell ropes		2
Two Bell ropes weighing 15 pounds and an halfe	10	4
Robert Siggens for mending a Bell Clapper	7	0
Peter Fuller for a Bell Roape at 8d per pound	6	10

buy a "Damask table cloth and napkin for the Communion Table, £1 13s 6d". Earlier, a pewter plate had cost 1s 3d but a "silver and gilt dish for gathering money for the poore at Communion" required £5 6s. No expenditure on communion vessels was needed; Duchess Dudley gave a covered bowl to St Peter's c.1667 and William Crosfield gave a large paten inscribed with his name to the Abbey in 1697.[9]

Allocation of pews fell to the churchwardens and, at St Peter's as elsewhere, they were linked to a particular house or farm[10]; for example, Lady Jennings's

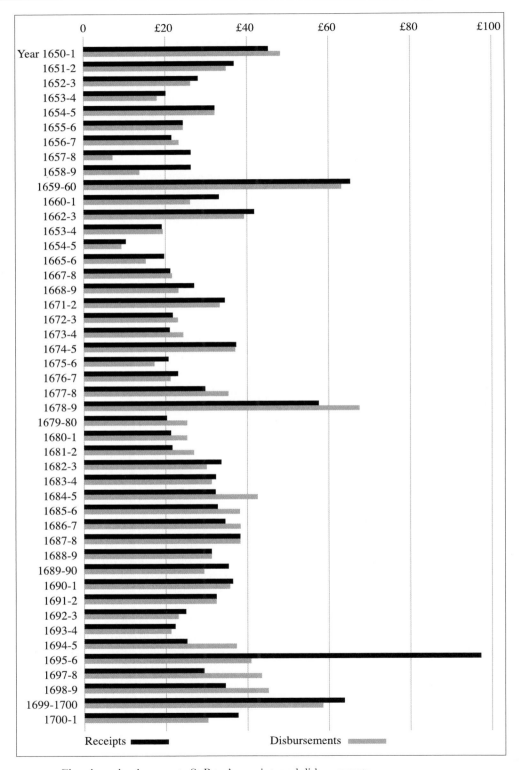

4.1 Churchwardens' accounts, St Peter's; receipts and disbursements.

seat and Mrs Markham's pew are repaired. In a society insistent upon status, individuals whose duties or possessions caused them to move between houses might arrange for suitable persons to take their place, as implied by a memorandum of 1666:

> Whereas Sr. Harry Coningsby of St Peters kt. hath heeretofore … given leave unto … Robert Robotham to use and sett in the seate … belonging to the saide Sr. Harry so long and untill the saide Sr: Harry shall redemand the same now the saide Robert Robotham is Willing & content that Dr Impie & his family shall use & sett in the saide seate untill it shall be redemanded as aforesd.

Another entry establishes the connection between land purchase and pew and incidentally throws some light on the pews of the period:

> Whereas Sir Samuel Grimston Knight Bt of Gorhambury in the parish of St Michaels … hath a seate in the parish church of St Peter … (where Mr Robert Sadleir of Sopwell formerly satt) with a chair or deske which stood in the midst of it (now reserved in the vestry house for him) belonging to him and hath heretofore at the request of John Rochford vic of the said church given the said John Rochford leave to use it himself or sett any that he shall please in the said seate so long until the said Sir Samuel shall redemand it Now the said John Rochford is willing and content that Edward Seabrooke Alderman with his family shall use and sett in one part of it (that nearest the pulpitt) and Mr William Hickeman and his family in the other part (it being now divided with a low partition to be removed at the aforesaid Sir Samuel pleasure) untill it shall be redemanded as above specified.

It must have been a large pew to be capable after division of accommodating two leading citizens and their families, in the sense of a conjugal family and its servants; and high-backed to prevent their inferiors from observing them. The servants no doubt sat on a fixed bench at the rear; where Sir Samuel's wife and children sat is uncertain, possibly on the high-backed chairs of the period; and Sir Samuel himself had a large freestanding chair with an integral prie-dieu which it would have been pointless to move out of the church: all very appropriate to the principal landholder of the parish.

The smooth running of the church services is exemplified by recurring entries in the accounts. Regular payments for bread and wine for communion ("5 quarters of Muskadell for the Sacrament, 8s 4d") suggest the sacrament was taken about five times a year. Wine was provided by the Selioke family for at least thirty years, bread by Zachariah Fitch and other bakers. For washing the church linen an annual payment of 13s 4d was made to the sexton.

THE KEEPING OF ACCOUNTS

The accounts run from Easter each year. The chief source of income was the rent from church property. Although the rent should have remained fairly constant it can be seen from a summary of the annual income that the actual amount of money received differed considerably from year to year (Fig. 4.1)[11] and must have been difficult to forecast. One potential source of income was the Church Rate. This had developed over the years from a series of special rates, although it had no statutory basis except for an ordinance of 1647 which was repealed at the Restoration. Only one rate was raised under this ordinance, in 1658, probably because, then and later, such special levies were unpopular and, as experience showed in 1670/1, hard to collect. The vestry minutes give no hint of disagreement over financial matters and in these as other matters the parish, throughout the period, carried on its affairs without dissent.

Given the many and varied types of expenditure throughout the year whose amounts could not be foreseen, it is remarkable that the churchwardens achieved such a reasonable balance at audit when they left office.

How the building in 1661/2 of 'two Church Houses' was financed has been mentioned earlier and the detail of the episode illustrates the burdens churchwardens were expected to bear. It seems that when the vestry first became aware of the size of How's debt on the almshouse account (£149 6s 7d), it was agreed that he should be repaid out of the church rents at the rate of £20 a year for seven years. The meeting which decided this was clearly seen to be an important one, for sixteen people signed the minutes. When the next meeting came round a month later How and his fellow wardens had borrowed £100 from John Clark to repay the debt, presumably because they did not have the ready money. Thereupon the vestry ordered the churchwardens to assign the leases of specified properties to Clark for the number of years required to settle the account. So, although the churchwarden carried out the orders of the vestry and signed legal documents on its behalf, he was ultimately responsible for the debts entailed until reimbursed by a vestry order. It is interesting that How, a well-to-do lathrender, appears not to have had money enough to hand to pay his debt, although he and his fellows must have had a fairly clear idea of the final costs when they made the contract. The date of the contract is not known but it is likely that building began in the spring immediately after signing, that is, at the beginning of How's term of office.

To assist them, the churchwardens had sidesmen, about whom little is recorded in St Albans. Ranking next in importance after the churchwardens were the overseers of the poor, whose work is described below, and surveyors of the roads who were appointed annually, although no reports of their activities are extant.

THE COSTS OF ESTABLISHMENT

Certain expenses arose directly from belonging to the Church of England by law established, as, for example, the requirement to display the royal arms and update them for successive sovereigns. Thus in 1650/1, "whight washing pt. of the armes out" – that is, C[arolus] R[ex], the crown above the coat and perhaps a date – cost 8d, but in 1659/60 Robert Babbs, painter, received £2 10s for "setting up the King's Arms in the church and writing the Commandments". Yet successive churchwardens at St Michael's thriftily avoided altering the arrangement, recorded about 1800: "over where the rood loft used to be, the ceiling is richly carved and painted and gilt, and here is placed the King's Arms dated CR 1660 on one side a Rose crowned, on the other a thistle…".[12] Contrast the care taken at the Gildhall in King's Lynn, where the royal arms were altered for each successive reign.[13] More serious was the cost of ringing the bells to commemorate national events, both annual ones and those such as thanksgivings for deliverance from the Rye House or other plots, when special prayers were decreed and service books had to be bought.

The accession of a ruler had necessarily to be marked by the ringing of bells and usually more. In 1658, when the Lord Protector was proclaimed, 3s were spent on "Faggotts for a bonfire the night", but 1660 was more expensive. First, the bells greeted Monck's arrival at St Albans during his march on London; then on 12 May 1660, when "the King was proclaimed" – four days after Parliament had done so – "3s 6d spent drink at the Boonfire" and again on 29 May to mark the King's birthday and entry into London. A more decorous note was struck by paying a Mr Hanslope £1 for three sermons in honour of the happy occasion. Following the Observance Day Act of 1660, the royal birthday was marked throughout our period, and from 1689 further ringing commemorated on April 11th the anniversary of the joint coronation of William and Mary. Mary's birthday was also celebrated.

Bell ringing formed part of the general rejoicing that accompanied military and naval victories, for example, in 1665 when a peal was rung "for the victory at sea" – the Duke of York's defeat of the Dutch in the Battle of Lowestoft. More heartfelt, perhaps, were celebrations marking the avoidance of the calamity everyone feared, the renewal of civil war, with the defeat of Monmouth's rebellion recorded in payment "to the Ringers for the victory in the West against the Rebells", while a few years later fears that the exiled James II might use Irish troops to regain the throne were lifted by the "good news from Iyorland" – the battle of the Boyne, 1690. Further rejoicings followed William III's return from Ireland, when he must have passed through St Albans; with yet more in 1692 for the French defeat at the sea battle of la Hogue, which ended James II's hopes of return.

Sometimes there was a purely local celebration, as in 1694: "To the ringers for My Lord Marlborough when he had the honnor to kiss His Majesty's hand .. 5s."; a recognition of a change in the fortunes of the most eminent parishioner.

Bells needed repair, ropes renewal, but the heaviest costs of ringing went in paying the ringers. A vestry order of 1679 confirmed a long-standing payment of five shillings a time, "excepting on the 5th of 9ber shall be allowed 6s 8d". The payment, about a shilling a time for each ringer, may be compared with a day's wage for an artisan of 1s 6d. Special events paid better, notably at the proclamation of Charles II as king, when they received £1.

Apart from the Burial Register, completed by the parish clerk, some details of burials can be found in the churchwardens' accounts. These range from prominent parishioners and their children to paupers, the former being distinguished usually by an entry reading "for breaking up the ground in the church". The 6s 8d charged for this, which appears as income, was inadequate to cover the long-term damage, here as elsewhere, to paving stones and through subsidence. During our period, forty-three people of all ages were mentioned in this context, with a further seven as "breaking the ground for … "(presumably in the church), and some references to mending of the pews and their floors may be connected with this practice.

Most parishioners were, of course, buried in the churchyard, and for a few, including some of those in receipt of a parish pension, the churchwardens of St Peter's bore the cost not only of shrouds but coffins (6s). A vestry in 1683 agreed that nobody buried at the parish charge should be buried "in Coffin & shroud both but only in a Coffin or shroud which of the two shall seeme most meete …". In most of the cases, though, where only the sexton's fees were recorded for the burial of (say) "two poore people", a coffin was provided for use during the service only; and the payment in 1690 to Robert Wood of 17s 6d for "coffins for the poore" suggests this was often the case.

The churchwardens' provision of as dignified a burial as the parishioners could be expected to pay for seems to be typical of a humane attitude to the poor who came into their care, untinged by distinctions between the deserving and undeserving that sometimes appear in charitable benefactions. Thanks to the generally tolerant attitudes of magistrates and incumbents in religious matters its officers were able to run the parish smoothly despite wide divergence of opinion among the parishioners, who, united in their common concerns to maintain the church, perform their Christian duties to the sick and poor and fulfil such secular obligations as establishment imposed.

THE POOR

Throughout Europe during the sixteenth century the poor were increasingly perceived as a problem, perhaps because of a rising population without compensating improvements in food production. In England this was exacerbated by the conversion of tracts of arable land to sheep ranches and the removal of the traditional charity of the church consequent upon its reformation. Thus in Tudor times, when the problem of the poor became pressing, the country became familiar with roaming bands of 'sturdy beggars' without work, money or hope, and it was against this background that in 1586 the mayor's court ordered the constables to search out "such newcomers ... as being poor may be chargeable" so that orders could be given to send them away.[14] Given so obvious an apparent danger to the stability of the country, a succession of laws was passed culminating in the Poor Law passed in the reign of Elizabeth,[15] which then continued basically unchanged for more than 200 years.

THE POOR LAW

Under this law, each parish became responsible for the relief of its resident paupers and had to raise money from its better-off parishioners to support the poorer. Originally, the idea was to use the money to set up work for them but such schemes always failed and, eventually, money was simply paid to the pauper, either on a regular basis or to meet exceptional needs. This law obviously provided a safety net for the poor but, with its parish basis, also acted against them.

Since parishioners provided the money for poor relief, it was in their interest to keep down the number of poor within the parish and this was achieved by refusing to allow outsiders to settle there if there seemed any possibility that they might require assistance at any time. Since legal settlement could be achieved by apprenticeship to a local inhabitant or by working for one of them for a certain length of time, there was little likelihood of work being offered to a travelling poor man. These conditions were reinforced by the Act of Settlement 1662, whereby a person who could not find work in his own parish was unable to go elsewhere to better his lot unless supplied by his parish with a certificate accepting responsibility for him. In fact, great efforts were made to move on persons who might become a charge on the parish and any local resident who gave them shelter was chided or even fined. In 1664/5 a tinker's wife died while staying at a St Albans alehouse and her husband decamped, leaving three children behind.[16] The Abbey parish paid for their keep temporarily but sent representatives to study the parish registers of Hillingdon (Middx.) and of Witney and Abingdon (Oxon.) to see if the children had been baptised at any of these places, seeking meanwhile to apprehend the missing father. Eventually, two of the children were sent to Witney, the third to Hillingdon and the father was taken. The whole exercise, admittedly an extreme example, had cost the ratepayers seven guineas (almost 5 per cent of the year's rate) but had protected the parish against an open-ended commitment to the upkeep of the children.

Many of the people forced to return to their place of last settlement will have been almost destitute and required some assistance on their journey to prevent them from starving. St Peter's churchwardens' accounts mention payments to people passing through: payments that were properly the responsibility of the overseers of the poor who, here, contrived to confine their disbursements to parishioners. Thus the churchwardens gave up to 12s total in some years, usually in the sum of 6d, to "a poore man", "a poore souldjer" or – the price of living in a thoroughfare town – "a man out of Irland" (several men and women from there). Two other kinds of payment were made, evidently to different categories of person because they are distinguished both from one another and from those to people described as poor. One is to men or women "with a pass" who may have been migrant workers with a definite destination; the other, to persons "with a letter of request" for assistance, was perhaps intended to help those thought specially deserving of help.

THE POOR RATE

In order to administer the system the vestrymen of each parish elected annually a number of 'overseers of the poor'. These were responsible for assessing those parishioners who were sufficiently wealthy to contribute to the poor rate, collecting it, and spending it as they considered fit, although the magistrates could, and occasionally did, order that a certain person should receive help. In general, the assessment was based on the notional annual rent of the premises occupied (the 'rack rent') but the Abbey parish was unusual in that the amount of goods owned was also estimated and the assessment made on the higher of the figures for rent and goods. A useful addition to the Abbey parish rates was the contribution from the bailiffs, whose 'farm' of the market tolls were considered equivalent to an annual rent of £40 and charged accordingly. A small amount of extra income was generated from fines for such offences as "swearing profanely", "travelling on the Lords day", "keeping an unlicensed alehouse" or "suffering their children to sport and play on the Lords day" (all mostly before 1663). If money was left at the end of the year it was added to the next year's income but, if the overseers overspent their collection, they had to find the extra money from their own purse (pockets not yet being common). They would eventually be repaid from the rate. For each year the two or three assessments made were recorded with the overseers' annual accounts, giving the amount collected from each assessed person and how the money had been spent. These accounts had to be approved by the magistrates but their accuracy is certainly not up to modern auditing standards.

The assessments and accounts provide the names of the heads of the richer households and some of the poorest persons in the parish but between the two were a good number of people of modest income who were hardly recorded. Some of these will appear in either the richer or poorer group as their fortunes fluctuate over time but the number never appearing in either category is totally unknown. However, a study of a number of Norfolk parishes during our period indicates that more than half of the households were excused from paying the poor rate and the proportion of households in Aldenham (Herts.) paying was estimated at a similar level.[7] In the Abbey parish, an average of 175 people were assessed to pay personal poor rate each year and this would suggest that the parish held a total population of at least 1,550 persons (but see below for more population estimates). The two overseers of the Abbey parish collected between £100 (1655/6) and £166 (1659/60), with expenditure rising sharply between these years and then falling slowly to £136 in 1671/2. Not surprisingly, every year it was necessary to obtain a warrant to force some people to pay.

SUPPORT OF THE POOR

The largest part of the poor rate went to providing some people with a regular income – a pension in today's terminology but 'in the collection' then. To come into collection it was apparently necessary to be quite destitute and a few persons had their possessions sold by the overseers before they were entitled to relief, the proceeds being added to the poor rate receipts. In 1658/9 it was ordered that in the Abbey parish "no poor person shall be received into the collection for the poor hereafter but such as shall be allowed of by the Justices at their monthly meetings", this being, probably, a reaction to the sharply increasing cost of the poor rate. The amount of money received monthly varied widely from individual to individual and, without knowledge of the circumstances, it is not possible to see why this was so. Perhaps some people could earn a little money themselves or perhaps it was simply that some people's needs were greater – more children, for example. And since the poor rate was local and distributed face-to-face rather than through a bureaucracy holding consistency as a prime virtue, each case could be decided on its own perceived merits.

The relief received by a collectioner in the Abbey parish generally lay between two and twelve shillings per month. At the time it was believed that

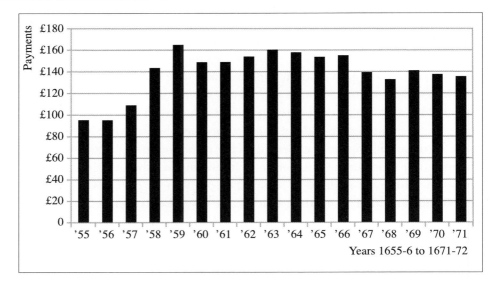

4.2 Payments to the poor, Abbey parish.

one or two shillings a week were necessary for a single person to have a basic but adequate living and so the lower amounts of relief must have been considered as a supplement to other means of subsistence, rather than the sole income. In the hard winter of 1647/8, an eighty-year-old Norfolk man, lame and almost blind, petitioned that he "is allowed but six pence by the week from the towne wherein he inhabiteth, which in these hard times of dearth and scarcitye will not buy any considerable or competent maintenance for his reliefe" and was granted one shilling per week by the justices.[18]

The variation in the amount paid to each collectioner hides the reason for the rapid increase in the total poor rate of the Abbey parish between 1655/6 and 1659/60 (Fig. 4.2) but further study shows two major causes. Between these years the number of people in collection, starting at thirty-two, increased by more than 20 per cent, and the average amount paid increased by 60 per cent; most of the increase in both measures occurred between 1657/8 and 1658/9. The increase in the average payment was not achieved by increasing all payments by a fixed proportion, as some of the amounts stayed constant while others increased in differing degree. For instance, Clare Woolhead (or Wooley) received £6 10s every year from 1656 to 1672: while between 1657/8 and 1658/9 Elizabeth Silke's collection rose from 18s to 26s; Robert Fisher's from £2 12s to £2 16s 6d and William Johnson's from £2 12s to £3 16s. Study of a number of economic indicators did not explain the complete pattern of changes in the level of the collection between 1655/6 and 1671/2 but an index reflecting the price of consumables[19] was a statistically significant indicator of this level[20]. In other words, the overseers had to distribute more money because the price of food, etc. had risen, forcing more people onto the parish and making their basic keep more expensive. It should be noted that the harvest of 1654 was outstandingly good and the following two harvests above average, leading to unusually low prices of bread in the mid-1650s.[21]

That part of the poor rate left after the collectioners were paid was mainly spent on a range of one-off problems, except for the one per cent or so devoted to administration. Many small sums were given to a person "in his time of need" or "in her extremity of sickness". The sick might also receive medical attention, medicine (physick) or nursing and be looked after by someone (sometimes themselves in collection) paid from the poor rate. Orphaned children (and sick adults) would be lodged with a named person who was paid for their keep, and they might well receive new clothing from the parish occasionally. Some people had part, or all, of their funeral expenses paid by the parish. In the Abbey parish at the most generous, overseers would provide a winding sheet, pall bearers, the fees of the minister, parish clerk and sexton, the knell (passing bell) and bread and beer for the funeral meal (wood was also supplied in one case – perhaps for a fire at the meal?).

Quite large sums were spent in order to apprentice poor children (both boys and girls) and, often, to equip them with a full set of clothes at this time. Many were indentured to local masters but several went to London tradesmen. These apprenticeships were clearly intended to reduce the amount of poor rate required but they also had the effect of establishing the youngsters in a trade, which might be more than they could have expected if their parents had been somewhat richer. The standard indentures laid down strict conditions for the apprentice's conduct and not all could meet the requirements. Francis Abott "a poore child of [St Peter's] parish" had been apprenticed to Samuel Hall, weaver, by the vestry but, when he "behaved himself towards his Master contrary to the law", Samuel returned the £3 10s that he had received from the parish, together with the boy's wearing apparel. The Abbey parish also spent money giving some education to a few of the poor children of the parish.

ONE POOR BOY

As an example of what the record reveals of a period of a person's life, we may take the case of "Goldstone's boy" in the Abbey parish. This is the only name by which we know him – his given name never being mentioned – and his surname is spelt indifferently as "Gouldston", "Goldston" or "Gouldstone". His parents do not appear in the records, although he might have been the son of the Elizabeth Golestone buried at the Abbey on 11 August 1648. If she died bearing him (death in childbirth being common enough at this period), he would have been about seven years old when he appears in the first surviving poor law record of 1655/6. Certainly he is unlikely to have been much older than ten at this time. His birth is not registered at the Abbey and no mention of the family occurs there, except for the burial already referred to.

Thus the first that we know of Goldstone's boy was in 1655/6 when he was kept for fourteen weeks by Goodwife Burton, who received 18s for this, and for thirty-eight weeks by Widow Burton for £2 11s 4d, so he was kept for the full fifty-two weeks at a cost of £3 9s 4d or 1s 4d per week. It is probable, but not certain, that the Goodwife and the Widow are the same person, both names recurring throughout the boy's record. Besides his keep, in 1655/6 the boy received a suit of clothes costing 13s 3d and Widow Burton was given 6s 8d to buy him a pair of shoes and for mending his clothes. In 1656/7 he was kept by Widow Burton for the whole year, again at a cost of £3 9s 4d, and was given shoes, stockings, breeches and shirts costing 13s. The following year he was kept for nine months by Goodwife Burton and no other keep is mentioned. However, in 1659/60 Widow Burton received 17s 4d for arrears of the boy's keep and this is the year that must be involved, since the year's keep then again totals £3 9s 4d. Alongside the entry for his keep is the annotation "to be put apprentice" and this may have been the reason that 1657/8 saw a number of entries for new clothing for the boy – it being normal for a youngster being put out apprentice to be provided with a decent, if limited, wardrobe. William Gibson was paid 2s 2d for a pair of shoes, John Clarke supplied 5 ells of lock-rome (a linen fabric) to make 3 shirts (6s 7d) and "2 yards and a half and half a quarter" of cloth to make a suit at 3s 4d per yard (8s 9d). Also bought for the suit were 3 dozen buttons at 3d and a penny-worth of thread, another penny-worth of hooks, one pair of skins (1s 6d) and filleting (3d). Finally, William Merriden was paid 3s for making-up the suit. Holland was bought for making his bands[22] (9d) and Goodwife Burton was paid 1s for making these bands, the three shirts and for buttoning and mending his old clothes. Thus, his clothes cost £1 6s 5d on top of the £3 9s 4d for his keep but, in spite of the outlay, he was not apprenticed at this time.

The following year (1658/9), Widow Burton again kept the boy for the whole year, receiving the standard recompense. This entry was once again marked "to be put apprentice" and more clothing supplied. Widow Burton was given 1s 2d for a pair of stockings for him and 2s 6d for a doublet, while John Ayleward was paid 4s for a pair of shoes and for mending them several times. Robert New provided a suit of clothes for 10s 2d and two shirts for 4s 8d. Again the boy was not made an apprentice and appears once more in the poor law records for 1659/60.

This year was considered to have thirteen months and Widow Burton was paid £3 18s for his keep. Strangely, this is not equivalent to the standard amount for his year's keep (5s 4d a month) but the slightly more generous figure of 6s per month. The only other relevant entry for the year was the 10s paid to Widow Burton for keeping Goldstone's and Sparling's boys while they were sick with smallpox. At last in 1660/1 the overseers' plans for apprenticing Goldstone's boy came to fruition when Abraham Darvoll, probably a carpenter, was given a premium of £4 4s for taking him and the fee of 2s 6d for making his indentures and for enrolling him into the borough records were paid. Widow Burton was paid £1 2s 6d for his keep that year, which suggests that it was about August 1660 when his apprenticeship started and he went to live in his master's house. If things proceeded smoothly, the boy would have finished his service, probably, in 1667 but the apprenticeship records for this period are lost and he disappears from view in 1660. Over the five years for which Goldstone's boy appears in the surviving records he had cost the parish an average of £5 3s 6d per year.

RENT PAYMENTS

A type of aid that fell between the regular collection and one-off relief was the payment of rent, most commonly for the whole year and perhaps for several successive years, but it might be for a shorter period. Some cases receiving limited relief may have been due to changes in the person's circumstances during the year but others may indicate that the person had died. The number of people in Abbey parish receiving rent aid was four in a typical year but varied from six in 1662/3 to none in 1657/8 and 1669/70. The annual rent of a house between the years 1657/8 to 1671/2 was usually between 20s and 26s 8d, although rents of between 10s and 18s are recorded between 1661/2 and 1663/4. There is no evidence that these lower rents were for a whole house but equally no evidence that they were not. Judging from the rate assessments, possession of a house with a rentable value of £2 per annum qualified a person to pay into the poor rate and so the house must have been a quite good one. Where a particular house can be traced for a number of years the rent paid does not change. In one case, the apparently high rent of 30s per annum was first paid in 1667/8 and was still being paid in 1671/2 when records cease. The reason for such rent support is not usually stated but is no doubt temporary or permanent incapacity, as in the instance mentioned in the following section.

SICKNESS

Sickness was a frequent reason for receiving relief but the records are rarely specific about the type of illness, which is hardly surprising, given their original function. We know that "the town was visited" in 1665 (and Sopwell Lane is specifically mentioned); this phrase and the date indicate that this was the plague then raging in London. Some payments may have been for people whose whole family was quarantined under virtual house-arrest because one of its members was sick and, unable to earn a living, would need support. Small-pox was recorded in 1657/8, 1659/60 and 1671/2, each outbreak reported as affecting only a few of the poor. In 1669/70 a family of four and a single woman (with a female companion) had their expenses paid from the poor rate when they went to London to be touched for the King's Evil. This disease was scrofula (tuberculosis of the lymph gland in the neck) which was alleged to be cured by the king's touch, a duty King Charles II was assiduous in performing (dealing with more than 90,000 cases during his reign[23]), so that in St Peter's parish 9d was spent on "a Frame for the Kings Order touching the time for his healing the Evil". Several people needed treatment for sores and poor Robert Fisher had his sore leg dressed for five years; this treatment stopped a couple of years before his death so perhaps it was eventually successful. There is mention of other sore legs and a sore neck as well as lameness and a broken leg. Three women received assistance when they lay in and blood-letting was provided for two people. One poor boy was taken to a hospital but this was not situated in St Albans. The vestry of St Peters paid the rent of John Wethered's wife, "he being a lunatick person in the hospital of Bethlam [Bedlam] at the charge of the parish". Of the 'medical' men mentioned in the accounts, Francis Wilkes was capable of dressing and "looking to" a sore leg and Mr Napkin was a barber-surgeon. Mr Edward Nicholas was an apothecary and both Robert Rumford and Richard Ruth junior were on one occasion described as a "chirugeon". Incidentally, a Richard Ruth (possibly the father) was a sexton at the parish church, so the Ruths stood to gain both from the medical treatment and its failure.

ALMSHOUSES AND CHARITIES

It is known that, throughout the country, many charities disappeared over the years, through neglect or cupidity. In St Albans there is no comprehensive list-ing before the late nineteenth century and this account is based on this list of the survivors, as reported in the Victoria County History.[24]

Besides the official charity of the poor rate, other sources of relief were available to the pauper of which the most prized was probably a place in an almshouse, offering secure shelter and perhaps a little money each week. In the Abbey parish were three cottages in Spicer Street, endowed by Richard Rayn-shaw in 1569 and supported by the rent of his house called the Vine, which were to house "honest poor persons". In St Peter's John Clarke in 1605 built, on land conveyed to him by the corporation, almshouses for six poor persons

(Fig. 1.5), three each from St Peter's and the Abbey; and in 1627 Roger Pemberton set up almshouses for six poor widows, two from St Peter's, two from St
Stephen's, one from St Michael's and one from Shenley. Another group of
almshouses may have existed in St Peter's, those mentioned earlier in which
chimneys were built, although these may have been Clarke's. St Albans thus
had almshouses for only fifteen of its poor and old people, and competition for
a place was probably keen.

Few people endowed almshouses; more bequeathed property or money to
provide money or food for the poor. Property producing a rent income was the
commoner. Of this type was Thomas Lathbury's bequest to the corporation in
1579 of two tenements, one near the Clock Tower and the other in Dagnall
Lane, the rents to be for the proper use and behoof of the people of St Albans.
The Cross Keys Charity set up in 1618 provided a rent income from the inn of
that name, half of it to repair the Abbey church and the remainder to be
divided equally between the poor of the Abbey and St Peters parish. In 1636
Thomas Gawen's lands were to provide £40 each year to twenty of the poorest
people in the Abbey parish; and in 1642 Bray Norris's went to provide 45
shillings to forty-five poor widows of the Abbey parish and 5 shillings for five St
Michaels widows. Two charities distributed both money and food. In the
Abbey parish Robert Skelton's rents in 1628 provided 30 groats (1 groat = 4d)
to thirty poor widows every Whitsuntide and twenty-six penny loaves every
Sunday for the poor, while in St Peter's Sir Richard Coxe's Charity (1632), aug-
mented by Robert Robotham in 1670, gave money to the poor and also sixteen
wheaten penny loaves every Sunday. Only Mrs Anne Goldsmith chose, in 1641,
to leave money rather than rents: £20 per annum for the benefit of the poor,
money which was added to the receipts of the Abbey parish poor rate. While
the poor certainly got this money, the real beneficiaries may have been the
ratepayers who had a rather lower assessment because of it.

The linking of charity to the recipients' deserts, often explicit, was given
more specific form by Joshua Lomax's bequest of 1686 which provided for two
sermons at the Abbey on the Sunday after Easter Day, when a sum of £1 was
to be distributed to twenty poor housekeepers of the parish who attended these
services; and equivalent arrangements were made for St Peter's, St Michael's
and St Stephen's.

It is difficult to judge the extent to which these charitable donations allevi-
ated the lot of the poor. If nobody benefited twice, a minimum of 162 persons
might receive help, to which must be added an uncertain number aided by less
precisely worded bequests such as Lomax's – perhaps 200 all told. Whatever
the deficiencies of distribution, the donors' intentions suggest the scale of the
problem, although if the numbers of poor were as great as appears likely,
many went without help.

So the surviving records give us the names of the poorest people in St Albans and some details of the lowest points of their life, but in no case has it been possible to establish even a skeleton biography of a poor person. We know that some of them were children but whether the others were old or young is unknown. Many of those in collection were widows but whether after decades of marriage or only years is obscure. Even their full names may have been lost or rendered virtually untraceable; we find "Emmanuel Babb's widow", "Goodwife North", "Robert Tompson's son's children" and so on. There is also the large number of poor people who did not benefit from the poor rates; for these we have no names and do not even know how many of them there were. They had their lives, with the good and bad times, perhaps established families which still exist today, but no trace of that life has come down to us in the poor law records.

NOTES AND REFERENCES

1 HALS, D/P 93/5/2
2 Tate 1983, p.33
3 Tate 1983, p.31
4 HALS, ASA 17 1/3; D/Ex 977 File 7
5 Tate 1983, p.87
6 Richardson 1986, p.36
7 Richardson 1986, p.36
8 Dodds 1994, p.188
9 VCH, Vol.2, p.510
10 Gough 1701, pp.77ff.
11 The accounts for 1659/60 have page(s) missing, for 1667/7 are incomplete and for 1668–70 two years data are combined in a single set of records.
12 HALS, Oldfield drawings. Vol.8, No. 407
13 Parker 1971, p.145
14 Gibbs 1890, p.14
15 43 Eliz cap.2 (1601)
16 City 311 (assessments and accounts for the Abbey parish for 1655/6 to 1671/2)
17 Wales 1984 (Norfolk); Brown 1984 (Aldenham)
18 Norfolk CRO C/S3/38
19 Phelps Brown and Hopkins 1956
20 For the statistically inclined, the regression coefficient (r) was 0.795 with 15 degrees of freedom, giving $P<0.001$.
21 Hoskins 1968
22 A collar or ruff work round the neck (OED)
23 Tate 1969, p.158
24 VCH, Vol 2, pp.512–15

5

ESTABLISHMENT VERSUS DISSENT:
FROM CONVENTICLE TO CHAPEL

MODERN ST ALBANS with the cathedral and its culture conveys at first sight a sense of a town steeped in the traditions of the established Church of England, yet in fact the townspeople have shown from the fifteenth century onwards an independence in religious matters which manifested itself strongly in the seventeenth century.

FROM REFORMATION TO RESTORATION

In the wake of the dissolution of the great monastery in May 1553 the town purchased from the crown, together with its first charter, the abbey church and the right to present to the living, so that henceforth the inhabitants – not just the parishioners of the Abbey parish – were in the unusual situation of having, through their governing oligarchy, some influence in appointing a rector. The acquisition of the advowson came just in time; two months later the accession of Mary might have blocked it. The decision to run their own parish church was encouraged by Sir Nicholas and Lady Ann Bacon who had purchased the local seat of Gorhambury in 1550. Sir Nicholas was one of the foremost early puritans, responsible for the appointment of the ministers of St Michael's and also influential in the affairs of the Abbey. Already by 1583 local opinion was in conflict with the established church, as John Aylmer, bishop of London, complained to the archdeacon of St Albans, saying that "many ministers within your Archdeaconry do seldom wear the surplice, and some of them little or nothing observe the Book of Common Prayer".[1] In 1637, in a letter from Archbishop Laud to Charles I, comes the first mention of Kensworth (then in Hertfordshire); "there and in some other places", he writes, "many go from their own churches by troupes after other ministers which is a common fault in the Southern part of that diocese [Lincoln] where the people are said to be very giddy in matters of Religion";[2] and St Albans was one of the 'other places'.

Laud's information on Kensworth refers to an early Baptist congregation and a meeting place for Quakers. Nonconformity was strong right across the Chilterns and St Albans linked into this. A register of members of the Baptist church at Kensworth dated 1675 has survived which lists 217 men and women from twelve widely scattered places, among them twenty seven members from St Albans.[3]

The support offered by St Albans to parliament during the Civil War implies a strong puritan element in a number of prominent families. They included the prosperous ironmonger, William Hickman, who acted as treasurer for wartime and post-war committees. From wills, strong association has been found between the Hickmans and another puritan family, the Pembertons (see p.174). John Marsh, a local innholder, was commander of the parliamentary infantry. Alban Cox who owned a large house and estate just outside the town was colonel in the local militia. Links with families of similar propensity are found in the marriage of two of his sons to daughters of well-known dissenting families, the Cowleys and the Aylewards.

The rise of puritan and anti-establishment feeling generally culminated in the severe regime imposed during the rule of the major-generals in 1655–56, when attempts were made to enforce the legislation of the Long Parliament in matters or morality. This highly unpopular intrusion of government into people's personal lives was an important factor, in conjunction with the economic crisis of the late 1650s, in the collapse of the Commonwealth, strengthening feeling against the whole body of opinion opposed to an Episcopal established church and weakening the support of those broadly sympathetic to it. Some such shift must account for the ease with which the leading inhabitants adapted to the restoration of the established church, whilst the willingness thereafter of people of different shades of opinion to collaborate in parochial administration shows that the divisions of the 1640s and 50s were by then less sharp and were diminished by uniting against those sects seen as a threat to the social order.

AFTER THE RESTORATION

The continuity in the town corporation from the Commonwealth to the Restoration ensured some restraint in appointing a new rector to the Abbey following the Act of Uniformity in 1662; too zealous a royalist church would have disturbed many of the burgesses and run contrary to the long-standing puritan sentiment of the parish. The minister at the Abbey since 1657 had been Nathaniel Partridge (Fig. 5.1). He refused to conform to the Act and moved to London where he addressed a meeting in The Blazing Star, Old Street, which was broken up by soldiers and his maid wounded. By 1676 he was in Newgate Prison.[4] In the Abbey, Edward Carter followed Partridge, a learned man who had been educated at Peterhouse Cambridge. He was devoted to his library and very much the deeply read man of religion sought

5.1 Nathaniel Partridge, minister of the Abbey parish prior to the Restoration.

after by churchmen and dissenters alike. His views appear to have been moderate despite his college years under the successive masterships of two zealous Laudians, Matthew Wren and John Cosin.[5]

At St Peter's the patron, who was none other than Matthew Wren, lately reinstated to the see of Ely and keen to 'purge his diocese of dissenters',[6] might have been expected to put in a man after his own heart; instead he appointed the son of a previous incumbent. Presumably John Rechford's views had moved somewhat beyond those of his father, who had already come closer to establishment than some of his parishioners wished, and his marriage to Anne Aldersley, granddaughter of Robert Robotham, the lord of the manor of Newland Squillers, improved his status. But Robert later had his will witnessed by two nonconformists and several leading parishioners had dissenting sympathies, so local opinion was far different from Wren's. Possibly the social status of these people swayed the bishop's decision but it would be interesting to know just what considerations caused him to respect parochial sentiment to this extent.

At St Michael's Abraham Spencer, ejected in 1642, returned as of right, the churchwardens buying him a surplice for £2 15s. His death a year later appears to have been foreseen by Joshua Lomax, who in that very year purchased three fourths of the rectory[7] to enable him to install the young John Cole who eventually succeeded Carter at the Abbey and may have been of similar temper. The only clue we have is that he was married to a member of a well-known dissenting family. His man in place (for fifty years, as it turned out), in 1664 Lomax sold his share of the rectory to Sir Harbottle Grimston.

All these changes fell far short of restoring a Laudian church. Even the £1 paid to Francis Hanslape, schoolmaster of St Albans School from 1657 to 1661, by St Peter's churchwardens for "three sermons one whereof was preached upon the thanksgiving day for the King's most happy return to England"[8] may not be quite the hint of triumphalism it appears, for Hanslape was almost certainly a puritan lecturer. His disappearance after Michaelmas 1661 was no doubt due to Restoration persecution.

On the whole, the people of St Albans, diverse though they were in their religious views, lived and worked in relative harmony in parish and corporation. Though one incident, recorded by an outraged anonymous writer, describes the most brutal manifestation of feeling against those who rejected the established church came from an ex-Cavalier major, Edward Crosby. It appears that when Elizabeth Tyrill died, her husband, relatives and members of a nonconformist congregation wanted their own preacher, the ejected minister, William Haworth, to conduct the funeral.[9] On Sunday, 4 May 1662, the group met in "a place called either the Cloyster or the Schoolwhite" – probably the passage that formerly ran across the antechapel of the Abbey. After a hymn, a Bible reading and prayers, Haworth was standing on a bench preaching when Crosby rushed in, calling them rogues and rebels and cried "Come down; Why prate you there? Come down, or I will pull you down". To which Haworth replied, "If you have any authority to command me down, I will obey it, but otherwise not". As they were pushing through the mourners towards Haworth one John Townsend said "Noble Major, pray make no disturbance, consider it is the Sabbath day", whereupon Crosby turned in anger and shot him dead. The constable, ignoring calls to arrest Crosby, instead arrested Haworth.

The hearing about the death took place at the Old Bailey on 11 and 12 August 1662 before Sir Harbottle Grimston as Master of the Rolls (Fig. 5.2); but his personal interest in St Albans may account for constable Ratcliffe's being made foreman of the jury rather than being tried as an accessory to the wilful murder with which Crosby was charged. Ratcliffe notwithstanding, the jury found Crosby guilty; so, asking the jury "Will you hang a man upon supposition? Can you prove that he came with a full intent to kill him?", Grimston bade them withdraw and reconsider. This time the jury brought in a verdict of *Ignoramus* and Major Edward Crosby, a man of the gentry and doubtless acquainted with Grimston, was freed. The murder, compounded by rigging of the jury and an unjust verdict reached under pressure, illustrates a darker side of Restoration England only revealed by chance references like this. As the anonymous author of the tract complained bitterly "… what quietness can the minds of Englishmen have … when the Justices … (and no less than a quondam speaker of parliament) shall countenance the Murderer? … Or … when such shall be made Foreman of the Jury to try Capital Offence, who were themselves accessory to the Crimes committed?"

For all his partisanship in the Crosby case, Sir Harbottle Grimston chose not to harry local dissenters too diligently, mindful, perhaps, that he himself had once attacked archbishop Laud in strong terms.[10] Among the Gorhambury papers is one dated 1665 headed "Evidence against the Phanatique Party" which names a number of leading inhabitants who had acted against the King during the Commonwealth.[11] The 'Phanatique Party' was a derogatory term often used for religious dissenters and not an organised group as 'party' suggests. One such person was the lawyer, soon to be a country gentleman, Joshua Lomax, who was "… always accounted a ffreind & assistant to ye Phanatique partie & when an unlawfull assembly was in St Albans hee did in open Courte affirme itt to bee Lawfull and pleaded what hee coude for ye meinteyninge of itt. And when a sermon was preached by Sir Harbotle Grimstons Chaplaine for the submission to and owninge of Government and Governors hee reported itt to bee a railinge sermon". Similarly of Thomas Cowley the elder, then in his third mayoralty, complaint is made that "Hee

Harding del.

Clamp

SⁱᵗHAREBOTTLE GRIMSTON.

from an Original Picture by SⁱᵗP.Lely in the Collection of

Lord Verulam.

Pubᵈ 1 May 1796 by E.W.Harding Pall Mall.

5.2 Sir Harbottle Grimston, sometime Master of the Rolls

hath allwayes joined with and shewed what countenance hee coulde to ye Phanatique partie and hath upheld one Partridge [see above] to preach which was never called to ye Ministrie & hath denyed others". There is nothing to show that Grimston ever acted on these allegations, which have the ring of truth about them, nor anything to show why he chose not to act, but he may have preferred to leave well alone in a town not keen to inquire who did what under the previous regime, and when action against a member of a gentry class more fearful of social upheaval than of religious difference would have been divisive.

OCCASIONAL CONFORMITY AND SOCIAL STABILITY

So as to maintain continuity and stability in the various aspects of town life, those inhabitants with leanings towards the nonconformist congregations, may have attended their parish churches once or twice a year, enough to keep themselves out of trouble. Regular attendance at church was required by law and non-attenders could be presented to the church courts and punishments meted out as thought appropriate. Occasional conformity is clear in the case of Joshua Lomax, reputedly of the 'Phanatique Party' in 1665 and indicted in 1683 for not attending communion but he must have received communion in the year he was sheriff, and for someone of his opinions to do so in order to hold the highest office in the county implies widespread tolerance of the practice among his peers. Such occasional communion for the sake of office was generally deplored by the higher clergy but must have been accepted by incumbents at parish level, by the archdeacon of St Albans and perhaps tacitly even by two successive bishops of London, who can hardly have been totally unaware of such happenings in their diocese.

St Peter's parish shows how close were the links between dissenters and Anglicans. Dr Thomas Arris, an eminent and wealthy physician, officiated at St Peter's church during the Commonwealth as auditor of the accounts, churchwarden or signatory to the appointment of officers. His political and religious opinions at that period are uncertain but become clear after the king's return when, as member of parliament for the borough from 1661 to 1679 and as a member of the committee for the Conventicles Bill in 1669, he was very much an establishment man. Nevertheless his signature continues to appear in the churchwardens' records on the same page as that of William Ayleward whose own house, according to the return to the archbishop in that very year 1669, was used as a conventicle.[12] Someone as visible in town and parish life as Arris cannot conceivably have been ignorant of a prominent yeoman's religious leanings, yet he suppressed his dislike of dissenting tendencies for fear, presumably, of disrupting his own parish and town; and no doubt he made exceptions to a general condemnation for people whose probity he recognised. Many lesser men certainly did the same; a vengeful Crosby was rare.

There are other examples of integration between dissenters and Anglicans. For instance, Edmund Howe, lathrender and property owner, married the sister of John Clarke in 1637. Clarke, a draper and well-known Quaker who, in 1672, gave land for a new meeting house and was later buried in the Quaker burial ground. Howe's son signed the trust deeds for the meeting house. Despite the strong inference that he was a dissenter, Edmund Howe senior was a churchwarden at St Peter's in 1645, 1646 and 1662 and signed the accounts regularly between 1647 and 1663. It is interesting to note that the churchwardens of St Peter's borrowed from John Clarke substantial sums of money in 1661/62 and 1670.[13]

Ellen Passmore's will written in 1672 illustrates well the passive association between the various shades of religious opinion in post-restoration St Albans society. Her choice of preamble is unique in the St Albans wills and suggests strong religious views. Ellen's first three legatees are the ministers of the three parish churches aforementioned, Edward Carter, John Rechford and John Cole – a bequest reminiscent of Lomax's later provision for sermons (see Chapter 10). She then lists twelve female friends, three of whom have surnames associated with dissent, and it is suspected that her 'friends' are members of a congregation. She names dissenters, Thomas Heywood and William Pembroke, as legatees and Joshua Lomax acts as her witness, although he might have been engaged in his capacity as a lawyer notwithstanding his religious beliefs.

Establishment and dissent may not have been quite so close in the Abbey parish, yet the absence of obvious friction between them shows that Edward Carter was not actively hostile to nonconformity. In both parishes, which between them covered most of the borough, the patron of the living played a crucial part in enabling a town with a history of resistance to church and crown to come to terms with a regime with which the likes of Edward Crosby felt comfortable.

PERSECUTION AND TOLERATION

In 1669 Charles II's need to persuade parliament to grant him more money compelled him reluctantly to approve the Conventicle Act of 1670 which introduced very severe penalties for clandestine meetings. To what extent this affected St Albans is uncertain as the Quarter Sessions records for St Albans have not survived but since the composition of the bench largely reflected that of the corporation, caution and even inactivity may have prevailed.

In 1672 Charles sought to buttress an unpopular foreign policy with harmony at home by issuing under his prerogative the Declaration of Indulgence, which suspended penal laws and allowed public worship to all protestant dissenters who requested and were issued with licences. Such a licence was granted to Robert Pemberton for meetings to be held at his house (see Chapter 10) and the Quakers of St Albans, many of them released from prison, built a meeting house.[14] The respite was short-lived; in the following year parliament enforced withdrawal of the Declaration in 1673 although locally justices of the peace were prevailed upon not to recall the licences for conventicles until parliament's insistence on their doing so in 1675.

Thereafter dissenters continued to meet secretly and in relative calm among generally tolerant neighbours until politics again became entangled with religion. The Whigs and their dissenter allies in the parliament of 1679 – in which the St Albans members were John Gape, an Anglican, and Thomas Pope Blount, "a good Commonwealth man"[15] – provoked a crisis by endeavouring to exclude James, Duke of York, from the succession as a Roman Catholic. After much parliamentary turbulence came the 1680 election in which John Gape was replaced by Sir Samuel Grimston, a Whig, and the ensuing royal campaign to replace the strengthened exclusionist Whigs from the boroughs by loyalists coincided with renewed attacks on dissenters. The atmosphere of the time is caught twice, first in his diary (14 February 1682) by the minister, Oliver Heywood: "I visited my son John … [who] … had a wonderful deliverence in preaching for Mr Grew in his meeting place at St Albans. Three Justices, three Constables, four Soldiers came to the foregate. Not going in, went to the back gates. That while people slipped out at fore-door, he was let down at a trap door, so they all escaped";[16] and secondly in the dry mayoral record of payment in 1683 for a lantern for the guards required to break open the barricaded door of the Quaker meeting house.[17]

These events mark the end of active persecution of dissenters. Toleration towards them was James II's tactic to gain acceptance for his fellow Roman Catholics and Tory control of the corporation ensured his wishes were followed. William III's accession brought a more positive toleration, so that from then until the end of the century quietness reigned.

NONCONFORMIST GROUPS IN 1669 AND AFTER

Quakers without exception were prepared to stand by their beliefs and take the consequences. Their steadfastness makes them the first clearly discernible and coherent of the nonconformist sects with a strong meeting emerging in St Albans soon after the Restoration. In 1669 an informant providing information to the archbishop about the various groups of dissenters reckoned that sixty Quakers met "at a hyred house for ye purpose, every Sunday and Wednesday" who had two teachers, one, John Crook who lived at Hertford, being a national figure, the other, Elizabeth Humble, being related to Stephen Humble, the draper, a man of some substance in the town.[18] Most local adherents were tradesmen, among them Richard Mote, carpenter, Thomas Richardson, tanner, Edmund How, lathrender, John Clarke, draper, John Mitchell, maltster and Richard Reading, husbandman. Quakers' conspicuous witness to their beliefs by dress and bearing was matched by their being the first nonconformists to build a meeting house.

According to the archbishop's informant, 100 Presbyterians – probably the congregation who left the Abbey when Nathaniel Partridge was ejected – were meeting "at Mrs Bachelor's". One of their three teachers, all ejected clergymen, was Dr Edmund Staunton, former president of Corpus Christi college, Oxford, who was then, following successive restrictions on nonconformist ministers, living privately at Bovingdon and preaching secretly in St Albans and nearby towns. Defiance in the face of persecution is conveyed by his remark that "seeing I cannot preach in a church to many, I will preach in a chamber to a few".[19] Jonathan Grew, living the same life, dared to shelter in St Albans under the protection of a prosperous ironmonger's widow, Catherine Hickman, who, more importantly, was a baronet's daughter.

Details were also provided about a third, more shadowy group of undefined doctrinal allegiance who met "at the house of William Aylward, yeoman, called New House"(Fig.1.5). Its numbers are not stated but the preachers and teachers were Mr Lownes, nonconformist Minister, Scott, an Oliverian Captain, Thomas Flindell, cooper and Thomas Heywood, shopkeeper. The interesting information is added that "a great number of sufficient men" met at this venue, a dark hint of potential subversion suggesting that the informant had in mind successors to the 'Phanatique party'. It appears that William Ayleward himself moved to London where he married in St Mary the Virgin, Aldermanbury, a strongly puritan City parish where his sister Hannah also married; and two of his children were married in St James, Duke Place, which had a similar reputation.

A final St Albans group, so secretive that its meetings were said to be "not constant to time or place", was described as 'Anabaptist' and fifty in number, its teachers being "One Heyward, a woodman; One Heyward, of Hertford, a scholler". Ironically, the survival of their church book means that the names of its members are now better known than those of most other sects. The uncertainty about its meetings may be because its primary centre was the Baptist stronghold of Kensworth, for not until 1714 was the house of Thomas Heyward in St Peter's parish certified for worship "by Protestant dissenters commonly called Baptists".[20]

HOW MANY NONCONFORMISTS?

In the absence of a local return to the Compton census of nonconformists in 1676, an attempt has been made during the process of family reconstruction, using the many sources listed in Chapter 6, to identify dissenters. As explained in that chapter, whilst assembling the families, an estimate has been made of the population size on the 31 December 1675 and this is approximately 3,500 of whom 1,192 were adult males. Of these, 263 men have been identified as dissenters – some 22 per cent. This figure compares with a suggested national average of 4-5 per cent.[21] A check on the number for St Albans can be made from other sources. According to Urwick the Congregationalists and Presbyterians of St Albans united in the building of a meeting house also in Dagnall Lane in 1696 which was designed to seat 400. The number of St Albans members of the Baptist church at Kensworth was 27 in 1675. To these totals might be added the 60 Quakers reported to the Archbishop in 1669, making a total of 487 members which is not too distant from the 263 identified in the current project, doubled so as to include women.

Dissenters have been identified by using a number of different sources and these have been approached cautiously, as will appear from the following examples. The church book of the Baptist congregation has already been mentioned though not all members have been identified because no Christian names were given. Those presented for not attending communion in 1683 have been included but only with supporting evidence. The extant list of voters in the 1690 election has proved to be a very valuable source.[22] The candidates were George Churchill, Tory, Samuel Grimston, Whig, and Joshua Lomax, Whig and dissenter. Each elector had two votes. It has been assumed that the fifty-one electors who voted for Lomax and did not cast their second vote were committed dissenters. A further 158 voted for Lomax, using their second votes for either Grimston (74) or Churchill (84). These electors have only been counted as nonconformists when additional evidence tends to confirm they were so.

More positively, wills and inventories reveal the recurrent association of certain names with known dissenters. Where the deceased used two well-known dissenters as witnesses or appraisers it has been assumed that he or she was also a dissenter and nearly always another source or a marriage link supports the assumption. Similarly with legatees, Catherine Hickman, a woman of strong dissenting principles and sister of the notable Cambridge divine, Benjamin Whichcote, included Jonathan Grew (first minister of the Presbyterian meeting house), Robert Pemberton (licensed to hold meetings 1672) and Abraham Cowley (presented for not attending communion 1683) among her legatees; and her witnesses were the first two of these, together with William

Pembroke (presented for not attending communion in 1683 and trustee of the Presbyterian chapel in 1690) and Thomas Clarke, of the Quaker family. Robert Robotham, lord of the manor of Newland Squillers, who might be assumed to be an establishment figure, used the nonconformists William Pembroke and Robert Swenston as witnesses. Can he be regarded as a nonconformist?

The extent of nonconformity in St Albans can largely be attributed to its geographical position. Good communication was crucial to the spread of dissent. Our research has shown that there was a close relationship between St Albans and the City of London. Publications written by dissenters might easily have been circulated. Merchants travelling through could spread the message of dissent. It has been noted also that the migration pattern into the town comes from the north-west. This route traversed the Chilterns where, as we have seen, there was a strong dissenting community which may also be a factor.

It may be that numbers rose following the Toleration Act of 1688 and the subsequent building of a place for nonconformist worship that was entirely separate from the parish church would be likely to draw away those who previously had feared an illegal division and those beliefs could be accommodated within a tolerant establishment. Certainly seating capacity of 400 implies confidence in the future, a confidence that was reflected socially among the names of the trustees signing the foundation deed. The times of persecution were remote when one of them was the landed gentleman and former sheriff, Joshua Lomax, whose fellow signatories included the locally important William Pembroke and Jabez Earle who was at the beginning of a long and distinguished career as a Presbyterian minister.[23] The other less eminent trustees, John Eeles, Matthew Iremonger, Thomas Jones, William Grunwin, William Smith, William Knowlton and Ralph Thrale, were solid citizens and fairly prosperous tradesmen who were no doubt more representative of the congregation.

WHO WERE THE DISSENTERS?

Of the 375 men who have been identified over the whole period of the present study, it has been possible to determine the occupation of 229 and these have been analysed in Table 5.1:

The proportions of trades to one another roughly follow the pattern for the town overall. It is possible that more labourers than have been identified were nonconformist but documentary evidence is sparse for this social group. However, in the 1690 election 58 per cent of labourers who voted, voted for Joshua Lomax.

Table 5.1 The occupational distribution of identified nonconformists in relation to the known occupations of the whole town[24].

| Occupation | Dissenters | | Whole town | |
	Number	Percentage	Number	Percentage
Agriculture	44	19.2	160	15.1
Food and drink	67	29.3	344	32.5
Transport	6	2.6	55	5.2
Building	23	10.0	100	9.5
Leather	25	10.9	104	9.8
Textiles	27	11.8	97	9.2
Household goods	14	6.1	52	5.0
Professions	14	6.1	73	7.0
Labourers	7	3.1	61	5.8
Others	2	0.9	11	1.0
Total	229	100.0	1057	100.0

In relation to their total numbers lawyers seem to be particularly well represented among dissenters. It would have been in their interest for the law to be removed from the authority of the church. The most prominent lawyer in St Albans was Joshua Lomax who rose professionally and socially to become sheriff. Another lawyer, John Charnocke, was, like Lomax, reputedly of the 'Phanatique Party' and their contemporary William Foxwist, recorder to the corporation during the whole Commonwealth period, evinced strong puritan leanings in his will. John Leigh, like the younger Joshua Lomax, was a signatory to the Presbyterian chapel deeds and, judging by the preambles to the wills written by him, it is clear that he was employed by nonconformist testators because of his religious convictions. A fifth, Nathaniel Bull, was presented for non-communion in 1683, and Jonathan Grew, who, during the period of persecution, preached to secretly convened congregations, and became the first minister at Dagnall Lane in 1697.

One of the more important gentry families with nonconformist connections were the Pembertons, though not all of them remained of that mind. The Roger Pemberton who founded almshouses in St Peter's Street in 1627 was a puritan and his younger son Ralph, a Cromwellian major, followed his father's thinking. So did his elder son, John, two of whose daughters married nonconformists and whose own son, Robert, grandson of Roger, requested a licence for permission to use his house for a congregational meeting in 1672. But Francis, son of the Cromwellian major and a Cambridge-educated lawyer, adapted easily to the Restoration; he married a baronet's daughter, was knighted in 1675 and in 1681 became chief justice of the King's Bench.

Mention has already been made of Thomas Cowley, thrice mayor and latterly alderman under Charles II's charter; his religious views can be judged from his support of Nathaniel Partridge, the unbending minister ejected from the Abbey. Cowley's son, Thomas, who, like his father, served the corporation for forty-odd years and was thrice mayor, was presented for non-attendance at church in 1683 and in 1689 was a trustee of the Presbyterian meeting house in Dagnall Lane. In contrast, the elder Thomas's younger son, Abraham, played no part in civic life despite being a wealthy draper; probably his religious convictions were less flexible than his father's and brother's, as appears from his failure to take communion in 1683 and his friendship, attested in her will, with Catherine Hickman.

THE ESTABLISHED CHURCH

Despite long-standing efforts to achieve a better-educated clergy and puritan demands for a preaching ministry, it is hard to imagine a man of Edward Carter's standing becoming rector of the Abbey parish without the impetus for change provided, in the established church as in other aspects of society, by the short-lived puritan ascendancy. Carter became archdeacon of St Albans and received some recognition in being made a prebendary of St Paul's; an appointment which in itself suggests he was not only learned but reasonably effective as a preacher. John Evelyn's description of his library as "a very good collection, especially divinity" implies religious learning as deep as that of his predecessor, John Geree, and of greater width.[25] He had no successor in that regard.

As part of James II's attempts to conciliate other denominations while improving the position of his co-religionists he endeavoured to augment the income of the rector, by then John Cole. This he did by a charter dated 25 February 1687 and exercised through trustees, whereby the advowson of either St Mary Northchurch or Great Munden rectories should pass to the rector of St Albans, whichever first became vacant,[26] but James's abandonment of his throne caused it to lapse before taking effect.

If the appointments patrons made to the town's four livings prevented religious discord at a critical time, the conciliatory attitude of the bishops of London made it easy for the local clergy to show their sympathy towards dissenters. Whereas the first post-Restoration bishop, Gilbert Sheldon, strongly favoured uniformity, his successor in 1663, Humphrey Henchman, did not give "trouble or disturbance" to nonconformists; and, following him in 1675, Henry Compton "sought to minimise the differences between himself and the nonconformists".[27] William Rechford could not have put it better.

NOTES AND REFERENCES

1   Urwick 1884, p.90
2   Haines 1987, citing Lambeth MSS 943
3   HALS Off. Acc. 1162
4   DNB, Nathaniel Partridge
5   Walker 1912, p.52
6   DNB, Matthew Wren
7   VCH, Vol.1, n.223
8   HALS 5/2 443 (St Peter's Churchwardens' Accounts)
9   Anon 1662. A postscript to a letter of 6 May 1662 from John Humfrey to Richard
    Baxter confirms what happened; Baxter Letters IV, fo.219 (In Dr William's
    Library).
10 DNB, Harbottle Grimston
11 HALS VIIIB/67
12 Turner 1911, p.92
13 HALS 5/2 443
14 PRO SP44 38a
15 Beds. CRO FR24/18
16 Henning 1983, Pope Blount
17 Urwick 1884, p.187
18 Turner 1911, p.92
19 DNB, Edmund Staunton
20 HALS ASA 21/1
21 Spufford 1995, pp.21–2
22 HALS 9243
23 DNB, Jabez Earle
24 Howe 2002, p.21
25 Evelyn Diary, Vol.4, p.589
26 Chauncy 1826, Vol.2, p.300
27 DNB Henchman; Compton

6

POPULATION, FAMILY

RECONSTRUCTION AND

OCCUPATIONAL STRUCTURE

H OW MANY PEOPLE lived in St Albans? It is the kind of question that has long exercised the minds of those in authority and already in the reign of Charles II the earliest statisticians were anxious that the number of people should not outstrip the resources available to feed them. In 1695 the Lancaster Herald, Gregory King, estimated the total population of England and Wales as 5.183 million and he reckoned that rather more people were decreasing the wealth of the kingdom than were increasing it.[1] At a local level the authorities were well aware of the discontents arising from unemployment and the danger to health posed by overcrowding; numbers mattered to them, especially the parish officers seeking to exclude from their alms those such as vagrants or women with illegitimate children who could be shown to be some-one else's proper concern.

This is the background that makes it important to know how many people lived in St Albans and whether the population was static or changing. Unless we have some idea of the total numbers there is a risk that entire sections of the community, particularly the poor who rarely appear in the records, will be overlooked. How the old, the sick and the destitute were cared for has been described above, but did some or many fall outside the safety net? Did a Caroline town swarm with children? At what age did they marry and how large were their families? These are some of the questions addressed in the research and this chapter.

THE COMPUTER DATABASE

The better to address them, a computer database was set up in order to create a directory of people whose names occur in St Albans records of the second half of the seventeenth century, with the intention, initially, of linking scattered items of information to individuals and using as many sources as possible. They comprise parish registers, marriage licences, wills, probate

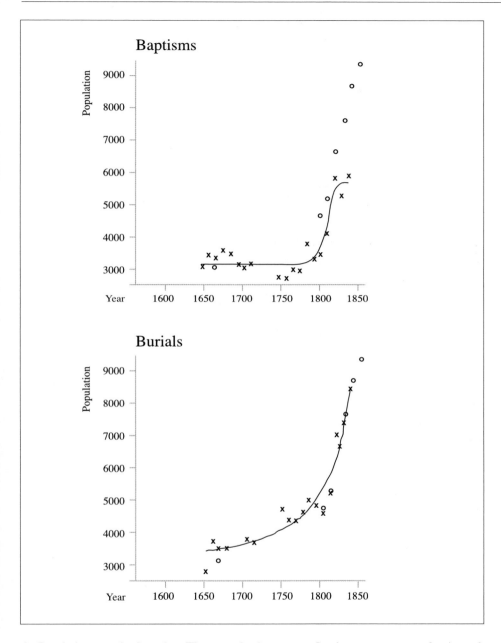

6.1 Population growth 1650–1850. These graphs show curves fitted to 9-year means of estimated populations. Also shown are the 9-year means using the symbol 'x' and populations derived in other ways using the symbol 'o'.

inventories, corporation records, title deeds, hearth tax assessments, protestation oath returns of 1642 and 1696, a list of voters in the election of 1689, archdeacons' records, manorial records and church memorials. Unfortunately, neither the Compton census of religious affiliation in 1676 nor returns of the Marriage Duty Act of 1695 exist for St Albans and some of the registers of the Abbey parish were lost in a fire.

The basic process of entering data produced so many names that it became obvious many must be duplicates. It transpired that the best way to remove duplicates was family reconstitution, a procedure which leads to the production of (often partial) family trees for a sizeable proportion of the town's population. This ultimately refined the data and consequently the calculations based on it. The data can also be ameliorated by the use of statistical techniques described elsewhere.[2] These make it possible to distinguish differences (between parishes say) which are probably due to random fluctuation from those where this is unlikely. The latter, which indicate that there is (probably) a genuine divergence between the results (e.g. counts or averages), will be referred to as *significant* differences.

ESTIMATES OF TOTAL POPULATION[3]

Population estimates can be obtained from the returns for the Hearth Tax which listed heads of households who were liable for, or exempt from, taxes on each hearth. It is believed that the 1663 returns give the most accurate count of the taxpayers but the 1673 returns are the most reliable for those in the Abbey parish exempted from the tax. Since there was no great change in the population between these two dates, they have been combined to give a figure of 54 per cent of households paying the tax. This means that the number of taxpayers must be increased by a factor of 100/54 (= 1.85) to allow for those exempt when calculating the total number of households. It has been assumed that there were on average 4.3 persons per household[4] and so the total population is estimated as:

$$4.3 \times P \times 1.85 \qquad \text{if P households paid tax.}$$

Estimates of total population for each year can also be obtained using counts from the registers of baptisms and burials. The calculation is:

$$\text{Total population} = \text{Annual count} \times 1000 \ / \ \text{crude rate}$$

Birth and death rates will vary with age but crude rates are calculated over all ages. The rates used are for England and Wales as a whole[5] which may not be appropriate for St Albans. Such population estimates varied widely from year to year and an average taken over nine years was considered to be more reliable. Counts of baptisms and burials between 1644 and 1836 (corrected for possible under-registration) were used to obtain a long-term pattern of population growth and the graphs are shown in Fig. 6.1. Also plotted are the estimates obtained from the Hearth Tax returns and counts from censuses conducted in the first half of the nineteenth century.

The fitted line for populations estimated from counts of baptisms runs fairly close to the estimate derived from the Hearth Tax returns and to the figures from the first two censuses of 1801 and 1811 but it tails off before the date of the third census (1821) and well before 1837 when civil registration was introduced. The curve derived from counts of burials does not run close to the Hearth Tax estimate but it fits very well with figures from the censuses of 1801, 1811, 1821, 1831, 1841 and probably 1851 and does not tail off. This implies that most people continued to use the parish churchyard for burials right up to 1837 and beyond but that many did not use it for baptisms which may have been performed in nonconformist chapels, private houses or not carried out at all. Here it should be remembered that, although marriages and baptisms could be celebrated elsewhere, the church had almost exclusive control of the burial grounds. Both curves indicate that the population stayed fairly static during the latter half of the seventeenth century and did not rise steeply until late in the eighteenth century.

To see how the estimates of population in the latter half of the seventeenth century fitted into the pattern of long term growth, the various estimates are compared in Table 6.1. The figures in the 'Estimated' columns for baptisms and burials are the averages of the population estimates for nine years centred on 1666. The figures in the 'Equation fit' row are calculated from the equations of the two fitted curves.

The estimates derived from counts of burials were slightly higher than those derived from counts of baptisms. The estimates derived from counts in the parish registers were higher than those derived from the Hearth Tax returns (8 per cent for baptisms and 12 per cent for burials) but perhaps this represents a fair measure of agreement considering the inadequacies of the data. It seems reasonable to suppose that the total population of the urban Abbey parish and the semi-urban St Michael's and St Peter's parishes in the latter half of the seventeenth century varied around 3,200.

Two of the most obvious factors affecting population size, immigration and emigration, have not so far been mentioned because they are ones for which it is most difficult to find adequate information, especially the latter. It is possible, though, to show from which parts of the country most immigrants came by listing all the personal names that are also place-names which occur in the fifty years covered by this study in whatever context (Fig.6.2). These are place-names that are either unique or, if the name occurs in more than one county, it can be assigned to a particular one with strong probability. The map does not show that all the people with locative surnames arrived in St Albans between 1650 and 1700, only the parts of England from which they or their forebears came.

Table 6.1 Estimates of population from hearth tax returns, baptisms and burials

Parish	Hearth tax	Estimated from:	
		baptisms	burials
Abbey	1585	1665	1871
St Michael's	536	575	808
St Peter's	945	1080	765
Total	3066	3320	3444
Equation fit	3182	3418	

Common names like Aston or Hockley are excluded except where, as with Eccleston, its inclusion in one county or another (Cheshire or Lancashire) would not affect the overall distribution. It is very clear how closely movement was tied to the road system even at a time when many must have migrated in stages, travelling on foot or by horse and thus theoretically were not bound to it. Newcomers came very largely from towns and villages served by the Chester road and its branches, with notable concentrations in Lancashire and the West Riding of Yorkshire, but an east-west road and its branches also drew a few people. Probably the chance of finding work, whether casual for those intent on a more distant destination, or permanent for those willing to settle where opportunity offered, was greater in thoroughfare towns with their day to day fluctuation of traffic.

A check can be made on this map by listing surnames that are new to St Albans between 1650 and 1700; they total 92, of which 21 are also place-names. Of the 21, 13 are from north-west England, four from places in east Hertfordshire or East Anglia, one from Gloucestershire and one from Berkshire via London (Antony Faringdon, who arrived via the Inns of Court). The correspondence between the two distribution patterns is close.

Nothing like this can be done for emigration which cannot be estimated beyond pointing to the obvious pull of London, a connection repeatedly mentioned in this book, while for some immigrant families life in St Albans may well have proved to be only a stage towards the capital. To attach meaningful numbers to these movements is impossible; only the impression remains that inward and outward movements were not very different when averaged over a half-century.

AGE STRUCTURE OF POPULATION

As has been described, population sizes can be estimated using simple counts taken from the parish registers. To study such matters as age structure, average age at marriage and family size the registers must be examined in more detail.

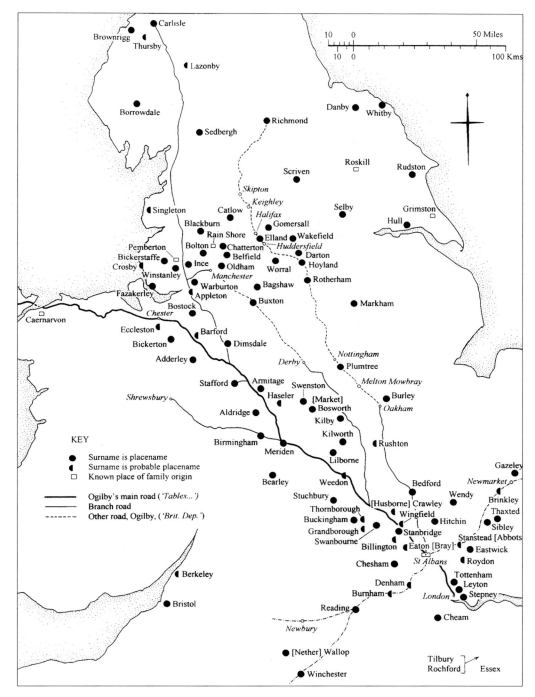

6.2 Map showing locative surnames appearing in St Albans records between 1650 and 1700.
The distribution shows the catchment area from which people came to live in the town over the
period c.1550-1700, not necessarily in a single move, and illustrates how closely migration was
bound by the transport system. Probable place-names are either such as Burnham, which is
more likely to be that in Buckinghamshire than those in Lincolnshire or Norfolk; or such as
Eccleston, which might be in Cheshire (as here) or in Lancashire and where the alternative
would not alter the distribution pattern. The map hints at the importance of transport services
connecting with those shown in Fig.7.1.

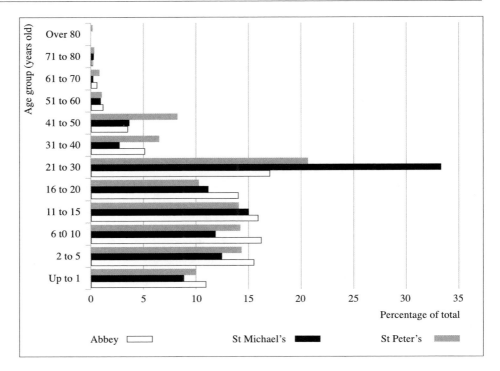

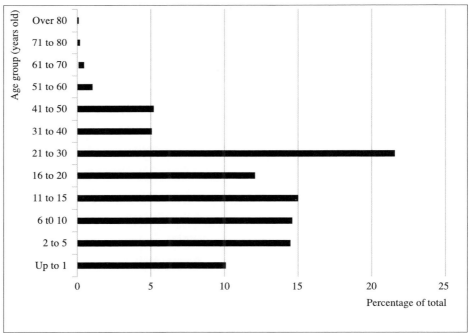

6.3 Age structure of the population, 1675; (a) each parish, (b) all three parishes.

This is relatively time-consuming and, as compared with about 300 years for counts, the more detailed information has been collected for shorter periods only. The period for St Peter's parish extended over eighty years but the periods for the Abbey parish (where registers were destroyed in a fire) and for St Michael's parish (where no records survive before 1644) were inadequate for estimating age structure from dates of baptism and burial alone. A date about halfway through the period was chosen (31 December 1675) and an attempt was made to estimate the numbers of people of different ages living at that date. Where dates of baptism and burial were known this presented no problem but, if they were not, other data such as dates of marriage and baptisms of children were used to arrive at an estimate of age. Fig. 6.3 contains diagrams showing the proportion of people in each age group for each parish and over all three parishes.

Because of the longer period of recording it was expected that the data from St Peter's parish would present the most reliable picture of age structure but there was a similar pattern for the other two parishes. Apparently, the majority of people were in their teens or twenties — much younger than is the case today.

THE FAMILY: MARRIAGE

To study age at marriage, dates of baptism and marriage must be known and both dates are known for only a few people (426). Table 6.2 shows how the counts of marriages in this small sample are apportioned.

Table 6.2 Number of marriages

Parish	Men	Women	Total
Abbey	74	82	156
St Michael's	45	67	112
St Peter's	69	89	158
Total	188	238	426

Table 6.3 Average age at marriage

Parish	Men	Women	Total
Abbey	24.7	23.8	24.2
St Michael's	26.5	22.7	24.5
St Peter's	25.9	24.0	24.9
Total	25.6	23.7	24.5

Table 6.4 Home parish of bride and groom

Parish		Abbey	St Michael's	St Peter's	Total
Same parish	Bride	529	259	756	1544
	Groom	532	247	756 1	535
Other parish	Bride	35	25	3	63
	Groom	38	67	4	109
Outside	Bride	92	50	10	152
St Albans	Groom	90	19	10	119
London	Bride	4	1	1	6
	Groom	0	2	0	2
Total	Marriages	660	335	770	1765

Dates of baptism are known for more women than men, perhaps because brides were more likely to marry in the parish where they were baptised than grooms.

The average age at marriage for men (25.6) was significantly higher than that for women (23.7). The average ages for the three parishes were not significantly different. These averages fall at the lower end of the scale for averages estimated for other small towns in England (24.9 to 30.5 for men and 22.2 to 28.4 for women).[6] In those days, it was customary to delay marriage until an opportunity arose to start a new household — for instance, when trade premises or farm land became available.[7] Perhaps opportunities for setting up new households would arise more frequently in a prosperous market town like St Albans than in the smaller communities studied elsewhere. The average ages were lower than they are today. By 1995 the average ages at marriage in England and Wales were 32.6 for men and 30.2 for women.[8]

Often both bride and groom came from within the same parish and this may be why their addresses were seldom entered in the register. Assuming that, if addresses were not given, the couple lived in the parish where they were married, Table 6.4 shows counts of those married within their own parish, of those coming from other St Albans parishes and of those coming from outside the town.

Not infrequently, a bride or groom came from another parish in Hertfordshire, many of them from places nearby such as Redbourn and Wheathampstead (Fig. 6.4). Occasionally both came from outside the town and Mary Cayley and Samuel Marow, who were married by licence in the Abbey church on 14 October 1669, came from as far away as Coventry (Fig. 6.5). Their appearance in St Albans may be explained by an unusual entry in the marriage register of Berkswell parish (near Coventry): "Ann Marrow daughter of Samuel and Mary Cawley born abt. 1668 Birkswell".[9] This states born, not

Table 6.5 Number of people marrying 1, 2 or 3 times

Marriages	1	2	3
Men	1676	126	11
Women	1705	38	0

Table 6.5 Number of people marrying 1, 2 or 3 times

Marriages	1	2	3
Men	1676	126	11
Women	1705	38	0

baptised, so the rector's disapproval of the extra-marital birth may well account for their marriage so far from home.

In the Abbey and St Michael's parishes around one in five of both brides and grooms did not come from the parish in which they were married which is, perhaps, not surprising. What is surprising is the very small proportion (2 per cent) of spouses in St Peter's parish who married outside their own parish.

Remarriage after the death of a spouse was not particularly frequent as Table 6.5 shows. Men took second or third spouses more frequently than women so there were more single marriages of women than men, as the first marriage of a women was more likely to be the second or third marriage of the groom.

THE FAMILY: CHILDREN

The number of children born to a couple ranged from 0 to 14. Table 6.6 shows the average number of children born to men who are known to have had children. Men were chosen as being more likely to be heads of families than women.

The average count for the St Michael's parish was significantly lower than the averages for Abbey and St Peter's parishes. However, these figures take no account of couples who had no children, of couples who had children baptised elsewhere, of children whose baptisms were not registered nor of children whose baptisms were registered outside the period under study. Families with

Table 6.6 Average number of children baptised per family

Parish	Abbey	St Michael's	St Peter's	All parishes
Average	3.25	2.73	3.12	3.08
Count	568	344	582	1494

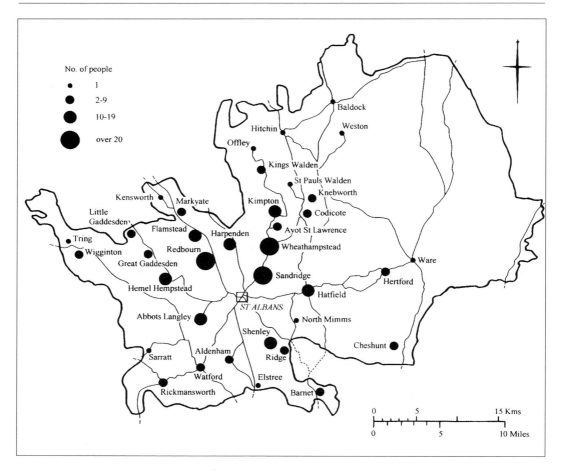

6.4 Places in Hertfordshire from which people came to be married in St Albans, showing the marked east-west division of the county.

3-5 children were not uncommon at that period[10] and these estimates for St Albans fall near the lower end of that range. It may be that families were slightly smaller in St Michael's parish than in the other two parishes but no reason for this is known.

HOUSEHOLD SIZE

The average size of household during the latter half of the seventeenth century has been calculated to be just over 4 persons,[10] the larger households including domestic and other servants. The average number of baptisms per family shown in Table 6.6 takes no account of children who died in infancy (less than one year old) who could not be considered as contributing to

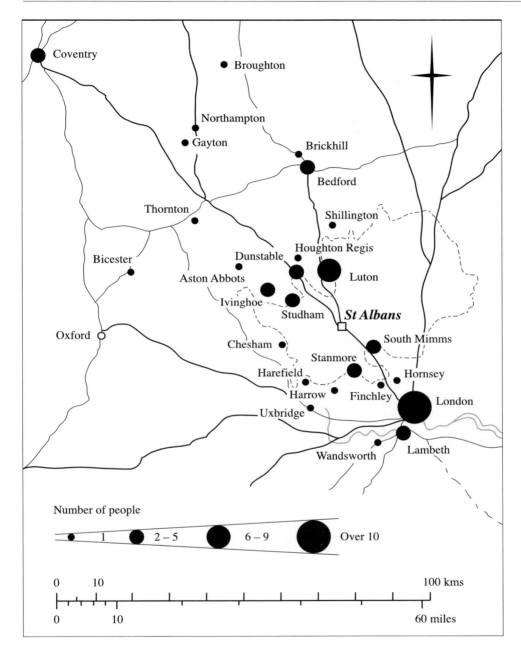

6.5 Places outside Hertfordshire from which people came to St Albans to marry. The numbers from Buckinghamshire show the strong link with a county known for dissent.

Table 6.7 Percentage of children dying in infancy and adjusted average number of children per family

	Parish Abbey	St Michael's	St Peter's	All parishes
Percentage	51.7	55.5	45.8	50.1
Adjusted average	1.65	1.45	2.08	1.76

Table 6.8 Average interval between successive baptisms

	Parish Abbey	St Michael's	St Peter's	All parishes
Interval (years)	2.69	2.68	3.11	2.84
No. of baptisms	352	202	311	865

Table 6.9 Average interval between marriage and first baptism

	Parish Abbey	St Michael's	St Peter's	All parishes
Interval (years)	1.62	1.79	2.13	1.84
Number	352	202	311	865

household size. The percentages of children who died in infancy are shown in Table 6.7 and the average number of children adjusted for these percentages.

Adding in two parents gives a average household size of between 3 and 4. Taking the number of childless couples (which is not known) into account would reduce the average and including those who are not members of the family would increase it. This estimated household size does not diverge widely from that considered usual at that time.

Table 6.8 shows average intervals between baptisms subsequent to the first and the number of baptisms used to calculate the averages which were all similar to that considered usual for those times (2.72).[12]

The average interval for St Peter's parish was significantly higher than those for the other two parishes. Birth intervals can be affected by several causes, for example, the duration of breast feeding, by coital frequency and by miscarriages. Maybe the longer interval between baptisms in St Peter's parish is a reflection of better care in that prosperous area which also had a strong nonconformist element.

Average periods between marriage and first baptisms are shown in Table 6.9. These are shorter than those between subsequent baptisms (Table 6.8) as there will have been no delay due to breast feeding; also there were some pre-nuptial conceptions (about 10 per cent in St Albans).

Again the average period for St Peter's parish was significantly longer than for the other two parishes.

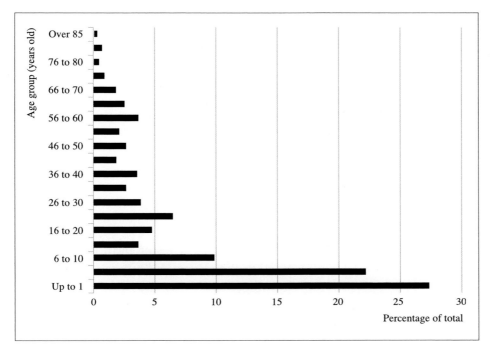

6.6 Age structure for burials, St Peter's parish.

DEATH

Mortality rates also govern the size of a population. Child deaths, it has been said, amounted by the age of ten to half of those born. The first year or even day of life is commonly thought to have been particularly dangerous, as was recognised by an eminent physician of the time, Sir Thomas Browne: "Nothing is more common with infants than to die on the day of their Nativity, and to behold the worldly Hours and by the Fractions thereof ...".[13] In recent years Peter Laslett in particular has challenged this "lugubrious view", arguing from studies of rural communities that the very high death rates alleged for the seventeenth and eighteenth centuries are much exaggerated: though he allowed that towns might be worse.[14] St Albans was certainly worse and it is impossible to know how many very brief lives or miscarriages went unrecorded. An extreme case is that of William and Ann Bailey, seven of whose eight children appear to have been buried within a day or two of their birth, with the eighth living less than five weeks. Even a well-to-do man like Abraham Cowley saw six children by his first wife predecease him, five before the age of five and the sixth at twenty-six.

Table 6.10 Number of burials and average age at death

Parish		Number		Average age
	Men	Women	Total	
Abbey	297	227	524	5.6
St Michael's	141	118	259	8.7
St Peter's	393	266	659	16.5
Total	831	611	1442	11.1
Average age	12.4	9.6	11.1	

AGE AT DEATH

Ages at death can be calculated by subtracting dates of birth from dates of death but these are seldom recorded in the registers. However, for the seventeenth century, it is considered that using dates of baptism and burial give reasonable approximations to the actual ages.[15] The counts of deaths, grouped by sex and parish, are shown in Table 6.10; also the average age at death for men and women and for the three parishes.

As has been described, only the period of recording for St Peter's parish is long enough to give reasonable estimates and even the average age at death for that parish looks low, possibly because there is no information about those entering and leaving the parish. Fig. 6.6 shows the proportion of deaths for different age groups in St Peter's parish.

Despite the inadequacies of the data the diagram does illustrate the appalling number of deaths in infancy — over 25 per cent of the total. From then on there was a slight improvement and life expectancy was around 34 years in those times.

CRISIS YEARS

A crisis year is one where the death rate is unexpectedly high, possibly due to the onset of disease. Death rates were calculated for the period 1562 to 1836 and examined to see if any diverged widely from the trend. In Table 6.11 the years when death rates were unexpectedly high are indicated by an entry of 'Yes'. The crisis years for England and Wales as a whole are similarly marked in the last column.[16] St Michael's parish has not been included as its registers have not survived before 1644 and the population was too small for satisfactory analysis.

Not all the crisis years detected nationally were apparent in St Albans but many of them were and there is a reasonable correspondence between the

Table 6.11 Years with high death rates

Year	Parish		National
	Abbey	St Peter's	
1562	–	Yes	–
1563	Yes	–	Yes
1578	Yes	Yes	Yes
1597	–	Yes	Yes
1598	Yes	–	Yes
1603	–	–	Yes
1604	Yes	Yes	–
1610	Yes	Yes	Yes
1616	Yes	–	Yes
1624	Yes	Yes	Yes
1625	Yes	Yes	Yes
1637	–	Yes	–
1638	–	Yes	Yes
1656	Yes	–	Yes
1657	Yes	–	Yes
1658	Yes	–	Yes
1665	Yes	–	Yes
1667	Yes	–	Yes
1673	Yes	–	–
1710	?	Yes	–
1725	?	Yes	–
1727	?	Yes	Yes
1729	?	Yes	Yes
1731	?	Yes	Yes
1738	?	Yes	–
1741	?	Yes	Yes
1742	?	Yes	Yes
1760	Yes	Yes	–

'Parish' and the 'National' columns during the late sixteenth and the seventeenth centuries. In the Abbey parish, registers for the first half of the eighteenth century are lost and '?' is entered for these years. There was mention of plague in the burial register of St Peter's parish in 1578. During 1665/6 the plague was raging in London and, in St Albans, the mayor's accounts for 1664/5 include an entry "Paid for a board to paste the bye-laws agst the plague upon". Road transport was one way the disease spread and fear of infection

Table 6.12 Number of burials

Parish	Abbey	St Michael's	St Peter's	Total
Same parish	1577	847	2301	4725
Other parish	0	93	43	136
St Albans*	0	36	0	36
London	3	40	125	168
Other areas	1	24	60	85
Total	1581	1040	2529	5150

* This was the address given in the register and it is not known if this was intended to indicate the parish that the deceased lived in or one of the other two parishes.

was said by excisemen to deter people from visiting inns and alehouses on major roads or in major towns.[17] In the Abbey parish, so dependent on transport, the death rate rose markedly in those years. St Peter's parish, less associated with the main road and largely rural, was not so seriously affected. In 1710 there was an outbreak of smallpox in St Peter's parish which does not seem to have spread as that year was not a crisis year nationally. Due to the lack of information, it is not known how much the Abbey parish was also affected, but a part of the town as crowded as Figs 2.6 and 6.7 suggest can hardly have escaped whatever infection was around.

BURIALS

Burials in the three parishes were not confined to the inhabitants of those parishes. This is shown in Table 6.12 where it has been assumed that, if no parish is entered in the register, the deceased had lived within the parish of burial.

Many of the outsiders buried in St Michael's or St Peter's parishes came from the other two parishes or from places near St Albans, pre-eminently Harpenden, Redbourn, Sandridge and Wheathampstead. A considerable number came from London amounting to no less than 125 in St Peter's parish which was the most popular parish of residence for those with London connections. The practice of sending infants out from London for wet-nursing may have affected these figures. Whereas only eight nurse children were buried in the Abbey parish between 1600 and 1674, thirty-one were buried in St Peter's parish between 1566 and 1739.[18] Few outsiders were buried in the Abbey parish but forty-eight burials of people in the upper layers of St Albans society were recorded twice, once in the Abbey register and once either St Peter's or St Michael's registers. This suggests that a link with the great church carried prestige even in death.

6.7 Looking North towards High Street, late 1890s, showing the crenellated Clock Tower and the chimney of the house over Waxhouse Gate (both top left) and the rooftop retreat added to the rear roofs above No. 13 High Street. Nearly all the buildings are pre-1700. The excessive building density was typical of the Abbey parish and resulted in an ill-ventilated and insanitary environment.

SEASONAL FLUCTUATIONS IN MARRIAGES, BAPTISMS AND BURIALS

It is considered that the seasonal pattern of vital events may throw light on the activities of a community.[19] In the last half of the seventeenth century the average counts of marriages for St Albans were significantly lower in August and significantly higher in September and October than the average over all 12 months. When the analysis was extended to include the subsequent period from 1701 to 1857 it was found that there were significantly fewer marriages in March and August and significantly more in October. The Church frowned on marriage during Lent and this may account for the low March figures. The low counts of marriages in August and the high counts in October are more likely to have been affected by the cycle of the farming year. For arable farmers August is a busy time with little opportunity for marriage which could be delayed until October after the harvest had been gathered in. This was more marked in the semi-rural parishes of St Michael and St Peter than in the Abbey parish.

For counts of baptisms there was no significant difference between the monthly averages during the late seventeenth century although, for the period extended to 1857, the monthly averages tied in with the monthly pattern of marriages in the semi-rural parishes but not in the Abbey parish.

Average counts of burials were consistently lowest in July for all three parishes. For the Abbey parish the average counts were highest in August and September whereas, for the semi-rural parishes, they were highest in May and high in the winter months. This implies that those living in the crowded Abbey parish were more susceptible to the intestinal complaints associated with hot weather and those in the more spacious parishes to the respiratory complaints common in winter. Possibly the May figure results from the privations of the months before the new harvest when the combination of high food prices and the severity of winter finally took effect. It has been shown that lower temperatures in winter and higher temperatures in summer did increase mortality until about 1840.[20]

POPULATION RECONSTRUCTION AND THE OCCUPATIONAL PROFILE

The data linkage made possible by the computer permitted extensive family reconstitution and also provided information about the numbers and composition of trade, professional and religious groups; indeed, only family reconstitution made possible serious discussion of the occupational structure in the absence of the freemen's or similar lists.

So far has family reconstitution proceeded that it is possible to match the age profile of the population for 1675 with an occupational profile for the same year which accounts for a substantial proportion of the adult males. To this can be added the number of people who received poor relief; and the whole can be related to the number of males of an age to earn their own living in that year. In order to reveal significant aspects of employment in St Albans, comparative information has been introduced from the two towns for which the best information is available, Uttoxeter, which had grown quite rapidly since the Reformation to about 3,000 inhabitants by the 1690s, and Shrewsbury, a county town and the economic focus of North Wales, which had twice that number and was on its way to becoming the town of fashion admired by Defoe.[21]

Trades, though grouped for the most part in the usual way by the materials worked, show some departures from convention in order to keep together those that are inextricably linked. Thus lastmakers and a heelmaker go with shoemakers in the leather trades, and wheelwrights and a collarmaker with other transport-related trades; members of these trades rose or fell together.

In view of the importance of coach and carrier traffic for St Albans it is surprising how few people were employed directly in transport, as coachman, waggoner or carrier, in 1675; only seven, with fifteen more in closely allied trades. These figures are certainly an underestimate but not necessarily by much. For comparison, Uttoxeter had five and the much larger town of Shrewsbury eight people in road transport. But the true economic effect of these comparatively small numbers is revealed by the trades catering mainly for travellers, the innkeepers, innholders, alehouse keepers, victuallers and tapsters, in which St Albans far exceeds Shrewsbury in the proportion of inhabitants involved; the former 10 per cent, the latter 4 per cent. That is what it meant to be a thoroughfare town.

From the age profile for 1675 it appears that close on 200 males were of an age, assumed to be 15 on average, to be earning their own keep, and that those aged 20 and over, numbering c.600, were potentially able to marry and, through their savings and earnings and those of a bride, to set up house and support a family. Of these 800 people the occupations of 410 (51 per cent) are known, and they include 69 of the 95 trades (73 per cent) recorded between 1650 and 1700. Since nearly all the remaining trades occur only once it can be assumed that linking names to them would not greatly increase the number of people employed in a specific year. Then there are those between the ages of fifteen and twenty, both male and female, of whom a proportion would have been servants — life-cycle servants, as they are called, who, characteristically, spent the years between sexual maturity and marriage in service; and apprentices and even journeymen were reckoned as servants. Their numbers increased in our period and it appears that they are likely to have been present in a quarter or a third of the households of a community.[22] Among them are the footboys like the one Pepys employed to attend him in public, ready to perform any errand. Every man of standing in the town is likely to have had such an attendant and some will have employed one on duties around the house.[23]

Inns, too, must have afforded employment in many minor tasks around the house and yard.

A calculation of the number of servants can be made by using data from Kendal which has been analysed by C.B. Phillips.[24] For that town, which had a population of about 2,200, two lists compiled under the Marriage Duty Act exist for 1695, one of freemen, the other of freemen together with the male and female servants, including apprentices and journeymen, in each family. The proportion of servants to freemen in each of the occupational groupings can be calculated; it varies from 44 per cent in the metal trades to 153 per cent in the distributive trades, the overall average being 90 per cent. It is hardly worth while trying to reconcile Phillips' grouping of trades with those used here because the occupations in the two towns differ so much, Kendal, for example, having 41 per cent in labour-intensive textiles and St Albans a mere 4 per cent; but the latter achieves balance through a larger number of occupations in the equally labour-intensive distributive and victualling trades. If, then, the figure of 90 per cent be accepted and applied to the 410 persons whose occupation is recorded, there were about 370 living-in servants of both sexes. Of them, between a third and a half may have been female if the Kendal proportion were applicable.

What proportion of the remainder followed a trade and what proportion were unskilled labourers? Comparison can be made with the exceptionally full recording of occupations at Shrewsbury in 1668,[25] when, in an obsolescent procedure called view of frankpledge, heads of households pledged to keep the peace. There, in a population of just below 7,000, the 'vast majority' of male householders were recorded, excluding only journeymen, to produce a total of 1,142 tradesmen in all working at 124 trades, and, if the proportion of males in the population aged fifteen and over was similar to St Albans, those listed made up rather more than half (58 per cent) of about 1,960 employable men and youths. Since it is unlikely that many tradesmen avoided the Shrewsbury listing, it is probable that most are accounted for in St Albans too, so that a sizeable residue of unskilled persons remains. In assessing their numbers the Shrewsbury listing is superior, for it seems that all kinds of working people subscribed their names and only the leisured classes are under-represented. Much the largest occupational group was that of labourers, 134 people, representing 11.7 per cent of the whole, whereas the 24 known labourers in St Albans, where the sources of information are likely to under-record them, amount to only half that proportion (5.8 per cent). Doubling the number of labourers and accepting the precarious estimate of servants and including, as Phillips did, apprentices and journeymen, accounts for virtually all the 800 or so males of employable age in St Albans in 1675.

Labourers, it must be presumed, earned a precarious living from working in a variety of trades as, for example, tanning, in which men with no particular skill but plenty of strength were needed to work the tan pits and move the heavy hides about during the various processes; and the building and associated trades, from the cutting up of logs to the erection of a timber or brick building, required unskilled labour at all stages. These labouring men with uncertain incomes did not contribute to poor rates; they, with the poorer tradesmen, correspond to the 55 per cent of households in Aldenham parish who were in that position.[26] By no means all of them are recorded as receiving poor relief but many must have fallen into poverty at some time, however briefly. Their numbers might be increased by the sons of craftsmen who failed in a trade or never had an apprenticeship. And, as is noted below (ch.9, p.193), the occasional labourer made good.

TRADES AND PROFESSIONS: SOME COMPARISONS

The important part transport played in the economy of the town has already been referred to, yet the number of people who can be identified as being directly employed in the industry in 1675 amounted to no more than seven — three coachman and four waggoners. That may be an understatement because one or two may have been missed, though comparison with Shrewsbury suggests not many. More important, though, were the people whose work maintained the local vehicles and the many others passing through the town on the road — the blacksmiths and wheelwrights, together with the saddlers, the collar-maker and the farriers and ostlers who looked after the horses and their harness. And there were the two coopers and two basketmakers, a fair proportion of whose products are likely to have been used in transporting goods by carrier or pedlar. Nor is it possible to quantify the contribution made by inn and alehouse keepers in the provision of food and beds, but again comparison with Shrewsbury is instructive. In 1675 St Albans the names of twenty-three innholders and innkeepers are known, amounting to only three-quarters of the true total since thirty-one inns are recorded at this period. Nevertheless, twenty-three is the number of innkeepers and innholders in a county and assize town which was more than twice as large as St Albans and was an important river port and regional centre for North Wales; and the total number of people employed in the provision of food and drink far outstrips those in Uttoxeter, a thriving and fashionable town of some 3,000 inhabitants.[27]

Comparison with the same two towns brings out two distinctive features in St Albans which arise from its proximity to London, although they have to be qualified because the different kinds of source document incorporate biases of different kinds. On the one hand the attraction of the town for

London doctors and lawyers is obvious from the number of residents of both professions as compared with Uttoxeter, where a parish clerk diligently recorded occupations in the registers over ten years; and probably St Albans compared favourably with Shrewsbury too, without it being possible to press the comparison, for there the professional classes appear largely to have ignored the view of frankpledge. On the other hand, the nearness of the capital appears to have stifled the growth of leisure and luxury trades: not a single musician is recorded, in contrast to the three in Uttoxeter and ten in Shrewsbury, and not until the closing years of the century does a dancing master appear. Country pursuits were provided for by a gunsmith, as in the other two towns and the pipemaker's essentially local products furnished inns and alehouses in St Albans and Shrewsbury alike but only in the latter did distillers produce what citizens of the former no doubt generally obtained from London.

A further comparison demonstrates in a negative way the importance of road transport in the economy of St Albans, where the manufacturing element relative to that of the other two towns is quite small. Thus cloth production had largely disappeared by 1675 and even the number of people employed in making clothing was proportionately smaller than in Uttoxeter and Shrewsbury. In comparison with those places, leather working in St Albans in all its forms, from tanning to the making of saddles and gloves, was important to the extent that it employed twice as many people as clothing but they still formed a smaller proportion of the total population than in the other two towns. This might be ascribed to the more strongly pastoral economies in the hinterlands of Uttoxeter and Shrewsbury except that leather and its products were in universal demand, as were those of the metalworking crafts; and in that branch of the economy St Albans kept pace with two towns which were much nearer the iron furnaces whence their material came.

CONCLUSION

St Albans in the last half of the seventeenth century is revealed as a town of predominantly young people. They married at a younger age than they do today and younger than was common in the late seventeenth century. This may have been because of the many opportunities for setting up new households in a thriving market town. There is some evidence that the Abbey church was a popular venue for marriage and, from the burial records, that St Peter's and, to a lesser extent, St Michael's parishes had contacts with London.

The total population of the three parishes of Abbey, St Michael's and St Peter's was probably around 3,200. There was certainly no 'population explosion' partly due to the many deaths in infancy but also to the number of children born to each family being at the lower end of the scale for that time. There may even have been a slight decrease in numbers during the period. Were St Albans parents careful to avoid larger families than they could support? Average household size seems to have been near to that considered usual but here several reservations must be made. The estimate takes no account of childless couples nor of servants who might have lived with the family.

Generally, the pattern of mortality in St Albans reflected what was going on in the country as a whole and particularly in London. For example, if London suffered from the plague, St Albans, on a main route into and out of the capital, would be infected also. The Abbey parish, which depended heavily on the transport system, was especially vulnerable.

Counts of burials, marriages and, to a lesser extent, baptisms were affected by the seasons. Judging by the number of burials, July was the healthiest month in all three parishes. In Abbey parish, August was the unhealthiest month probably because, in an overcrowded, unsanitary area, disease spreads rapidly in the hot weather. Dwellers in the more open parishes of St Michael and St Peter seem to have been more exposed to the privations of winter as in May and the months preceding there were higher number of burials. Marriages were often arranged to avoid the busy harvest months and the interdictions of the church. In the rural parishes baptisms reflected the pattern of marriages but this was less apparent in the urbanised Abbey parish.

NOTES AND REFERENCES

[1] Glass and Eversley 1965; Laslett 1972
[2] Snedecor and Cochran 1980; Ratkowsky 1983; Genstat 5 1988
[3] For more detail, see Alvey 2000
[4] Arkell 1982
[5] Wrigley and Schofield 1989, Appendix 3
[6] Wrigley et al 1997, Table 5.18
[7] Laslett 1983, pp.12, 100–1
[8] Statistics 1998, Table 2.11
[9] Marriage register Berkswell 1668
[10] Laslett and Wall 1972, pp.135–6
[11] Laslett and Wall 1972, pp.138–9
[12] Wrigley et al 1997, Table 7.36
[13] Browne 1690
[14] Laslett 1983, p.112
[15] Berry and Schofield 1971, pp.453–63
[16] Wrigley and Schofield 1989, Table 8.13
[17] Slack 1985, p.189
[18] Fildes 1988, Table 1
[19] Wrigley and Schofield 1989, pp.286–305

20 Wrigley and Schofield 1989, pp.384–98
21 McInnes 1987; McInnes 1988; Defoe 1927
22 Laslett 1983, pp.14–16
23 Pepys 1970-83, Vol.10, pp.193–4
24 Phillips 1984, p.104
25 McInnes 1988, pp.84–7
26 Brown 1984, p.409
27 McInnes 1987, p.115

7

THE ECONOMY: THOROUGHFARE TOWN
AND MARKET TOWN

S T ALBANS does not fit easily into the common categories of town. It was one of the largest of small towns and, although it hosted quarter sessions, was neither a major administrative centre, having declined opportunities to host the assizes, nor a truly regional centre, despite being as important in west Hertfordshire as the county town. More positively, it combined the two functions of thoroughfare and market town, each feeding the other and neither dominant, with possession of the finest church for miles around, which, long after the monastery that had created it had vanished, conferred on the town a special status and some economic advantage.

THE THOROUGHFARE TOWN

Although St Albans must always have been important in the transport system by virtue of its location on one of the country's major roads, the term 'thoroughfare town' in the sense of a place owing a substantial part of its prosperity to road traffic only becomes appropriate in the late sixteenth century and loses its force by the middle of the eighteenth. Growth begins in the reign of Elizabeth with the building of new inns and the improvement of old ones[1], so that by 1637 the mayor and burgesses could describe the town as consisting "chiefly of inns and victual-houses, who drive a trade upon the travelling of passengers".[2] In that year, too, carrier and other services were sufficiently numerous countrywide for John Taylor to list them in his book *The Carriers Cosmographie*, from which an estimate can be made, albeit with a considerable margin of error[3], of the volume of traffic passing through or originating in St Albans.

The traffic consisted largely of pack-horses, not a single waggon or wain being listed. It is a situation different from that on the other important roads. In the eastern counties Bury St Edmunds and other places sent vehicles to London, as did Winchester and "places in Gloucestershire", while even in Hertfordshire they went from Much Hadham, Ware and Watford. So great a difference seems unlikely to be due wholly to omission so, although it may be safe to assume that some carriers used waggons, we have to envisage some twenty-odd strings of horses passing through St Albans each week and three more in alternate weeks or irregularly.[4] Among the impressive number of destinations are six or seven county towns, some commercially important places like Coventry and Nantwich and a few more distant towns like Preston and Sheffield. Some places must have been served by connections but Nottingham and Halifax, with fortnightly and monthly departures respectively, probably had through services. Traffic was quiet in the first half of the week, amounting to only nine services each way weekly with two more in alternate weeks, while Saturday may have seen no more than one. Thursday, with a dozen carriers each way, was the busiest day and Friday saw seven or eight, all calling at one or other of the inns. Such a fluctuating volume of traffic demanded a staff large enough to cope with the peaks of demand, including the Wednesday and Saturday market days, but under-employed for the first two days of the week.

On the other hand, St Albans had the quite unusual provision of a twice-weekly coach service going every Friday to the Bell in Aldersgate Street and "the like coach is also there for the carriage of passengers every Tuesday"[5]; otherwise only Cambridge, Hatfield and Hertford had a "waggon or coach" going to London. Probably the three Hertfordshire services were patronised initially by the gentry and court officials living close to those towns, but soon ease of communication brought to St Albans a new kind of visitor, the Londoner – Taylor speaks of shopkeepers – making pleasure trips. To such people the abbey church was an attraction and to the townspeople a modest economic asset and, although its direct contribution to the economy can only have been small, the trade so generated helped the inns and may have raised standards. Perhaps William Smith's opinion that St Albans was the fairest and greatest of the Hertfordshire towns in 1588 had some foundation.[6]

A more important economic benefit of the coach service lay in its use for part of a journey from places not in direct connection with the capital. Thus on Friday 30 January 1642 "Mr. Coleman, secretary to Lord Chief Justice Bankes, lately come from Oxford, leaves his horse tonight at St Albans, thence comes up in one of the coaches, and returns on Thursday".[7] Evidently no coaches then ran from London to Oxford, and in 1650 Mary Verney sent her infant son and his wet-nurse with her sister by coach from London to meet her steward at St Albans, spend the night there and depart with her son the following day on horseback for Tring and Claydon (Bucks.).[8] The town functioned like a railhead and for about two decades provided a captive trade for innkeepers and ostlers until coaches reached more distant towns – Chester by 1657.

WAGGONS AND PACK-HORSES: TRANSPORT IN CHARLES II'S REIGN

After the short-term disruptions of the Civil War the concern for the repair of roads expressed in a Commonwealth ordinance found local application when, in 1652/3, "Mr Bastchon the bailiff … served a warrant upon the mayor upon process out of the crown office for defaults in our highways"; and continued with an Act of Parliament empowering authorities to raise a rate for the purpose, not exceeding 6d in the pound.[9] Such measures were evidently effective for the road from London to St Albans, along which Lord Chancellor Clarendon (visiting Gorhambury in 1665) expected to be drawn at a speed of six miles per hour.[10] Improvement was rapid, traffic increased and in 1676 John Ogilby depicted in his *Tables of the Measur'd Roads* the four 'Great Roads of England' and their branches for the increasing number of travellers who needed to know how to reach particular destinations. Through St Albans went the road to Chester, Holyhead and the Dublin packet, with principal branch roads leading to Derby, Shrewsbury and Carlisle (Fig.7.1), forming an artery through the Midlands to reach all of northern England west of the Pennines.

Already by 1681 two coaches were running from St Albans to London, those of Joseph Marshall (of the Fleur-de-Lys) and Anthony Wilson, also an innholder.[11] But coaches and waggons tended to operate from their terminuses and, given the steady improvement in journey times, they moved farther away from London. Consequently, the interest of the town's innholders lay as much in hiring horses to coach travellers needing to reach destinations to east or west as in providing food and drink while coaches halted.

But not all innkeepers did this and the variations of horse ownership throw some light on relations between them and the coachmen and carriers. Thus Thomas Eccleston, owner of the Bull, the most important inn in the town and the one used by the Chester coach and frequented by well-to-do travellers, died in 1687 owning only a horse and mare for his own use; their oats and beans were in the garden hayloft, not the inn yard. The extensive comings and goings of vehicles and horses he left to others to whom he appears to have leased the stables and other buildings around the yard, which are not mentioned in his inventory, although the ostler's and postilions' rooms are. So did Thomas Jones of the White Hart, another major inn, who likewise possessed only his own nag. It seems to have been the owners of the second-rank inns who invested in riding horses, perhaps because the business was not on a large enough scale to be worth contracting out. One such was James Ashton of the Chequer in Sopwell Lane, whose stables held "five Naggs and two Mares and all the Saddles Bridles Girts and horse Cloths"; hiring out riding horses was evidently a profitable business.

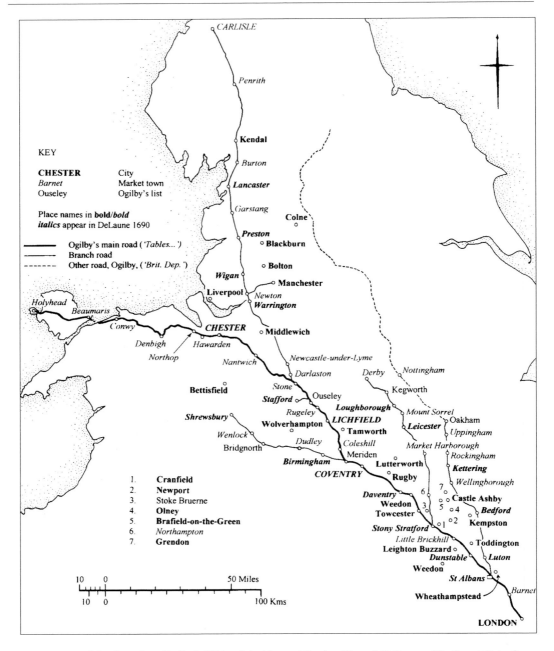

KEY

CHESTER   City
Barnet   Market town
Ouseley   Ogilby's list

Place names in **bold**/***bold
italics*** appear in DeLaune 1690

———— Ogilby's main road ('*Tables...* ')
——— Branch road
----- Other road, Ogilby, ('*Brit. Dep.* ')

1.   **Cranfield**
2.   **Newport**
3.   Stoke Bruerne
4.   **Olney**
5.   **Brafield-on-the-Green**
6.   *Northampton*
7.   **Grendon**

10   0   50 Miles

10   0   100 Kms

7.1 Map based on Ogilby's *Tables of the Measured Roads*, 1681, and DeLaune, *The Present State of London*, 1690, showing places from which coaches, waggons and carriers came through St Albans to London. It is not clear from the sources which route coaches took from London to Shrewsbury at this period.

7.2 Places from which wheeled vehicles came through St Albans to London in 1681. The carriers from other places shown in Fig.7.1 are assumed to have used horses although there will have been unrecorded exceptions. The Rugby 'caravan' and the Tamworth coach which operated in summer provide the only indications of seasonal traffic.

Comparison of the transport services listed in DeLaune's *The Present State of London* of 1690[12] with those in the *Carriers Cosmographie* reveals both a greater number of carriers and the extent to which coaches and waggons had by then supplanted horses (Fig.7.2). Chester and Nottingham were now the most distant towns to provide coaches and waggons to London, as did many intermediate places on or near the road, although carriers, presumably using pack-horses, still operated from five of them. Beyond Newcastle-under-Lyme

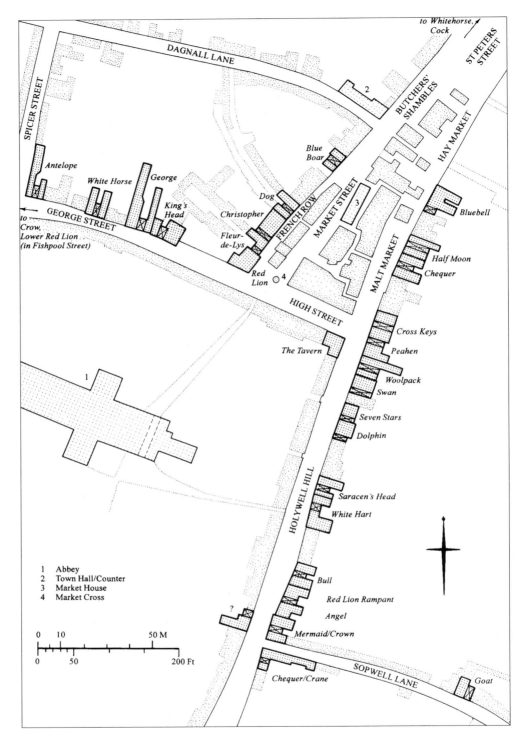

7.3 'A town chiefly of inns and victual houses': the location of inns, mostly on the line of the London–Chester road. The short plots abutting the abbey precinct wall prevented the establishment of inns there; only the Tavern which was forbidden to provide accommodation could flourish on that side. Several inventories of alehouse keepers show that they too put up travellers.

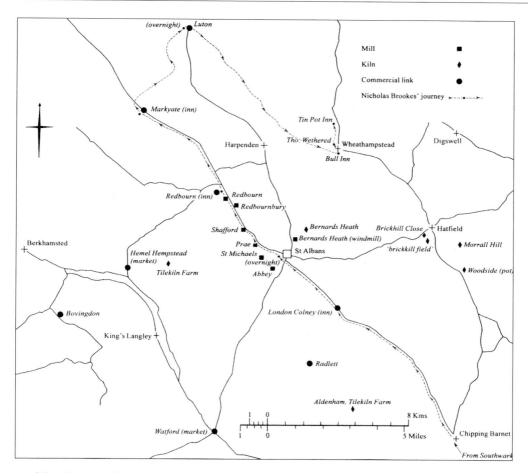

7.4: Map showing mills, brick/tile kilns and inns owned by St Albans men; places with links to St Albans; also Nicholas Brookes' journeys, 30 December 1664 – 2 January 1665.

and Nottingham pack-horses were universal[13] and strings of horses were still an everyday sight in the market-place at St Albans.

In 1690 fourteen coaches, twenty-one waggons and twenty-three carriers with pack-horses passed each way each week through St Albans, and there were also coaches and waggons starting and terminating there. Although daily traffic still fluctuated, Thursday remained the busiest day and Tuesday the quietest, but at both ends of the week traffic had increased markedly through vehicles staying in London on Friday night or Sunday. The town, by reason of its size and relative importance, will have provided a stop for all services, whether brief to pick up and set down, longer for dinner, or overnight, and the extent of its dependence on such trade is clear from a map (Fig.7.3) showing how inns dominated the most important artery through the town, those streets forming part of the London-Chester road. Nevertheless, by 1700 the inns of Redbourn and particularly London Colney, where two St Albans men, Thomas Miles and John Stanes, owned the Lion and Chequer respectively, were rivals, and are a sign of the development of alternative and quite nearby locations for the growing traffic. Road services were increasing, even if St Albans was no longer able to profit from its location quite so much.

In addition an unknown number of people arrived on horseback, as did Celia Fiennes from Dunstable, who was accompanied by her maid and a groom – two or three beds and three stalls at every stopping-place – or like Thomas Baskerville coming from the Watford direction[14] on one of those cross-country roads about whose traffic hardly anything is known. Nicholas Brookes, a London fishmonger, is another who, after going from St Albans to Markyate, used minor roads to Luton and on to Wheathampstead, where he was twice refused lodging before being taken in at the "Tin Pott" (Fig. 7.4).[15] The fact that this small village at a minor road junction had enough traffic to maintain three lodging-places is the only hint we have of a considerable volume of business generated in St Albans by travellers on secondary and cross-country routes which were not thought worth mention in the road-books.

Towards the end of the century the speed of road travel increased markedly. Whereas in 1681 Joseph Marshall's coach went to London on Mondays, Wednesdays and Fridays and returned on the following days, by 1690 DeLaune's continuator listed Humphry Cooper's waggon as making return journeys on those days, as in 1694 did "Newel, carrier" (who must also have used a waggon).[16] No doubt waggons were not as uniformly heavy and cumbersome as is commonly supposed, and Cooper and Newel were perhaps as keen to take passengers as goods, but it is nevertheless remarkable that the two-day return journey by coach in 1681 had given way only nine years later to a same-day return by carrier, and the contrast says as much about the growth as about the speed of traffic.

The same developments affected coaches. By 1690 Anthony Wilson's coach still plied from St Albans to London but by then Joseph Marshall was running a coach from Luton and another from Dunstable, each departing Monday, Wednesday and Friday and returning the following days. Four years later the town had dropped out of the advertisement for coaches in Houghton's Collection,[17] an omission implying what other evidence suggests, that the town was ceasing to be a starting-point. Although this in itself was a loss to the economy, it was certainly outweighed by the general increase in other kinds of transport activity, whose volume is hinted at by the ability to meet the twenty warrants issued in 1687/8 and again in 1690/1 for the impressment of carriages for soldiers without, presumably, completely disrupting normal traffic.

Nevertheless, the economy of the thoroughfare town was not a straightforward story of growth. The rapid development of the coaching system initially brought, as the inns demonstrate, considerable prosperity, yet by the 1680s the improved journey times resulting from better roads and coaches made an overnight stop no longer a necessity for the faster long-distance services and changed gradually the composition of the inn guests: travellers to and from London, who formed the cream of the business, stayed less in St Albans as their first day's journey made it feasible to sleep at Dunstable or beyond. This is reflected in John New's acquisition of an inn at Leighton Buzzard (ch 10, p.207), far enough away to profit from traffic stopping at a more distant location. Any such effect was balanced and perhaps for a time outweighed by the continued increase in travel as it became easier, and as more people rode into St Albans to eat, drink and stable their horses at an inn for a day or two while they took the coach to do business elsewhere. This practice may go some way to explaining why, by 1756, the inns of St Albans and two or three other Hertfordshire towns had stabling for three horses for every bed, whereas more market-dependent towns like Ware and Watford had a much smaller ratio.[18]

THE MARKET TOWN: ITS CATCHMENT AREA

What difference did the growing volume of traffic make to the town's economy in the late seventeenth century? St Albans might have performed no more than the ordinary functions of a market town had these not been modified successively by the presence of a great abbey and, after the Dissolution, transport growth. Unfortunately, no market records survive, so a first step in trying to disentangle the two facets of the economy is to consider the size of the area from which people habitually came to buy and sell in the town.

Probably the market exerted a greater pull to north than to south. In the Chester direction the first sizeable market town was Dunstable, which was also full of inns, while Luton was the nearest rival towards Bedford.[19] To the west Hemel Hempstead became a competitor after 1530 when its important corn market was established, yet competition cannot have been injurious to either in 1656 when a petition for an additional fair was supported by prominent inhabitants of St Albans.[20] Such co-operation implies a symbiosis between the two that may have existed between St Albans and other towns, albeit not expressed so directly.

Watford may have been one such. In their wills and inventories farmers in the southernmost parts of St Stephen's parish are sometimes described as "of Watford",[21] which is no doubt where they marketed their produce, even though for some St Albans was as near. Market specialisation may explain the choice. In all the belt from Watford to Cheshunt horse breeding was a staple of farming and as a natural consequence oats were the single most important crop. Pigs, chickens and geese "in great number" were also reared and were fattened on barley, peas and beans before going mostly to the London markets.[22] In the late sixteenth century these four arable crops, together with a much smaller quantity of rye, greatly surpassed the production of wheat, which was sold locally for cash; and certainly inventories of farms close to Watford, such as Waterdell and Hansteads, show quite large acreages of oats, beans, peas and vetches. The specialisation in oats, ascribed to the demands of mealmen, maltmen and travellers, has two implications. First, the corn market at Watford, being mainly in crops other than wheat, is unlikely to have affected that at St Albans which was pre-eminently in wheat.[23] Second, since no specialised horse market is known to have existed in the county, the horses which the south-west part of the county was noted for rearing must have been sold in small numbers in markets, or in greater numbers at fairs, notably Barnet, or in private bargains. In reality there was no market competition.

If the catchment area of St Albans market was limited to the south-west by agricultural specialisation, to the west by Hemel Hempstead corn market and to the north by Luton, what of the rest? For Wheathampstead in the very centre of the county St Albans was the nearest and best market, those at Codicote, Digswell and Welwyn being extinct by the sixteenth century, nor can Hatfield close by have offered much competition.[24] Not many miles beyond Wheathampstead the road pattern suggests that Stevenage or Hertford were more accessible places in which to buy and sell. Barnet was very much a market on the Great North Road and to south Elstree represents the likely reach of St Albans market. This gives an area of about 21 by 11km. (13 by 7 miles), well within the distance farmers might expect to habitually travel even in a county with as generous a provision of markets as Hertfordshire.[25]

In fact, the actual choice of market by those frequenting St Albans was certainly more eclectic than this, as the relations with Hemel Hempstead and Watford suggest – and vice versa. A documented instance is Samuel Hickman, ironmonger, who dealt in iron and steel by the gross. On his death in 1707 he left materials of his trade to a considerable value in premises at Hemel Hempstead and also debts due to him there amounting to £750, and although that total was less than half the sum due from St Albans, he clearly traded on a considerable scale in both places. It was a family business and it is likely that he lived and managed the Hemel Hempstead operation until taking over in St Albans on his father's death in 1700. The firm supplied iron to the blacksmiths and other metalworkers in the vicinity but presumably also to others over a wider area, to account for the size of their trade. Similarly, Elizabeth, widow of Henry Gould, mealman, had equipment at Wheathampstead belonging to her late husband's trade. But most dealings in the open market were more parochial than these instances might suggest, as a list of debts owing to Samuel Whelpley, mealman, shows: for although he himself, like the Hickmans, had wider connections, of his twenty-seven debtors, only two names have a place beside them, those of Goodman Dell of Radlett and Thomas Hall of Colney Street. Their dealings, like those of the Redbourn poulterer who paid a year's rent of three shillings for his standing under the Clockhouse, are representative of the local nature and small scale of many market transactions.

THE OPERATION OF THE MARKET

Freemen and foreigners – people from outside the borough – sold their goods in the market-place twice a week. All except those trading on the smallest scale needed a stall that allowed them to display their wares and offered some protection from rain. The form of stall allowed by the market authorities was important, as a legal case concerning Hemel Hempstead market place shows.

Crucial to the argument was whether the stalls in question were fixed to the ground or moveable, and a witness described them as follows: " ... some of the shambles and stalls ... about thirteene yeares agoe were fixed to the soyle ... by a brick ground penn and ... the same are since digged up and sett upon wheels"; a point confirmed by a second witness who said that the Shambles "are moveably stood on pattens till lately set on wheels". A third person attested that he had brought "about fifty years since ... timber and gravell to fasten the said Shambles to the ground".[26] Evidently the customary rule in a market place was for traders to bring their own stalls and remove them after the market had closed, but regular, established traders might observe the letter of the law by making the stalls just about moveable while breaching its spirit by making them semi-permanent. That appears to be the significance of digging up the "pattens"[27] and replacing them with wheels; people had been forced to comply with the letter, too.

Nearly all traders in St Albans market who had stalls provided them themselves – rudimentary structures, either brought in on a cart or stored somewhere near the market place, perhaps at an inn[28] – which they set up and took down each market day. Probably, as the term 'stall roomths' suggests, not all traders set up a stall, many being content to lay out their wares in baskets on the ground just as they did early in the twentieth century.[29] Only for butchers were five permanent stalls provided (ch.3, p.60), to be maintained by the Counter-keeper, and the Hemel Hempstead dispute suggests what they were like: a simple wood frame with a counter and probably a boarded roof, the posts and base plates being either fixed to the soil, in gravel or within a brick "penn". The five stalls were leased out successively to William and Martha Stone and George and Hannah Feild at £3 p.a. for sub-letting to country butchers,[30] while five "stall roomths" and two or three more – the exact number uncertain – were leased to individual town butchers at 10s p.a. A stall roomth was to contain in length seven feet and no more and leases contained a proviso that the stall was to be taken down by 9pm. This tight control of butchers' places of sale stemmed from a complaint made in 1588 by the wardens of the victuallers, that country butchers "wandered about the town with their meat, not keeping to the shambles".[31] Their competition was restricted if they were forced to sell in company with town butchers, who at that period were forbidden by a lost regulation to sell in any other place than the butchers' stalls on market days[32] but, by the 1690s, the rule was in abeyance because seven families of butchers who are not recorded as renting a stall or stall roomth evidently sold only from their shops. The butcher's shop Nos. 33/34 Market Place (p.27) may well be a symptom of this change.

The grouping together of butchers was a survival, along with the corn merchants in their ten corn shops above the market hall, of the trade groupings universal in medieval markets. First-floor accommodation for corn dealers protected grain from damage by damp or rats, and the segregation of butchers restricted the nuisance created by the noisome residues of animals slaughtered on the spot by country butchers. For the same reason fishmongers had their assigned place although the volume of their trade was so much smaller that its precise location is not certain. But the original motive for allocating trades to particular parts of the market place may have been to make quality and price control easier, and the continued concentration of these two may reflect a greater concern felt by corporations in these crucial areas of food supply.

Little is known about any other trading carried on in the market place. The pig market, which appears in the records only because it was a place to whip those who had committed petty larceny, as in 1673/4 and 1674/5, must have been considerable to judge by the number of hogs or pigs listed in innholders' probate inventories. The animals were fed, no doubt, on food waste and killed as required to feed travellers with fresh or salted meat. A sizeable market for cattle can be inferred from inventories and a concern to prevent its decline appears in an order of 1687 that it be held "before Mr Norris's rails and shambles and no cattle to be sold in any other place".[33] A supply of good leather was equally necessary to meet the needs of transport-related trades, of which William Jones, saddler and innholder of the Swan, is representative, and of shoemakers or cordwainers. The economic importance of leather is attested both by the searchers and sealers who ensured its quality and by payments in the mayors' accounts from 1656/7 to 1659/60 "for serving the distresses upon the butchers that brought not in [to market] their hides and tallows": an attempt to discourage forestalling. This mention of tallows is the only mention, apart from the names of nine tallow-chandlers, of what must have been a

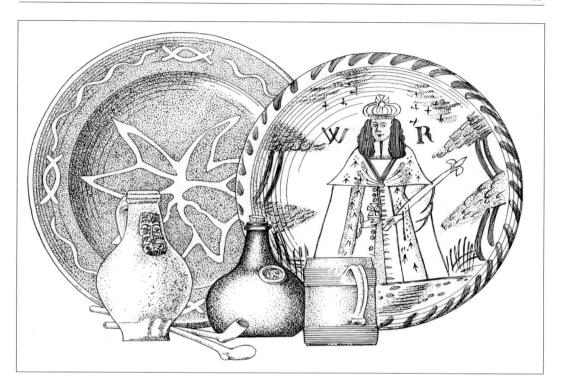

7.5 Pottery and glass of types used in St Albans between 1650 and 1700, mainly from archaeological sites in the town centre and St Michael's Street. Large plates or 'chargers' in red lead-glazed Metropolitan Slipware (with white slip decoration), and polychrome London Tin-glazed Earthenware ('Delft'), with William III (1694-1702). Rhenish Stoneware 'bellarmine' bottle, English 'black' glass wine bottle with seal, London Stoneware tankard, c 1690, and locally-made clay pipes of types current between 1680 and 1710. Diameter of larger plate 36 cm. (St Albans Museums)

quite considerable trade in candles. For many other trades there is not even that much evidence.

For what must have been a large trade in pottery there is only archaeological evidence. A coarse red ware used for cooking pots and other common vessels was made near Hatfield; a superior glazed product came from Harlow, Loughton (Essex) and near Towcester, and a further step up is represented by the slipwares popular in London and made at Harlow (Fig. 7.5). But the best pottery was either the famous blue and white Delft ware or the so-called Bellarmine jugs from the vicinity of Cologne, although by the 1690s these types may be Staffordshire or London copies. Pottery, to judge by its absence from tradesmen's probate inventories, appears to have been sold in the market by traders coming from wherever it was made.

REGULATION OF THE MARKET

The mayor was responsible for enforcing regulations governing the price of bread and ale and other victuals and the people appointed to check the quality of various other goods and commodities reported to his monthly court. Tasks of this kind – inspecting and tasting flesh and fish, examining leather and giving it the stamp of approval – were important in maintaining the reputation of the market. With this went the prevention of cheating and overcharging, and the seriousness of this business is shown by the regular payment made, as for example in 1658/9, "to the six men when the mayor gave them their oath to gather up the weights and measures".[34] Twenty years later, when a need for standardisation of the many different measures in use in southern England appears to have been widely felt[35], it was thought desirable to make a local check by sending to the capital John Guise who, in 1679/80, was paid "for his charges and pains in trying our brass bushel by the Standard of London". That was the same standard as the "Winchester copper measure brought ... from St Albans" against which the measures of four Bovingdon people "selling drinks as victuallers" were proved in 1690, following a complaint but they argued it was "there used as a corn measure only".[36]

Price regulation was particularly important when corn was scarce, with consequent effects on the cost of bread that might, and often did, lead to riot and disturbance.[37] Public order in St Albans was not affected in this way, no doubt because corn was available even in times of shortage elsewhere, but care was taken over the price of bread. Every year the mayor was reimbursed for money spent when he checked the weight of bread at bakers' shops on other than market days. Variations in the amount spent, as far as they can be known from the incomplete series of accounts, correspond fairly closely to the years of good and bad wheat harvests.[38] Spending in the 1650s was uneven until 1657/8 when it jumped to almost double that of the previous years after bad harvests. More bad harvests in 1673 and 1674 caused wheat to rise to half as much again as the previous year and in 1674/5 expenditure on weighing bread rose nearly as much. In March 1698 an order went out to bakers to ensure that their loaves at various prices from 1/2d [halfpenny] to 18d contain the correct weight by the London standard and that they not make "any loaf above the value of a penny to odd farthings or half pence ...". This order, like the purchase of a set of brass weights to weigh bread in the same mayoral year 1697/8, when wheat prices rose to unprecedented heights, displays a well-founded concern to prevent the sale of under-weight loaves.

The very small quantities implied by the halfpenny loaf and farthing-worths are reminiscent of Bunyan's indignation, in the character of Mr Wise-man, at the hucksters "who buy up butter, cheese, eggs, bacon, etc., by wholesale and sell it again ... by pennyworths, two pennyworths, a halfpenny-worth ... to the poor, all the week after the market is past". The mention of butter suggests it may at that time have been an item in the diet of poor people, which would explain why in 1692/3 the mayor for the first time weighed bread and butter, as again in 1699/1700. Mr Wiseman goes on: "they take usury for victuals ... and because they cannot so well do it on the market-day ... they do it ... when the market is over; for then the poor fall into their mouths".39 These remarks have the ring of truth undistorted by religious rhet-oric and bring to life the poor people who bought the little they could pay for in ready money from the baker or the women who sold their small amounts of butter and their few eggs at the market cross.

Quality regulation is only apparent in the records through the viewers' dis-covering unwholesome meat on sale. In 1696 when they found John Howson "selling meat, which was not marketable" the mayor's court bound him over to appear at Quarter Sessions; and in 1697/8 faggots were bought "to burn a side of mutton taken from White of Dunstable, butcher".40 Instances of defects in other commodities that did not present a potential danger to public health were not reported to the mayoral court; buyers of leather, for example, were warned off by the absence of the sealers' stamp.

FROM WORKSHOP TO RETAIL SHOP

Trading in the open market was only one element in the economy of St Albans and one to which it is easy to attach undue importance. Traders opened their shops every day except when their particular trade was conducted in the market, only bakers, it seems, being regulated, and the volume of shop busi-ness is likely to have equalled or exceeded that of the market. As earlier refer-ences to forestalling show, much trade went on outside markets or even shops.

Prior to 1700 most shops were much as they had been in the Middle Ages: workshops with a large front opening through which craftsmen could be seen producing the finished products they then set out on the boarded flaps that were raised to close the opening at night. The part of the building so occupied was often little larger in area than a market stall.41 Shops of this kind persisted for some trades, notably butchery and greengrocery, into the twentieth century. But gradually, as ready-made articles and goods began to be manufactured in quantity and distributed through an efficient transport system, shops were glazed and their owners became retailers.

Some probate inventories list goods that were certainly not made in the shop. Thomas Gill who died in 1678 was a haberdasher, though not so called in his inventory. His stock comprised more than thirty kinds of cloth, many kinds of ribbons, thread and lace, silk hoods, caps and masks, gloves, combs, needles and scissors, with many other articles for men, women and children. It would be interesting to know how he sold his goods; given their variety and the need for shelving from which to draw articles for examination, it was probably not in an open-fronted shop of the ordinary kind. Gill was essentially a new kind of tradesman, a shopkeeper buying his wares ready-made and selling them without alteration, no longer a craftsman whatever trade he may have been apprenticed to. Another such, in a much smaller way of business, was Jane Long, milliner, who in 1693 left a hamper of "redy made goods" unspecified, linen ready made up and yarn ready spun. A box of black hoods and "skarfs" lay ready to meet the constant and urgent demand for the trappings of mourning, a demand that was sometimes met by hiring, as when, for Sir Harbottle Grimston's funeral, his son paid for "the use of ten fine cloaks for gentlemen, and seventeen cloaks for servants".[42]

At this time the few people known to be engaged solely in retail trade comprised three milliners, three haberdashers and four who are described simply as shopkeepers. The one inventory for such people is that drawn up in 1682 in respect of Emanuel Kentish, whose occupation is not specified. His "Shopp goods" valued at £49 were of a very miscellaneous nature, the largest item being "Nayls of all sortts" worth £10, followed by "Sugar of all sortts" (£4 10s), "Butter & Cheese" and "Raysons & Corants" (each £3); then "Manchester wayer", soap, tobacco, beds, brooms, shot and powder – in all, some 36 items valued at £38. Clearly, Kentish cannot be categorised more closely than shopkeeper: he bought and sold anything likely to yield a modest profit. More restricted in their wares were the one or two booksellers in St Albans, who appear to have been essentially retailers of books and paper and are not known to have engaged in publishing. They may have had stalls in the market but most of their business lay outside it. How large their trade was is hard to judge but it may be relevant that in 1707 Thomas Dagnell mentioned in his will "the corn mills called the paper mills".

TRADE OUTSIDE THE MARKET

Trading in the open market was supplemented to an unquantifiable extent by private trading. Most of the larger St Albans businesses traded principally with London but there were exceptions such as the Hickmans who were ironmongers. Another may be Christopher Loft, who styled himself brewer in 1675 but chapman – in the sense, presumably, of a dealer or agent – in his will of 1688; and his bequests alone (p.169) show that he was no mere local trader.

In the late seventeenth century the growth of London provided an ever-expanding market that stimulated food production in all the Home Counties. The large quantities of corn required came from many parts of England, much of it carried by coastal shipping or along the Thames[43]; yet, as the brief issued in 1682 for the repair of the abbey church put it, St Albans "is perhaps the greatest for Corne of any Towne that is not a port in England". Its merchants presumably faced a price differential imposed by their dependence on waggons as compared with their competitors from, for example, Henley-on-Thames. Possibly the demand was so great that price was a minor consideration; otherwise, the good state of the London road may have helped, or the trade was conducted with lower wages and less profit than from more favoured places.[44]

Among other merchants looking to the capital was the mealman Samuel Whelpley whose will includes two significant bequests: to "my chapman, Mr Thomas Spicer of London, Baker, two Sackes of houshold Flower", and to "my Chapman Mr Giles of London, Baker one Sacke of Fine Flower". Presumably these men used some of Whelpley's flour in their own bakeries and sold on the rest for him as agents, performing a dual role that may not be reflected in other documents such as wills or lists of freemen and may pass unrecognised in St Albans. Some tanners had a London trade, for example John Salter, whose inventory includes debts owing for skins sold to a Widow Kempe as well as to a tanner in Watford. Evidence for direct connections with London is nevertheless sparse, even where they seem likely, for example, in the clothing trade. The inventory of John New III, ironmonger, who is described as "late of the parish of St Sepulchre's, London, but at St Albans", is divided into two parts, the second of which is headed "goods that were at St Albans", the other part being, presumably, for goods in London. A similar inference can be drawn in the case of Thomas Lucy, tanner, who, although he was a St Albans man living in Fishpool Street, died in London at a young age in 1675, having attained his freedom only two years before. Many of the family connections with London had commercial foundations, the details of which elude us.

Not all trade outside the market involved large transactions. The ready availability of horses was crucial to a town as dependent on road transport as St Albans and hardly less so to its merchants and traders. An important element of the economy was the buying and selling of horses which must have been carried on quite largely by bargaining between buyer and breeder at a farm or an inn. Coachmen and the carriers who could provide twenty waggons on demand needed a considerable number. Mealmen, maltsters and other traders required a horse to enable them to visit suppliers, for example, butchers riding out to buy live animals or tanners to get hides and skins. Several butchers had two horses and if the appraisers are to be believed most were in a sorry state: James Turner's were old, as were William Robinson's geldings, and George Robinson's were lame – though he had a mare and a little mare in reserve. On this showing a likelihood of collapse or sudden death increased the need for private bargaining over horses.

Horses were usually sold at fairs. For horses, that at Barnet may already have had a local reputation but not much is known about the St Albans fairs which seem gradually to have become limited to cattle. A decline in their importance is implied by their removal at some date unknown from Romeland, where they had been held from time immemorial, to the upper end of St Peter's Street. Decline, if not a move, is implied by the building of the row of houses lining the eastern fringe of Romeland and, more significantly, by encroachment on the formerly open space. In 1672 Robert Gregory, labourer, leased "a newly-built messuage between the highway and a void place of ground called Romeland", a house identifiable as one of a row formerly on the south side of Romeland Hill. An earlier timber-framed house with a jettied elevation facing down Fishpool Street may be comparable to the small unheated buildings which marked the beginnings of market encroachment in some Hertfordshire towns,[45] so that by then the ground available for the fair would have been more restricted than previously. But it certainly continued to be held somewhere, because in 1695 the mayor's court dealt with the stalls in the fair,[46] so that it still had some of the general trading found at the famous Stourbridge fair.

PRODUCTION IN ADVANCE OF DEMAND

Many trades can be said, in some sense, to have produced goods in advance of demand – butchers and bakers, for instance – but others demanded greater investment in raw materials and skilled labour before their work could be exposed for sale. Thomas Baskerville, passing through the town in 1671, noticed timber products, especially "gates for highways ready made to be sold";[47] words that are clarified by mention in the inventory of Edmund How, lathrender, of gate-heads, which were 'a frame or arch in which a gate is hung'.[48] Probably they were heavy gates set in a frame spanning the road through an estate of farm or leading to the stable yard of a manor house. This inventory includes ladders – no doubt long ones used to reach storage lofts like that Jeremy Fitch the baker was permitted to place in the Dolphin yard in 1665 – and quantities of laths and boards, besides barrel boards which were evidently half-prepared for the cooper.

Production in advance of demand was also used to some degree for both structural carpentry and joinery, whether for new buildings or the heightening and improvement of old ones. John Carter I, whose inventory of 1674 includes "his stocke of Timber not cut out And bords redy sawed and lathes" to the value of £80, out of a total of £140, is probably typical of the carpenters able to undertake the larger works, men who needed timber to hand of the right quality, in quantity and some prepared. Nearly two-thirds of William Nicholl's inventory value is in timber in various stages of preparation but it includes an important by-product, firewood ($£3$). The names of about fifty carpenters and sixteen joiners over the fifty-year period demonstrate the importance of these trades and some contracts which include work by Joseph Carter II at Holywell House in 1699[49] show that the craftsmen were capable of high-quality work. Their services were no doubt required some distance from St Albans.

Straw plaiting has left little trace in the records apart from Baskerville's cryptic mention of "St Albans straw tankards and pots"; terms that may be akin to the expression 'a bottle of hay', meaning a bundle of hay[50] of a specific size and named, presumably from the shape. Pointers to the early importance of the industry are two petitions against the import of foreign plait in 1689 and 1719.[51] Only the latter includes St Albans but mention in the earlier one of Redbourn reinforces the Baskerville reference.

An important element of the economy comprised small-scale manufactures about which very little is known. Brick- and tile-making is one. Bricks were made to individual demand where the quantity was large enough, and often on site or near it, as in 1649 when Sir John Wittewronge bought 184,000 for the refacing and enlargement of Rothamstead manor house, with another 32,000 in 1653 to finish the work.[52] For a town house something like the second figure was required and supply may well have been organised in the same way, whereas the many fewer bricks needed for refronting, the building of chimneys or the underbuilding of a jetty were probably met by stockpiling in advance of demand. The bricks were made just outside the borough at Bernards Heath, where the place-names Brickkyln and Brick Close are recorded in 1726[53], and in St Stephen's parish, where Thomas Higden, brickmaker, lived, and whose inventory in 1686 included "Brickes and tyles Burnt and unburnt" to the value of $£3$ 6s 6d. Possibly the large numbers of tiles that were all but ubiquitous for roofs, for which no local source is known, came from Tilekiln Farm, Hemel Hempstead or Tilehouse Farm, Aldenham.[54]

A smaller-scale manufacture was that of clay tobacco pipes which took place at a kiln half way down Holywell Hill from about 1680 to 1730. Several pipemakers appear to have shared its working because of the heavy cost of heating it to the high temperatures required. Those whose names are known from kiln waste include John Wilsher, whose pipes are found all over the town, William Tryant and William Hunt who married Sarah Tryant and was an innholder and clerk to the Abbey.

THE CHANGING ECONOMY

London's rapid growth governed the prosperity of St Albans as a market town. In the last quarter of the seventeenth century cereal crops, principally wheat and oats but also rye and barley, were grown more extensively in south-west Hertfordshire, much of it going to the capital.[55] An unquantifiable amount, though, went to meet growing local demand generated by road traffic. The many horses these services required and all those needed by people going about their business increased the demand for fodder that was met by farmers in the country between St Albans and Hendon specialising in hay;[56] and by 1699 hay had become a sufficiently important commodity for the mayor to weigh it.

Agricultural changes like these may explain why the Saturday market flourished in the late seventeenth century, despite the lack of contemporary evidence to show what was sold on that day or Wednesday. In the 1680s there are signs that the town's cattle trade was changing, with a falling-off in market dealing. In 1685 a toll of a penny a head from both buyer and seller was restored on cattle, having presumably been lifted earlier in the hope of stimulating trade. It was accompanied by an injunction that cattle should be sold only in the market and followed in January 1686 by a proclamation prohibiting the sale of cattle anywhere other than in the market. These restraints were intended to restore the profitability of the Wednesday market and do not connote a reduction in the cattle trade carried on by townspeople, some of whom evidently participated in the private dealing against which the measures were directed.

Not surprisingly, the increasing trade in corn in the last two decades of the seventeenth century also tended to be conducted outside the market-place. The only clear evidence of this appears at the very end of the century on 6 December 1699, when the mayor's court, faced with the bailiffs' difficulties in collecting toll (ch3, p.50), ordered that persons selling "grain and other things in the Markets and Fairs without paying toll" were to be prosecuted.[57] This, though, can hardly have been a sudden change. More likely, a general prosperity that allowed a high rent to be charged the bailiffs for their farm of the market from 1694 onwards conceals a steady growth in private bargaining.

A more specific decline, not merely a change of location in bargaining, is that of cloth-working. In the late sixteenth century people were brought before the mayor's court for buying and dressing flax or engaging in the fuller's trade without being a freeman[58]: or the mayor and aldermen paid for equipment to teach the poor spinning and weaving.[59] After 1650 the scarcity of references to cloth production coincides with the rise of the industry elsewhere and the beginnings of a retail trade in clothing.

Some of the effects the large transport business had on the economy have already been mentioned and insofar as they are quantitative, are obvious enough, principally the building of inns c.1570–1610 and their enlargement and improvement c.1660–1700. That may not have been quite the peak of prosperity for the innkeepers but it was not far off. The point has already been made that greater speed reduced the need for coaches to make stops of any length in St Albans, so that by the turn of the century the town was no longer a convenient first or last stop on journeys to or from the capital. And as inns farther out at places like Dunstable benefited from this change, so the new ones established in small places like London Colney, Redbourn or Markyate attracted traffic that might otherwise have gone to St Albans. Important though the carriers and coachmen were in making the town prosperous and stimulating several ancillary trades, some of the cream of the coaching trade had already gone elsewhere by the turn of the century.

NOTES AND REFERENCES

1   Above, ch.2. It is hoped to produce a fuller account of the inns elsewhere.
2   Petition against Ship Money quoted in Urwick 1884, p.122
3   Taylor 1637 (unpaginated), a book which "is almost certainly incomplete, as well as difficult to interpret"; Gerhold 1993, p.6
4   Very different figures are given in Crofts 1967, pp.11 and 125
5   Taylor 1637
6   Smith [1588], p.26
7   Records of the Committee for the Advance of Money
8   Verney and Verney 1907, p.361
9   Firth 1911, Vol.2, pp.861–9 (31 March 1654)
10 Hist. MSS Comm., Verulam, p.66
11 DeLaune 1681, p.386. Wilson is described as an innholder in the lease of a corn-shop in 1686.
12 1690 edition. For an assessment of DeLaune's book, which is generally reliable, see Gerhold 1988, pp.394–400.
13 Information from Professor David Hey.
14 At Watford, coming from Cassiobury, "the water was then so high ... we went another way to St Albans"; Hist. MSS Comm., Portland, p.305.
15 Hardy 1905, pp.170–1
16 DeLaune 1681, p.386; DeLaune 1690, p.402; 'List of Carriers' in Houghton 1692–1703. The advertisement for Cooper's waggon appeared from 3 August 1694 until at least 1 November 1695.
17 DeLaune 1690, pp.402,414,425; Houghton 1692–1703
18 Smith 1992, maps at pp.170–1
19 Flamstead is not listed as extant 1500–1640; Camb Agr Hist Vol.4, p.474. Defoe includes it among the ten market towns of Bedfordshire; Defoe 1968, Vol.2, p.513
20 Yaxley 1973, pp.177–8
21 Parker 1991, i,17, pp.107,130

22 This paragraph is based on Camb Agr Hist, Vol.4,pp.50–1, 509

23 It is not listed among specialised corn markets of the period 1500–1640, nor does any Hertfordshire town appear among the horse markets; Camb Agr Hist, Vol.4, pp.589–90.

24 Hatfield 1959–64, part 11A, pp.4–7, 11–13

25 Camb Agr Hist Vol.4, pp.496–8, with map.

26 Smith 1992, p.146

27 The sense of 'pattens' derives from a shoe into which the foot slips without fastening, e.g. clogs; OED. For its architectural application, Parker 1850, I, p.343; also 'The Carthouse…on Pattens' in the inventory of Samuel Turner, 1680. The witnesses in the Hemel Hempstead case appear to have had the impermanence of the first meaning in mind. A 'brick ground penn' was a low wall enclosing the feet of the stall. These comments partly supersede Smith 1992, p.146.

28 Cf. the 'carts and tumbrils unshod' that were the only vehicles allowed in the market at Ipswich; Camb Agr Hist, Vol.4, p.488.

29 Old photographs of St Albans market show this to have been a common practice; Mullins 1994, pp.10–14.

30 Gibbs 1890, p.36

31 Gibbs 1890, p.27

32 Special treatment of butchers was common. At Retford (Notts.) their trade is the only one mentioned in connection with market stalls; Marcombe 1993, pp.33–4, 84

33 Gibbs 1890, p.88

34 A painting in Norwich Castle Museum of the Market Place at Norwich in 1799, by Robert Deighton, showing a large weighing machine in use, implies a need for men to gather up the weights and measures.

35 Camb Agr Hist, Vol.5ii, p.820

36 Hardy 1905, p.392

37 'The moral economy of the crowd' and 'The moral economy reviewed', in Thompson 1991, pp.185–351

38 Wheat prices as Table 1, Camb Agr Hist, Vol.5ii, pp.828–30; harvests, Table XVI, p.864. The price indices are for harvest years, 29 September to 28 September; mayoral years run from 1 April to 31 March.

39 Bunyan 1928, pp.243–4

40 Gibbs 1890, p.94; mayors' accounts

41 Gretton 1929, p.173

42 Urwick 1884, p.122

43 Camb Agr Hist, Vol.5ii, pp.19, 155

44 In 1300 the cost of carrying wheat from St Albans to London permitted effective competition with many more distant places favoured by water transport. The same geographical conditions that made this possible pertained 400 years later; Campbell et al.,1993, 61–62, 76.

45 Smith 1992, pp.145–7

46 Gibbs 1890, p.88

47 Hist. MSS Comm., Portland, p.305. The local form of field gate is illustrated in a map of 1677; HALS IIIB.72.

48 OED

49 Harris 1987, p.34

50 OED

51 Grof 1988, p.14
52 Smith 1993, p.67
53 Map attached to survey of Sandridge 1726, repr. Rose 1999, p.25
54 EPNS Herts, pp.43, 63
55 Camb Agr Hist, Vol.5i, p.243
56 Camb Agr Hist, Vol.5i, p.247
57 Gibbs 1890, p.96
58 Gibbs 1890, p.27
59 Gibbs 1890, pp.28, 32

8

THE SOCIAL STRUCTURE:

GENTLEMEN AND MERCHANTS

WILLS, PROBATE INVENTORIES, hearth tax records and other local sources have yielded a mass of information concerning families and individuals living in and around St Albans in the late seventeenth century, some of which is collected in the following three chapters to give a picture of the social and occupational structure of the town. The present chapter is concerned with men who were accorded armigerous or gentry status and others who did not necessarily aspire to gentility but whose operations were on a large enough scale for them to be called merchants rather than traders. These last are the subject of Chapter 9, while Chapter 10 is devoted to ten 'biographies' of representative professional, mercantile, trading, artisan and yeoman families.

When William Harrison set out in 1577 to give a picture of the English society of his day, he divided it into four broad categories.[1] The first consisted of gentlemen, defined in general as "those whome their race and blood or at least their vertues doe make noble and knowne". He thus acknowledged that gentle status could be achieved as well as inherited: by obtaining a university degree, by appointment to governmental or military office, or by any man who "can live without manuell labour, and thereto is able and will beare the port, charge and countenance of a gentleman". Similarly, Sir Thomas Wilson, writing c.1600, explicitly placed a variety of professional men – lawyers, officers, graduates and middle-rank clergymen – among the gentry.[2]

For Gregory King in 1695 wealth corresponded closely to status and, in the form of land ownership, to gentility. Land was primary, pedigree, positions of authority and life-style secondary, but the two last attributes could be acquired by merchants, professional men and yeomen wealthy enough to purchase a modest landholding and ambitious of superior social status.[3]

LANDED AND ARMIGEROUS GENTRY

What part did wealth play in the establishment of gentility in St Albans in the seventeenth century? Between 1650 and 1700 some eighty families have so far been identified of which one or more members style themselves gentlemen or esquires or are so styled by others. Above this group in social rank were the two titled families in the area, the Grimstons and the Blounts.[4] Originally a family living on Humberside, the Grimstons had come south in the fifteenth century and had risen to prominence by service to the Crown and expertise in the law. Sir Harbottle Grimston was a leading member of the Long Parliament as MP for Colchester, but was caught between army and parliament in his attempts to mediate with the king and forced to retire from public life until he became Speaker of the Restoration Parliament. He bought the reversion of the Gorhambury estate in 1652, and was succeeded in 1684 by his son Samuel, who died in 1700.[5] Of the Blounts of Tyttenhanger there is little to be said. The will of Sir Thomas Pope Blount in 1654 shows few connections with St Albans and, apart from the important episode when his son Sir Thomas represented the borough in the parliaments of 1679 and 1680, the family played little part in its affairs.

Next below them in social status come those families which, according to the heralds' visitation in 1634, were entitled to bear arms. Of those which survived into the second half of the century, ten lived in or near St Albans – the Coxes of Beamont, the Jenyns of Sandridge, the Prestons of Childwick, the Sadleirs of Sopwell, and in the borough itself the Pembertons, Robothams, Rolfes, Gapes, Seliokes and Sympsons. All these families were entitled to the rank of esquire and to them should be added three lawyers – the recorders, William Foxwist and Anthony Farrington, and the attorney, Joshua Lomax, to whom the style of esquire was accorded as a courtesy. The use of this style rather than that of gentleman seems in practice to have been intermittent. Thus Thomas Coxe in his will of 1690 styles himself "of Beamonds" whereas his father and his son, both named Alban, content themselves in their wills with the style of gentleman; and while John Robotham is styled esquire in the will of William New in 1657, his son Robert in his own will in 1698 only calls himself gentleman, although the family were lords of the manor of Newland Squillers and Robert is one of the select quartet (Grimston, Churchill, Killigrew and Robotham) who sign themselves immediately after the Earl of Marlborough, High Steward, in the Declaration of Allegiance of 1696.

Some of these older gentry had gained their status through Crown employment: an unnamed Rolfe had served Henry VII, Sir Richard Coxe had been Master of the Household to Elizabeth and her two successors, and a Robert Robotham of Roskill (Yorks.) had served Edward VI, Mary and Elizabeth.[6] Others profited from the Dissolution: Ralph Jenyns of Church (Soms.) got Sandridge manor on marrying a daughter of Ralph Rowlatt, Sir Ralph Sadleir Sopwell on his marriage to Anne, daughter of Sir Richard Lee, the military engineer, both had shared in the break-up of the Abbey lands. Others had purchased land: the Prestons had been at Childwick since at least 1580[7] and Sir Goddard Pemberton, from Pemberton (Lancs.), "purchased a fair Estate and settled in this Burrough"; he became Sheriff in 1615 and was the father of Roger, who built almshouses opposite St Peter's church.[8] Only three of the families rose mainly through trade: the Gapes were tanners, the Seliokes brewers and the Sympsons look to have made their money in London where John I's father, Giles, a goldsmith, married into a titled family. But wealth itself seems not to have been a prime condition for advancement among these older families. No doubt they were prosperous enough but, apart from the Grimstons, neither their land holdings nor their other assets seem to have been particularly large.

POST-RESTORATION GENTRY

The heralds in 1669 added five new St Albans families to the ranks of the armigerous gentry – Crosbye, Ellis, Mountgomery, Rudstone and Wiseman. Edward Crosbye stands apart from the others, being described as "sometime major in the King's army" and he must therefore be the same Major Edward Crosbye who shot dead one John Townsend in a remarkable incident near the Abbey in 1662 (see p.100–101). Army service and life-style – he employed a huntsman, Charles Feild – recommended him for the style of esquire, rather than his small land holdings and modest estate of £200.[9] All the rest have in common a connection with London, no doubt the source of their wealth and standing.

John Ellis was a draper (merchant tailor) and alderman of the City of London who in 1643 bought the old monastic buildings at St Julians, pulled them down and built "a fair house" there before becoming Sheriff in 1668.[10] His brother James married Dorothy Sadleir from Sopwell and his daughter Rebecca married into the Arris family, who had become gentry through the professional standing of Edward Arris, a sergeant surgeon to Charles I. But the Ellises did not stay long at St Julians, which was sold in 1695 to the retired admiral, Sir Henry Killigrew.

The Mountgomerys were also related to the Arris family. When Lewys Montgomery I died in 1682 he left to his son Lewys, who had married Olive Arris, property in Aldersgate "that I purchased of the Goldsmiths". So it may well be that the Mountgomerys, like the Ellises, became gentlemen through their standing in the City, and the same may be true of the Rudstones and the Wisemans. The Rudstones had a house rated for Hearth Tax at eleven hearths, had plate valued at the remarkably high figure of £72, and were clearly wealthy. In her will in 1680 James's second wife Mary asked to be buried with her first husband in Little St Bartholomew's in London, and James's own background lay in Kent; but by the long list of minor legacies in Mary's will – to

Arrises, Ellises and a Mountgomery among others – it is evident that they were well integrated into the local gentry.

Of William Wiseman we know that his father came from Elsenham in Essex and that he himself married Mary, the daughter of William Scriven, an attorney in the Exchequer,[11] which may imply a London connection. He also was a wealthy man, living in a house in Fishpool Street rated at fourteen hearths, and it would probably not be unfair to attach the label of *nouveaux riches* to this small group of new families, since they were new not only to their status and wealth but also to St Albans.

Among the much wider class of non-armigerous gentry, there are similarly a few with probable London connections. Robert Barlee, for instance, who was born in Kimpton, had a sister married to William Scriven, the Exchequer attorney; and if Edward Nicholas was really the descendant of Sir Edward Nicholas, principal secretary of state to Charles I, who certainly had a son Edward, baptised in 1624, his background also lay in the metropolis. There were less exalted connections too. Thomas Eccleston, who about 1670 bought the Bull from the Sympson family, had a daughter married to a soap-boiler of London, and one of his brothers was a vinegar merchant in Wapping. Both Eccleston and Nicholas were wealthy men and Jane Nicholas, Edward's widow, founded the charity of that name.

CIVIC AND PROFESSIONAL GENTRY

The commonest way to gentrification among those living in the borough was undoubtedly through trade and civic office. Of the six families which amongst them held the mayoralty in half of the fifty years between 1650 and 1700 – New, Oxton, Pollard, Gape, Cowley and Marston – all except the last had held the mayoralty already before 1650, and William Marston held it in 1651. All styled themselves gentlemen. The News were pewterers, the Oxtons and the Gapes tanners, the Pollards brewers, the Cowleys mercers and the Marstons drapers, though some members of the families seem to have pursued other trades. All were wealthy but not all outstandingly so. The only really wealthy member of the New family was Robert who was Mayor in 1663 and almost certainly a draper. In his will in 1673 he describes himself as "gentleman of New Barnes" (later Sopwell House), and certainly he lived in considerable luxury. Thomas Oxton, who was four times mayor and died in 1677, lived in a substantial house in Fishpool Street rated at six hearths and had a total inventory of £399, while Philip, who was probably his elder brother and a maltster, built himself a house at Great Nast Hyde. John Gape the elder ceased tanning at the house he had built in Fishpool Street (Fig. 8.1) to become a country gentleman at Harpesfield Hall which he bought in 1676 from the Woolley

8.1 The Gape family house, now St Michael's Manor Hotel, in Fishpool Street.

family, another which had attained gentry status through civic office (Robert was Mayor in 1601 and 1608). But such examples of what, by small town standards, was conspicuous wealth were the exception rather than the rule.

In general, it would seem that within the borough reasonable wealth, normally acquired by trade, had to be allied with some standing in the local community, usually attained through civic office, and a certain ambition and life-style for a family to aspire to gentry status. These families joined the older gentry like the Jenyns, the Pembertons and the Robothams (though the two groups seem to have married largely within themselves rather than with each other) and the newly arrived gentlemen, some with London backgrounds, like the Ecclestons or the Rudstones. To these must be added the growing class of professional gentlemen such as lawyers, doctors and clergy.

Reference has already been made to the senior members of the legal profession in the town, to whom by custom the title of esquire was accorded. The three successive recorders were all benchers of their Inn of Court and two of them had Welsh connections. William Foxwist was a native of Caernarvon, to which town he left £20 in his will for the repair of the town church and £2 a year for the upkeep of the town conduit, while Anthony Farrington was justice for Cardigan, Pembroke and Carmarthen.[12] Foxwist lived in a large house in St Peters Street, rated for Hearth Tax at twelve hearths, and owned property in the town and land in Hertfordshire and near Caernarvon. In 1691 Farrington was granted a lease by the corporation of an old house in Spicer Street at a peppercorn rent, provided that he repaired it and the three neighbouring almshouse belonging to the Raynshaw Charity.[13] John Sympson, son of the John who owned the Bull, was living in 1662 at the Fleur de Lys, which the family had bought in 1642. But he sold the inn in 1671, and it is not clear where he lived for the last ten years of his life, in the course of which he received a knighthood. As he was also a judge in the sheriff's court in London, he may not have had a permanent home in St Albans.

The period around 1700 is notable for the drawing together of various groups of men active in the spheres of law and medicine into what are recognisably the beginnings of the two modern professions.[14] Besides attorneys, concerned mainly in drafting and executing wills and drawing up deeds and settlements of every kind, were also solicitors, acting in London as assistants to attorneys but in the provinces largely indistinguishable from them; notaries, dealing with bonds and contracts; and scriveners, dealing with conveyances. In seventeenth century St Albans the leading attorney was undoubtedly Joshua Lomax (see Chapter 10). Of the other lawyers little is known, and it is difficult even to know what they would have called themselves. The names of Thomas Richards, father and son, John Charnock and John Leigh occur regularly as witnesses on wills, and all three were accorded the title of Mr on at least one occasion.[15] Richards was Common Clerk of the borough from 1648 to 1678, a post in which he was succeeded by his son, and he married a sister of the mercer Abraham Cowley (see chapter 10), while Leigh was a trustee of the Dagnall Lane chapel in 1698.

In the medical field, the dominant figure was Thomas Arris (see Chapter 10) whose background lay with the barber-surgeons but who was granted the degree of MD by Cambridge University and became a member of the exclusive College of Physicians. The only other local doctor of equal standing is John King, a graduate of Leyden and Fellow of the College, who is best known as the father of a famous son, Sir John King, Solicitor-General to the Duke of York (the future James II).

The names of six apothecaries and twelve barber-surgeons are known in the fifty years from 1650 to 1700, and the apothecaries are markedly superior in wealth and standing. Formally qualified only to make up medicines to the physician's prescription, in practice apothecaries did the major part of medical treatment, especially in the provinces. Edward Nicholas has already been mentioned, and men like Henry Dobyns, Edward Horsell and Thomas Rotheram equally regarded themselves as gentlemen. All three were aldermen, and the first two went on to be mayor successively in 1690 and 1691. Rotheram, the only one for whom an inventory (totalling £587) is available, was a man of substance, owning lands and tenements in Sandridge and Windridge as well as a substantial house in the town well furnished with three looking glasses, some pictures, a pair of "Harpsicalls" and plate valued at £25.

The barber-surgeons make a poor showing in comparison and cannot be ranked as gentlemen. The ambiguity of the trade, which included on the medical side blood-letting and tooth-drawing and the treatment of boils, is shown by the combination in the case of John Doggett of barbering with wig-making; and a Robert Rumford, probably a son of Abel, is described in his marriage licence as barber and elsewhere as surgeon. With the possible exception of James Ramridge, who is once described when acting as surety for a marriage licence as a gentleman, it is doubtful whether any barber-surgeon would have so considered himself.

The clerical scene is dominated by the figure of Edward Carter, rector of the Abbey church from 1662 until his death from smallpox in 1687. He was also master of the grammar school till 1683 and became Archdeacon of St Albans in 1683 and a prebendary of St Paul's in 1684. He was a scholar and bibliophile, and in his diary John Evelyn records a visit made in 1688 with Dr Godolphin and his brother to St Albans "to see a library which he [would have] bought of the widow of Dr Cartwrite [sic] late Arch Deacon of St Albans, a very good collection of books, especially Divinity: he was to give 300 pounds".[16] Carter's successor as master of St Albans School was Dr Charles James, who in his long tenure of office from 1669 to 1695 revived the school's fortunes. He was undoubtedly regarded as a gentleman, and the only other known schoolmaster, Thomas Clarke, who ran what was probably a Quaker school in Fishpool Street, appears as Mr Clarke in both the 1663 Hearth Tax list and his own inventory in 1692. Thus, although it is too early in 1700 to speak of a professional class in the town, those described constitute the beginnings of such a class and were markedly more prominent than their predecessors before the Civil War.

It will be clear from what has been said of the professional gentry that they and the smaller number of civic office-holders represented in social terms the top level of what was otherwise a trading community. Not all the well-to-do merchants, of course, aspired to civic office and gentility. On the other hand, the merchant class virtually monopolised the mayoralty – it is noteworthy that though many traders and artisans became assistants, none seems to have become an alderman and so qualified for election as mayor, and this in spite of the fact that a number of them appear to have been as rich as the merchants who did. Clearly some social barrier prevented even the richest traders or artisans from proceeding to the higher civic offices and so achieving gentility.

By occupation the merchants of St Albans, who included many claiming gentry status, fall into four more or less well-defined groups: those dealing in food and drink – mealmen, millers, maltsters and brewers; in cloth and leather – drapers, mercers and tanners; in timber and metal – the lathrenders (timber merchants), cutlers and pewterers; and some general merchants who call themselves grocers or chandlers. But some problems of definition remain as, for example, with the ironmongers, who include both the large suppliers of metal goods and the retail shopkeepers; and where the latter can be identified with certainty they are considered in the following chapter. Of the four groups the first seems to be the most numerous and the second the most prosperous.

MEALMEN

In a brief issued for the repair of the Abbey Church in the 1680s the Saturday market is described as "perhaps the greatest of any Towne that is not a port in England", so it is no surprise to find mealmen among the most numerous of the town's merchants. Mealmen were essentially middlemen who bought corn from the farmers, some of which they sold on and some of which they ground either in their own mills or by taking it to one of the line of mills along the River Ver and the River Colne. So in a long list of debts owing to Samuel Whelpley of St Stephen's, which make up £652 of his inventory total of £812, there are several sums owing for loads of wheat, one for four loads "att the Windmill", and an item for thirteen loads "Tooke up in my Shoppe". But there are also a number of debts for bran and several loads of flour – seven in the warehouse, four of "household", one of "Course" and one of "wheaten". Obviously Whelpley, by the scale of his trade and his bequests of sacks of flour to two London "chapmen" – both bakers – dealt with more than a local market.

Three other mealmen also had considerable sums owing to them: Adam Potter (£220), who lived in the old Castle Inn on the corner of Shropshire Lane (later Victoria Street), rated at five hearths in 1663 and with two acres of land behind it, according to his will in 1669; Thomas Knight of St Stephen's (£150); and John Sampson of Holywell ward (£240 in bonds and bills). Both the latter had their own flour mills, with cloths and sacks, and their inventories include twenty loads of meal and fourteen loads of wheat respectively. Michael Sanders owned his own windmill on Barnet (Bernards) Heath, besides two houses in the borough. But although some mealmen took a notable part in civic life – Richard Millard, who lived in a large house in Fishpool Street (six hearths) was an assistant from 1651 till 1682 and John Cowley I for even longer (1677-1713) – no mealman seems to have moved on to aldermanic rank. Both John Cowley and John Sampson were wardens of the Victuallers Company, and Cowley, together with William Stone I, even earned a memorial tablet in the Abbey. But it was left to Stone's son William to move up the social scale –

his mother refers to him (no doubt with pride) as 'gentleman' in her will of 1691, and he became an alderman in 1702.

MILLERS

Of the millers Peter Medowes at Shafford is much the most impressive. As well as the mill at Shafford, which he leased from the Grimstons, he was also in 1669 working another Grimston mill at Redbournbury.[17] His inventory runs to £786, including £655 in debts "both at home and abroad" and the inclusion in it of thirteen acres of wheat and barley and six acres of Lent grain shows that, like some other millers, he had a substantial land holding. The inventory also includes a flour shop, with nine sacks of household flour, four sacks of "Corse" and a flour mill; so Medowes also sold direct to the public without the services of a mealman.

The only other miller who comes near Medowes in wealth is Thomas Dagnall. When he made his will in 1707, as well as being tenant of the Grimstons at Redbourn mill, with the mill-house "lately erected", he also leased from them "the corn mills called the paper mills", the corn mills "where I now dwell" (location not clear) and a field called Millfield in which he had recently built a windmill. He was tenant of other lands in St Peter's and St Stephen's parishes and a copyholder of a house in Abbots Langley.

MALTSTERS

Like the mealmen, the maltsters were middlemen, buying barley and converting it to malt for sale either to brewers or to those who brewed their own ale, including the inns, and from the nature of their trade they tended to live outside the borough. This is certainly true of the two Philip Oxtons, father and son, who were gentry and lived at Great Nast Hyde near Hatfield.[18] Philip I's will in 1661 makes clear that he was a considerable landowner, and Philip II's in 1687 makes bequests totalling more than £700, with a specific requirement that the sum of £200 to be paid to his son Edward shall come "out of my stock of mault & money due for mault". Similarly the inclusion in John Mitchell's inventory of a millhouse, yard, malthouse, farm animals and implements, malt and dried and green oats valued in all at £283 suggests that he lived outside the borough. But he had also barns and yards in St Peters Street with wheat, barley and pease, some in barns and some on the ground, valued, together with farm implements, at £68 in a total of £463.

BREWERS

Brewers too were men of considerable wealth, and included individuals of eminence in the borough. Robert Crosfeild I owned a messuage and brewhouse in Fishpool Street, together with three other messuages. When he died in 1660 these came under the trusteeship of his father-in-law, Thomas Oxton, and his brother-in-law, John Gape I, both tanners and near neighbours, until such time as Robert's son, Thomas, came of age; and the brewhouse was duly assessed in their name in the poor rates of 1660/1 to 1665/6. Robert was also related through his sister, Margaret, to the influential New family (see Chapter 10). In due course Thomas Crosfeild held the offices of constable, bailiff, assistant and alderman, and was mayor in 1683 and 1699.

The Pollards were equally eminent and were related to the Crosfields by marriage. Ralph Pollard I (who was the brother of Robert and father of Roger) had been three times mayor in the first half of the century, and owned the Christopher Inn and the Black Boy alehouse in addition to a messuage and brewhouse in Fishpool Street, which he left to Roger. Now Roger already owned the Angel in Holywell Street and Ralph's other son, Ralph II, already owned the White Horse, so they evidently sought to control outlets for their ale as well as invest in property. Ralph Pollard II was equally eminent in public life, being twice mayor (1665 and 1676); he was rich too, owning three properties in Holywell Street, and in his will bequests totalled over £200, with any residue to go to Edward Carter and the churchwardens of the Abbey church for lending in sums of £5 and £10 for three years to poor decayed tradesmen.

Among his legatees was his godson, Matthew Loft, son of Christopher Loft. Ralph Loft I and his wife, Mary, owned the Maremaid in Holywell Street. Of their four sons, Christopher, who is described as a brewer in a conveyance of 1675[19], had a house and brewhouse in Holywell Street and left bequests to his children amounting to over £1,000, while Samuel became an alderman in 1689 and mayor in 1699 and 1703, and is commemorated with his wife, Martha, on a memorial stone in the Abbey.

Thus the brewers seem to represent an extreme example of a wealthy and influential group in the borough, bound together by family ties.

MERCERS AND DRAPERS

The distinction between the two trade descriptions is not always clear, for although, properly speaking, mercers dealt with a wider range of goods, such as silks and satins, than drapers, who were essentially cloth merchants, a mercer can often be described as a draper.

The Cowley family, described below (Chapter 10), undoubtedly led in this

field although other individual drapers come near them in wealth and standing. Robert New I, who broke away from the family trade of pewterer and
built himself a house at New Barnes which he furnished in handsome style,
was obviously a wealthy man, as were William Jackson I with an inventory in
1681 of £1,343 and John Clarke I, who owned at least eleven houses in the
town; and although William Marston I's inventory total of £154 does not look
impressive, his Poor Rate assessment of £2 8s in 1663 and his Hearth Tax
rating at five hearths indicate substantial wealth. He was an Alderman for
more than forty years and was three times mayor. The elder Gawyn Crosfeild,
who died in 1666, was also three times mayor. Margaret New was a Crosfeild,
and one of her sisters married a Marston, so here again the families were
united by marriage ties.

It is not entirely clear how the drapers and mercers operated. Since there is
little evidence of cloth manufacture in the town – the names of only eight
weavers and two silk weavers are known – the assumption must be that cloth
was brought in from elsewhere by the big merchants like the Cowleys. In this
connection William Jackson's inventory is particularly interesting as containing
a list of materials "in the Shopp" but also finished articles such as gloves, stockings, waistcoats and muffs, and an item of £117 for lace (a William Jackson
appears as surety in a marriage licence of 1675, described as a laceman). In
sum, these items account for about half his inventory total, and a further £550
is owed to him in debts. So perhaps Jackson was more of a retailer than a merchant, as also more obviously was Solomon Smyth, described in his inventory as
a dyer but elsewhere as a draper. His inventory, too, contains a detailed list of
materials "in the Shopp", valued at £89. Whether these men bought from the
Cowleys or direct from some outside source, probably London, we do not know.

John Clarke is of interest as representing the strong Dissenting element in
the cloth trade. Abraham Cowley was a Dissenter, and John Clarke sold three
poles of land in Dagnall Lane in 1672 for the building of a Quaker meeting-
house. In 1683 he was presented for non-communion but claimed that he was
"no longer a resident, having sold up". A note added in 1684 claims that he is
"now at Holborn, has received and is orderly behaved" but he must have
returned to St Albans, for it is almost certainly he who is buried in the Friends'
burial ground in Victoria Street. His sister, Elizabeth, married Edmund How I,
lathrender, also a leading Dissenter. Stephen Humble was also connected with
the foundation of the Quaker meeting-house and was presented for non-communion in 1683, and the Thomas Jones to whom Abraham Cowley left his
shop fittings in 1690 was a trustee for the foundation of the Dagnall Lane
Chapel in 1698. Solomon Smyth mentioned above is named in 1661 as a
member of the Phanatique Party, but as he was a bailiff continuously from
1660 to 1674 he must have been at least an occasional communicant.

TANNERS, CURRIERS AND FELLMONGERS

Two families of tanners, the Gapes and the Oxtons, figure among the six which largely controlled the borough between 1650 and 1700. Both John Gape I and Thomas Oxton were aldermen for more than forty years and both were four times Mayor. Both were wealthy also, living in large houses in Fishpool Street (Fig. 8.1), and the families were joined by the marriage to John Gape of Thomas Oxton's daughter Anne.

The tanners bought hides direct from the butchers after the animals were slaughtered and sold the skins after tanning to the shoemakers, glovers and other leather workers in the Leather Market. Tanners are one of only two or three groups which congregate in a particular part of the town and the necessity for running water to fill their tanning pits drew them to Fishpool Street but not all of them were prosperous on the scale of the Gapes and Oxtons. George Edlyn, for example, was rated at only two hearths on his house in Fishpool Street, though he owned the Three Cranes alehouse next door, and John Graye at only one hearth, though he seems to have owned two other messuages. Nor were they all of comparable distinction, though John Doggett I, who lived at a large house in Fishpool Street (now Manor Garden House), was mayor in 1675, both Nathaniel Ewer I and Thomas Tanner were assistants for thirty-one and twenty-two years respectively and Ewer was warden of the Innholders in 1663. It is interesting that neither of them proceeded further in civic life, as both were of considerable wealth – Ewer's house was rated for Hearth Tax at seven hearths in 1663, and Tanner was able to leave £100 each to five of his seven daughters.

Trades related to the tanners include two curriers who dressed leather from the tanners and five fellmongers. The two fellmongers of whom something is known dealt in wool, Robert Davy being described also as a wool merchant, and Godfrey Scholfeild I, who lived in lower Fishpool Street and owned the Three Horseshoes alehouse there, owned also some premises described in his will as a woolshop, with a chamber over it, and a second woolshop over the house next door. The fact that Scholfeild was also a waggoner, with an item of £31 in his inventory for horses, suggests that he may have carried on a trade in wool outside St Albans. Scholfeild was quite a wealthy man, with an inventory of £172, and he owned two closes of land in Fishpool Street and rented a cornshop.

LATHRENDERS

When Thomas Baskerville visited St Albans in 1682, he commented: "Here is also in this town a great deal of timber to be bought and sold", particularly the ready-made gates (ch.7 p.154). This accords with the existence in the town of three obviously wealthy lathrenders (timber merchants), James Feild and the two Edmund Hows, father and son, and of a large number of carpenters and joiners.

The Feild and How families seem to have been friends. James Feild, not long before his death in 1685, entered into an agreement with the younger Edmund How by which he surrendered to How 50 acres of land at Tewin in return for the promise of an annuity of £30 a year to be paid to Feild's wife Susan. Feild also owned eleven messuages or tenements in St Peter's Street and Dagnall Lane, together with the Dog Inn in French Row, all of which he left to Susan (they had no children). His inventory of £281 reveals a well-furnished house and a fascinating list of stock-in-trade which includes all manner of timber from "spoakes" (300), "hart laths" (1,400) and elm boards (550) to 100 feet of "eves", 1,200 of "quarters, studd & rafters", 700 of "Thachen laths" and four gates (c.f. Baskerville above). The whole is valued at around £85, and Feild has debts owing to him of £101.

The will of Edmund How I in 1687 reveals much the same pattern.[20] He also owned eleven messuages or tenements, some in St Peter's Street and some in Romeland, and had the lease of a further house in St Peter's Street. His own house, probably the one rated at four hearths in 1663, had a woodhouse and yard attached to it, and he refers in his will to six barns and a room over the gatehouse which are attached to his houses in St Peter's Street. Some of these were probably used for the storage of timber, which, according to his inventory (total £189), included 6,000 laths, 1,100 feet of board and 1,700 barrel boards, besides items such as gate heads and six ladders, to a total value of £52. He also had a lease of the well-house in St Peter's Street, which he passed on to his widow. The younger Edmund inherited the stock of timber and the business, and one or other Edmund was associated with the foundation of the Quaker meeting-house in the 1670s. Another son James was a butcher and a third, Thomas, a watchmaker in London.

The only other two lathrenders known, William Hensman and Edmund Royden, were much less wealthy.

IRONMONGERS

The difficulty of classification arises in an acute form with the ironmongers. Whereas the Hickman family deal in iron and steel in gross, several of the others described as ironmongers are shopkeepers and one or two of them are sometimes described as grocers. In between comes a man like William Pembroke, who is well-to-do and has connections with the merchant group, so is clearly more than a shopkeeper but is also called both ironmonger and grocer.

The elder William Hickman was an active Parliamentarian during the Commonwealth and lived in 1663 in a large house (eight hearths) in St Peters Street. His second wife was the daughter of Sir Jeremy Whichcot Bt. of Hendon, and, according to her will in 1679, it would seem that the Hickmans had moved between 1663 and 1677 to a capital messuage in Spicer Street which had been divided into three parts, of which the Hickmans occupied one. In 1677 William, who was dead by the time Katherine made her will, had leased the house and his other property in St Albans (unspecified) in Spicer Street, Dagnall Lane and School Lane to his father-in-law and brother-in-law to provide an income for his widow, who was to decide their future. She gave instructions for them to be sold with their contents, and she bequeaths the proceeds in a number of legacies totalling (with two codicils) around £300. Her inventory, which would cover only that part of the house she occupied, mentions hall, two parlours, five chambers, buttery and kitchen, and totalled £103.

William's son, another William, was certainly an ironmonger and presumably inherited his father's business. His will of 1700 makes it clear that he was a man of property, with a house at St Albans, arable and meadow ground at Redbourn and lands and tenements at Kings Langley. He appointed three friends to help his widow in the administration since "I have no kindred to call to the assistance of my loveing wife" – this despite mention of his son, Samuel, in the will – but the remark is explained by the probability that Samuel then ran the smaller Hemel Hempstead side of the business. Samuel's inventory of 1707, the largest in total value seen (just under £4,000), speaks of him as "late of the Town of St Albans" and the debts owed to him are divided between "St Albans Booke" and "Hempstead Book". Their scale indicates that his trade extended over a wide area.

In what form did metal come to Samuel and in what form did he sell it? His stock, to a total value of £236, is disappointingly lacking in detail, consisting only of 11½ tons of iron at St Albans, 6¼ tons of iron at Hemel Hempstead, three Fagotts – bundles of rods weighing 120 lb. – and three quarters of steel, 69 lb. of German steel, four toe irons and five hammers, together with seven grinding stones and a lot of weights. Only the three 'Fagotts', providing the comparatively small quantities needed by blacksmiths and others, appear to be ready for sale, so presumably a slitting mill, not owned by him, existed locally, although its location is unknown.

Unfortunately, there is no other inventory extant for an ironmonger of the Hickman type. William Pembroke first appears in 1659/60 when he was assessed for the Poor Rate on a house in Middle ward with a rentable value of £6 and goods to the value of £80, these values fluctuating over the years. In the 1663 Hearth Tax list his dwelling is rated for six hearths. Also in that year he served as a warden for the Mercers company. In 1667 "Mr Pembroke" appears in the St Albans School accounts as supplying a lock and nails, and this fits with his description as an ironmonger in a deed of 1677 by which he bought two houses in Wheat Market from Abraham Cowley.[21] By 1677 he had demolished these and built himself a new house abutting southwards on Leather Market on the site of the present No. 6 Market Place. His name occurs in the wills of Katherine Hickman, for whom he acted as witness, and Robert Pemberton, who left him a ring, and he is a witness and appraiser in 1680 for the draper William Jackson. There is no doubt that this level of the wealthy merchants is the one to which he belongs with strong Dissenting connections. He was himself presented for non-communion in 1683 but as William Pembroke, grocer, and this trade description occurs again in 1689, when his apprentice Joseph Eeles was made free. Eeles was certainly a grocer, lived in a house owned by Pembroke and was one of the executors for his will in 1708, the other being the grocer Thomas Heyward. Both were noted Dissenters, and Pembroke himself was a trustee for the Dagnall Lane chapel in 1698.

By the time that he makes his will in 1708, Pembroke is living in a copyhold farm at Hill End and describes himself as gentleman. The will includes the house occupied by Joseph Eeles, probably the one built in the 1670s, land in St Peter's parish, and the Upper Half Moon inn. His wife, Mary, was daughter of Thomas Flindell, cooper, another Dissenter. By 1732 William's son, Joshua, was buying a house in The Vintry[22] and then and in his will of 1739 he is Joshua Pembroke Esquire.

What did William Pembroke buy and sell and on what scale? Clearly he was not an ironmonger on the pattern of Samuel Hickman. Equally, he seems to be of a higher status than, for instance, Samuel Waterton and who is much nearer to what we would call an ironmonger, i.e. essentially a shopkeeper selling a wide range of goods, though Waterton, like Pembroke, is also called both ironmonger and grocer. Perhaps Pembroke dealt in a similar range of goods but in the gross. The same may be true of two others styled 'ironmonger', Thomas Hayward I (not to be confused with the grocer Thomas Heyward) and James Arnold. Hayward followed a civic career – Assistant in 1648, Alderman in 1668, Mayor in 1678 and 1689. In 1663 his Poor Rate assessment was £1 10s. Arnold, with an assessment of £1 2s, was a cousin of both Edmund How II the lathrender and John Clarke the draper, and it is to this milieu of well-to-do ungentrified merchants that he seems to belong. Neither in Hayward's nor in Arnold's case is there any clue to how they operated their business, except that "Mr Hayward" supplied nails, locks and coals to St Albans School and the Corporation and occasionally coals for soldiers.

CUTLERS AND PEWTERERS

Although there is one family of cutlers, the Scotts, and one family of pewterers, the News, in the borough, in neither case is it clear whether they were concerned in the manufacture or only in the merchandising of their products; but almost certainly the latter. They differ greatly in status and prosperity. Whereas the Scotts lived at a modest level and took no part in civic life, the News were rich and powerful and more is said of them in Chapter 10. John Scott lived in a house which he owned in Holywell ward rated at two hearths in 1663, when his Poor Rate was 4s. William New I, who is quoted as a pewterer in apprenticeship lists of 1630 and 1635 when his sons, Abraham and Robert, were apprenticed to him, made his will in 1657, by which time he describes himself as gentleman, having held the mayoralty in 1641 and 1649. His will shows him to have been a man of property and wealth, owning messuages in Cook Row, most of which he had bought from the Robotham family, a further one in Malt Market, and two more in Hertford. His bequests totalled £300, besides some bonds and obligations unspecified. His son, John the elder, carried on the civic tradition as assistant in 1634, alderman in 1655 and mayor in 1659, 1670 and 1682. Although he describes himself as gentleman in his will in 1684, the likelihood is that he carried on the family trade also and that he is the John New, pewterer, who acts as surety for the marriage licence of Isaac Halsey and Mary Gape in 1669. But neither William's nor John's will gives any indication of involvement in pewtering.

CHANDLERS AND GROCERS

If it is difficult to distinguish grocers from ironmongers, it is still more difficult to distinguish them from chandlers and within each group to separate those dealing with merchandise in gross from those who were essentially shopkeepers. All but two of the chandlers are tallow chandlers, and are therefore concerned in the manufacture and/or sale of candles, though some of them may well have dealt in other goods. Edward Camfeild, for example, with a house of nine hearths in Middle ward and a Poor Rate assessment of £1 18s, is sometimes called a tallow chandler and sometimes a grocer. Similarly, Edward Eames, who is quoted as a chandler in a 1629 apprenticeship, may or may not have been a tallow chandler. The fact that his apprentice was a member of the Aldwin family, who were certainly tallow chandlers, makes it likely that Eames was himself one. His wealth is even greater than Camfeild's (a Hearth Tax rating of eight hearths and a Poor Rate assessment of £2 8s) and he was an Alderman in 1629 and Mayor in 1632, 1643 and 1654. The close trade connection between chandlers and butchers is reflected in the marriage of Humphrey

Aldwin to a member of the Seabrooke family, most of whom were butchers, and in the fact that at least one Seabrooke, Edward, Mayor in 1687 and 1701, was a tallow chandler.[23] According to his will, Aldwin owned substantial property in St Peters Street and Butchers' Shambles – he quotes eight occupiers, including himself. His will, though, does not indicate any great wealth and he does not display complete confidence that the sale of his houses will do more than pay his debts, but makes small bequests (five shillings each to his grandchildren) if it does. His widow (his second wife) comes off badly: she is left only the goods which she brought into the marriage.

Besides Edward Eames and Edward Seabrooke, one other tallow chandler, John Tisdall, held the mayoralty (in 1693). No grocer seems to have done so, though James Bradbury was an Assistant from 1685 to 1694, when he was dismissed for reasons unknown, and Ralph Marston II, to whom his grandfather, Roger Pollard, left the Christopher Inn in 1663, from 1682 to c.1708. Both Edward Camfeild and Mathew Iremonger held the wardenship of the Mercers company, and Camfeild is described at least once as gentleman when acting as surety for a marriage licence, as is Jeremiah Cowley, who lived in a house in Fishpool Street rated at five hearths, when acting as appraiser for Godfrey Scholfeild the fellmonger. No doubt the distinction between what we would describe as wholesale and retail was often blurred but most of the grocers were probably nearer to what we would understand as a grocer, and will be dealt with in the next chapter.

NOTES AND REFERENCES

1   Furnivall 1887, Pt.i, Ch.5
2   Wilson 1600
3   Wrightson 1982
4   A third titled family is represented by Sir Thomas and Sir John Cotton, who had a large house (12 hearthers) in St Michaels. They seem likely to be the son and grandson of Sir Robert Cotton, founder of the Cottonian library.
5   King 1983, pp.30, 41
6   Heraldic Visitation 1634; VCH Vol.2, p.414; Chauncy 1826, Vol.2, p.307
7   VCH Vol.2, p.398
8   Chauncy 1826, Vol.2, pp.308, 324, 399
9   PRO C8 227/88
10 Chauncy 1826, Vol.2, p.305
11 Visitation 1669
12 Chauncy 1826, Vol.2, p.302
13 City 756
14 See especially Holmes 1982
15 Charnock's name turns up also in a curious context: in 1692 Anthony Boys, a bookbinder, was given leave by the Corporation to buy Mrs Charnock's books at valuation (City 290).

16 Evelyn Diary, Vol.4, p.589
17 Featherstone 1993, p.28
18 Smith 1993, pp.69-70
19 Although in his will he describes himself by the odd title 'chapman'
20 Interestingly, he calls himself 'timberman', though he is called 'lathrender' else-
     where.
21 HCRO D/ECc T20
22 The site of the present public house and restaurant of that name.
23 It was after his second mayoralty that he was deprived of the rank of alderman for
     having made several persons free during his year of office without the consent of
     the other aldermen and for failing to hand over the civic plate. But he seems to
     have been reinstated subsequently.

9

THE SOCIAL STRUCTURE:
TRADERS AND ARTISANS

IT WILL ALREADY be clear that inns and alehouses formed the biggest element in the economy of the town. Some thirty inns and forty alehouses have been identified as active in the period, and no doubt the second of these figures is an underestimate. The distinction between inns and alehouses is not always clear: while inns offered accommodation and alehouses generally did not, this is not to say that one or two beds were not available in many alehouses; and there was also the Corner Tavern, offering wine but forbidden to offer accommodation, which, with its rating at six hearths in 1663, was as big as a middle-ranking inn.

The size of the inns varied greatly, as did the type of tenure. The Bull, with its eight parlours and twenty-three chambers, was in a class by itself; the traveller Baskerville described it in 1682 as "the greatest that I have seen in England". Next in size were the Christopher and the Red Lion with about fourteen chambers each, and the White Hart with eleven. Below them came a large group of sixteen inns with five to ten chambers and below them again a group of five small inns with less than five chambers. The three largest inns were owned by gentry who also lived in them, the Bull by the Sympsons and after 1670 by the Ecclestons, the Christopher by the Pollards and their descendants and the Red Lion by the Seliokes. So too was the George, owned and occupied by the Gladmans (Fig. 9.1). Eight others belonged to gentry who did not live in them, and in these cases the innkeeper seems to have been responsible for furnishing the inn: a major part of the inventories of Thomas Jones, who occupied the White Hart, and James Ashton who occupied the Chequer/Crane, consists of the inn furniture. Otherwise, apart from four inns with non-resident owners who were either not gentry or were of unknown status, the remainder belonged to owner-occupiers not of the gentry class.

Although owners and occupiers changed over the half-century, the balance between non-resident owners and owner-occupiers varied little. This would imply that either way the owning of an inn was a profitable business – a profitable investment for the gentry who formed the great majority of the non-resident owners, and a substantial livelihood for the owner-occupiers. How

9.1 Trade tokens of the 1660s: brass halfpennies issued by Henry Gladman, innkeeper at the *George*, and John Cowley, baker (with scales). Gladman's token is 18 mm in diameter (St Albans Museums).

substantial is difficult to gauge, especially as some of the owner-occupiers carried on another trade: the Stevens family at the Chequer/Exchequer, for example, were coopers, the Walter Cowleys at the White Hart in Cook Row were bakers, and William Jones at the Swan was a saddler. But the general impression is of a wide range. Thus William Bailey, who owned and occupied the Goat, had an inventory in 1684 of £301, which would put him in the top 20 per cent of the inventory range, while three more owner-occupiers – William Blithman at the Crow, Daniel Ireland at the George and Nicholas Goulding at the Dolphin – had inventories between £99 and £108, which puts them in the next 20 per cent, and Nicholas Goulding owned land in St Peter's parish. But Thomas Rotherham's inventory at the Blue Boar came to only £43. There is a similar range in the 1663 Poor Rate assessments: Robert Fletcher, who occupied the Chequer/Crane before James Ashton, was assessed

at £2 18s, well towards the top of the range but Joshua Carpenter at the Cross
Keys at the moderate figure of £1 2s and William Jones at the Swan at only
10s. To some extent, of course, the value of the innholder's inventory and his
poor rate assessment depended on the size of the inn: the Chequer/Crane was
assessed for Hearth Tax at eight hearths, while the Dolphin and the Cross
Keys were assessed at seven and the Blue Boar and the Swan at five. William
Bailey's inventory figure at the Goat, which was assessed at only four hearths, is
inflated by items other than the inn furnishings.

The pattern in the alehouses is rather different. In only four cases do the
premises seem to belong to the occupier. Of the outside owners, seven are gentlemen and of the twelve others whose trades are known, five are butchers.
None resides in the alehouse. Clearly, owning an alehouse must have been a
profitable business, just as owning an inn was, but for a slightly lower level of
society.

In both inns and alehouses women figure quite largely. When Gilbert
Selioke died in 1652 his widow, Martha, seems to have carried on the Red Lion
until 1670, when her son John took over. Likewise Sarah Sympson continued to
run the Bull after her husband's death in 1655 until her own death in 1670; and
when her successor, Thomas Eccleston, died in 1687, his widow Mary took
over the inn. The same is true of Judith Ashton at the Chequer/Crane, Mary
Blithman at the Crow, Mary Loft at the Maremaid and Mary Trustram at the
Saracen's Head. The names of four women appear among the alehouse
owners, and no fewer than eleven among the alehouse keepers. For widows, in
particular, keeping an alehouse must have been a welcome supplement to a
straitened livelihood.

In addition to the owners and keepers, both inns and alehouses provided a
livelihood for a multitude of ancillary occupations, quite apart from those like
butchers, bakers, mealmen or maltsters who were involved in the provision of
food and drink for the customers, or those like the farriers, saddlers and
wheelwrights whose trade was enhanced by the presence of so many horses
and waggons in the town. Unfortunately, very few of the inn servants had
assets large enough to justify the making of inventories. But there is one
inventory for an ostler, William Lickley (£30), and one for a tapster, John
Poole, (£87, including £80 in sperate and desperate debts) to represent a large
army of inn servants.

One other small group whose trade was pursued in close relationship to the
inns were the coachmen. Of the four known, much the most colourful is
Joseph Marshall, of whom some account appears in the following chapter. But
not all were as enterprising or as prosperous as the Marshalls. Stephen
Pricklove occupied premises between the King's Head and the Red Lion in
Cook Row.[1] In his inventory are listed two grey stoned horses and one black

one, valued together at £15, an old black stoned horse (i.e. stallion), a "bro" (?brown) bald horse and a lame gelding, valued together at £15, and two bay geldings, one moon-eyed and one lame, where the valuation is illegible. His vehicles are no better: two old coaches, and three old wheels. Nor was he much of a businessman: "there is certaine Bills", says a note on his inventory, "and some Debts in ye booke which are all or the most parte but desperat debts which wee doe thinke may be worth in time something but for present as they stand but £5". Nevertheless, his inventory totalled £103. When the inventory of his widow, Elizabeth, was drawn up nine years later, this sum had increased to £139. It included £30 for a coach, a "charrett", four horses and two geldings, with harness and trappings, so presumably she had carried on the business and improved it and, as she was a member of the Gladman family from the George, she was probably well qualified to do so. A sum of £33 was still outstanding for desperate debts, so perhaps Stephen's executors had not been entirely successful in their efforts to recover his money. In her will Elizabeth speaks of messuages and lands in St Albans without specifying their location or extent; but these seem on the whole more likely to have come to her through the Gladman connection than through Stephen's trade.

Of the three other coachmen whose names have turned up, Edward Chambers, who had seven children baptised in St Albans between 1659 and 1674, was discovered only through his marriage at St Botolph without Aldersgate and of Edward Eling and John Watts, nothing material is known, nor is anything known of five waggoners, one of whom was the Widow Trott, whose were operating from St Albans in 1681.[2] The only waggoner who appears in another context is Godfrey Scholfeild, the fellmonger in Fishpool Street. All six of them ran at least one weekly service to and from specified inns in Aldersgate Street or Old Street in the City.

From this point onwards it will be convenient to treat the traders and artisans in the same four categories as the merchants – those concerned with the food and drink trades, with cloth and leather, and with wood and metal, with a general section to conclude.

BUTCHERS

As with several other trades, butchering was dominated by a small number of families, in this case the Seabrookes, the Kinders and the Robinsons. Three Edward Seabrookes were butchers, while the Kinders produced two Gilberts, two Roberts, an Edward and a George, and the Robinsons two Georges, two Roberts, an Edward and a John and a Thomas. Unfortunately only one inventory is available for each family but the fact that Edward Seabrooke II, who died in 1680, had an inventory of £514 and lived in a large house in St

Michael's, with crops worth £192, animals worth £80 and debts owing to him of £150 shows how profitable the trade of butcher and grazier could be. Gilbert Kinder's inventory (1681) is much more modest (£135) and George Robinson's (also 1681) more modest still (£82). But these figures still put them in the top 50 per cent of inventories; and a man like John Cullett owned four houses and the Blewbell Inn and was able to bequeath more than £800, while Edward Kinder bequeathed £600, together with twenty-four pieces of old gold and three silver cups. No butcher held aldermanic office and so attained the rank of gentleman although Edward Seabrooke who was mayor in 1687 and 1701 and followed the related trade of tallow chandler did.

The butchers were segregated in the Butchers' or Flesh Shambles which extended from the Market House to the pillory just south of Dagnall Lane and somewhere thereabouts was the Bull Ring.[3] On the east side of this part of the Shambles was a line of buildings with three breaks in them, two being the present Lamb Alley and Sovereign Way with a third slightly north of that, and. it was here that several families of butchers lived. A series of property transactions link Thomas Watts, two members of the Robinson family, two members of the Kinder family and William Beastney.[4] Moreover, the property which William Beastney owned previously belonged to Henry Gape, butcher, and the alehouse next door, which belonged to Beastney and had probably belonged also to Gape, was in 1692 occupied by William Christmas, another butcher;[5] and by 1710 Mary Gilbert, the widow of John Gilbert, butcher, is sharing a property in Flesh Shambles with yet another butcher, John Cock. Although the Seabrookes did not live in Flesh Shambles, the eldest of the family, the first Edward Seabrooke, owned a house and barns not far away in St Peters Street, with another house next door leased to James Turner, butcher.

With so many butchers living right in the middle of the town, it is no surprise to find them owning or leasing land on the outskirts as temporary pasture for beasts which they had bought in the market but were not yet ready to slaughter. Thus, according to the St Peter's parish Poor Rate returns, John Gilbert, William Rowney, Robert Robinson, Gilbert Kinder and Edward Seabrooke all leased land in the parish. Likewise slaughter-houses were at a premium. Some butchers had their own on their premises but a family as prominent in the trade as the Kinders had to lease one from the Corporation in Dagnall Lane. No doubt William Rowney and Robert Robinson, who were presented at the Court Leet in 1663 for having piles of "stinckinge goare" in their "goare yard"– were representative of a much larger group creating the same hardly avoidable nuisance.

BAKERS

The number of bakers as compared with the butchers was small. This may indicate the extent to which households baked their own bread yet, since the architectural evidence for ovens is slight, it more likely reflects the greater intensity of use that was possible in the bakers' premises. Whatever the case, several of the bakers were wealthy and influential. Thomas Besouth, for example, owned a house rated at six hearths in Middle ward, land in St Peter's ward and was warden in 1663 of the Victuallers Company. Likewise, the elder Walter Cowley, as well as owning the house in Cook Row, owned also two other properties in Fishpool ward and was assessed for Poor Rate at £1 4s. When he died in 1664 he had been an assistant for thirty-three years. Further up Cook Row, some at least of the Gladman family who owned the George were bakers. The elder Ralph was an active parliamentarian in the Civil War who at his death in 1670 was living in a large house in Holywell ward. He was a man of considerable wealth, who had been mayor in 1652. A second Ralph, probably his grandson, was certainly a baker, and a trustee of the workhouse agreement of 1680[6], but not so Henry, the elder Ralph's brother, who took over the George and had an inventory value of £700 in 1675. So it is impossible to say how much of the family wealth came from baking.

About the Grubb and Fitch family, however, there is no doubt. As if to make it abundantly clear, Thomas Grubb occupied a property in Holywell Hill in 1684 called the Bakehouse. He was not particularly wealthy (poor rate assessment 16s) but he was an assistant for 30 years and a trustee for the workhouse agreement. Further up Holywell Hill, Jeremy Fitch owned a messuage rated at four hearths next to the Dolphin, access to whose yard was necessary for the conduct of his trade.[7] Evidently he prospered enough to acquire a nearby messuage subsequently.[8]

TAILORS AND ANCILLARY TRADES

In spite of their number, some fifty-five, the tailors in the town seem not to have been a very prosperous group. The only possible exception is Henry Smith of St Michael's who, in his will, bequeaths "all lands and messuages in the counties of Herts and Beds" to his four daughters. Although he describes himself as a tailor, one wonders whether he was not rather a dealer in cloth, and his inventory gives the impression of a man living in the country with horses, carts and farm animals, and with corn in the barns at Caddington[9] and Langley.

Of the twelve other tailors for whom information is available, only two own their own houses, and in no case does the poor rate assessment exceed 10s. On the other hand, three tailors, John Edmonds, Robert Hasell and Joseph Tarbox, served as assistants, Samuel Jewell was registrar at the Abbey in 1653, and Christopher Tayler was one of the trustees for the workhouse agreement.

Two milliners are known, both women. Mary Merritt has the distinction of being the only female freeman so far identified: she was made free in 1694 after being threatened with expulsion. Unfortunately, nothing more is known of her. Jane Long described herself in her will only as "widow" but it is clear from the stock of trading goods in her inventory that she worked as a milliner. It includes a box of "luys" (lace), a box of hoods and "skarfs", a box of linen "Redy made up" and a hamper of "Redy made goods" besides yarn "Redy spun" and twenty remnants of linen cloth. She also owned the Three Tuns alehouse in the middle of the town which had belonged to her first husband, the butcher William Beastney.

Other ancillary trades comprise two bodice makers (described, alarmingly, as "body makers"), three collar makers, one garter weaver and one hosier. Three of these are known to have lived in shared property, and the only known poor rate assessment, that for Francis Ellis the bodice maker, is for 4s. But the general picture of these trades is of small operators working in rented accommodation.

CORDWAINERS AND SHOEMAKERS

The fact that the shoemakers formed one of the original four trade companies or guilds in the town indicates their importance; whether their elimination as a separate company when the number was reduced to two in 1664 indicates a declining importance remains uncertain. Together with other leather workers they constituted the end of the economic line from the butchers through the tanners. To judge from the inventory of Edward Grunwyn the tanner, which includes an item for sole leather and upper leather, the tanners brought the leather to a condition where it could be sold direct to the shoemakers in the Leather Market.[10]

Unfortunately, only three inventories for shoemakers have survived, so it is difficult to form an overall picture of them. Only one of these mentions stock-in-trade. George Sleape appears to live in one room, and apart from a bond totalling £24 12s his other assets amount to only £3 11s 8d, including leather, 5s for working gear and heels (not 'tools', as one might expect), and 6s 8d. for a "last and" (where a word is missing). At the other extreme Andrew Whelpley, cordwainer, owns his own house in Abbey parish and another one in St Peters Street which he lets out to the baker, Walter Cowley II. His house has a hall, four chambers, a kitchen and a shop and is well furnished, though many items are described as old including a looking glass and, unusually, five pictures. He has plate and ready money totalling £25 and linen valued at £17 in an inventory of £82. Curiously, the only shop goods valued are twelve pounds of tobacco; perhaps he retired to keep an alehouse, especially as there is a sum of £7 for beer and wood.

This is the more probable because at least two shoemakers owned alehouses: Robert Haile the Saracen's Head in Bowgate (not to be confused with its namesake in Holywell Hill) and Thomas Woodward the Cock and Pye in St Peter's Street. Other prominent shoemakers were Richard Street and his son, John, Richard owned his own house in Market Place and both he and John were assistants – Richard for twenty-seven years – while John was warden of the Mercers in 1691.

Two wills are of particular interest. John Wethered was a Quaker, concerned in the foundation of the Quaker meeting-house in 1672.[11] He was comfortably off, living in his own house in Fishpool Street rated at four hearths and with a Poor Rate assessment of 9s. The house contained a hall, two chambers, a kitchen and a shop, and was left to his son James. But it also contained a cellar, and John was able to give to his son Stephen "the yuse of that ynd of the seller where now the rabetes are kept so long as he shall continer unmarred with the yus of the two pigeon houses". The shop contained leather shoes and other goods valued at £10. Both Stephen and James followed their father's trade.

As a sort of dependant on the shoemaking trade stands a translator, defined as 'a cobbler of low class who manufactures boots and shoes from the material of old ones, selling them at a low price to second-hand dealers'. Low class or not, Christopher Flanders owned his own house in Fishpool Street, which he left to his wife, Anne.

GLOVERS AND SADDLERS

The profile of the twelve glovers is not unlike that of the shoemakers. The three inventories available are fairly modest ones – £82 (including £56 for bonds, debts and ready money) for Richard Richardson, which is just on the 50 per cent line for inventories, £47 for Richard White and £28 for Henry Rugesby II, which would put him just into the bottom 25 per cent. The four Hearth Tax assessments are one for five hearths in Middle ward (John Mott), two for three hearths (Robert Scott in Fishpool ward and John Ruth in Holywell ward) and one for two hearths (Richard Richardson in Middle ward). Richardson's poor rate assessment is for 8s, Scott's only 3s. Three wills, for Henry Rugesby, father and son, and Richard White, indicate that none of the three owned his own house, and White is known to have rented a house in Fishpool Street[12], as did Anthony Polkinhorne in the Leather Market.[13] Two glovers served as assistants – William Moore in 1653 and John Ruth for a remarkable forty-five years from 1628 till 1673. Although his father, Richard Ruth, describes himself in his will as a gentleman, John did not aspire to follow him, though he did own his house in Sopwell Lane, left to him by his father, and had a poor rate assessment of 12s. He also married Ellen, the daughter of Ralph Pollard, thrice mayor of the borough.

Two inventories are of special interest. Richard White's house in Fishpool Street contained (besides a parlour, two chambers and a kitchen) a shop and a stable with two horses in it, and it is known from another will to have had an orchard attached to it.[14] In the shop was "a press to put gloves in" and a stock of leather, valued at £2 10s, and in the weighing room "the wool lying therein, scales and weights", valued at £20. This is reminiscent of Godfrey Scholfeild the fellmonger. Yet White, who is certainly described in his inventory as a glover, may, like Scholfeild, have traded his wool outside St Albans and been much like a fellmonger.

The most interesting inventory is that of Henry Rugesby II. He had inherited from his father in 1642 a stock of leather and "all things belonging to my trade", together with an apprentice for the remaining term of his apprenticeship. When he himself died in 1650 his appraisers made a detailed list of his stock-in-trade. This included 200 small white leather sheepskins, three dozen tanned sheep's leather, one and a half dozen white sheep's leather, two dozen skins of calves leather, ten beaver skins, two dozen small sheep's leather, one dozen dogs leather gloves, twenty-two pairs of sheep's leather gloves and five dozen and a half of half-handed gloves. All this was valued at £7 7s. A separate item of "one hundred of small white leather gloves" was designated in Rugesby's will as a gift to Richard White. To his own wife he left (right at the end of his will) one shilling.

Of the other users of leather, the saddlers (six in number), little is known. William Jones at the Swan kept a saddler's shop, with a stock of saddles, bridles, whips and other wares valued at £6 but it is impossible to say how much the shop contributed to his livelihood as an innholder. There is an inventory also for Thomas Redman, whose shop contains six saddles, two dozen of girths and "ties", five saddle cloths, leatherware, sixteen [saddle] trees and whips to a total value of £3 5s 6d. But his Poor Rate assessment of 4s does not make him look a very prosperous tradesman, nor does that of 4s 6d for Thomas Dalloway, of whom nothing otherwise is known, though he may be the Thomas Dalloway who is fined in 1659/60 for selling beer without a licence. Allied to the saddlers in making horse trappings is Peter Fullwood the collar-maker, who lived in his own house in or near Market Place. This business he combined with rope-making, being a regular supplier of ropes for the St Albans school bell over some thirty years.

CARPENTERS AND JOINERS

At a time when houses were still generally timber-framed carpenters were responsible not only for the timberwork of a new building but also its design and for organising the work of other tradesmen: they were part way to performing the function of an architect. One carpenter can be recognised in this capacity. Joseph Carter I contracted with Sir Harbottle Grimston in 1655 to rebuild part of Maynes Farm on the Gorhambury estate which had been damaged by fire, subcontracting the building of the walls, which were to be of brick, to a bricklayer; and again in 1673 to re-roof and improve the approach to the chapel at Gorhambury.[15] His son, Joseph Carter II, though, did not advance further along the professional road in his only ascribable work; he was almost certainly the "good, honest" man employed by the Marlboroughs in the remodelling of Holywell House in the 1690s under the architect Thomas Talman.[16]

Six inventories are available for carpenters and joiners, two of which stand out from the others. Although John Carter, a carpenter, lived in a modest house with a hall, parlour and two chambers, he kept a considerable stock of ready-sawn timber valued at £80 out of a total of £140, and William Nicholls, a joiner, lived in a very similar house, with a stock of timber of similar value (£78) in a total inventory of £129. Most of this is described as "sawed Stuffe", whch is in the yards, in the house "both above Staires and belowe", in the garden and in the street. There is also "Timber" – presumably logs – stored in the street, and it is no wonder that Nicholls and his son, William, are among a small group of carpenters and joiners living in St Peters Street who are presented at the 1663 Court Leet for obstructing the King's highway by having a pile of timber in front of their houses (and for having a sawpit in the roadway).

The other four inventories range from £93 down to £6.[17] The lowest – no doubt because he had retired – is for the elder John Branch, who had been able, nevertheless, according to his son's will, to buy land in Fishpool Street. By the time the younger John made his will, he owned property in St Peter's Street (he quotes six occupants in all) and he leaves to his wife, Alice, his plate, jewels and gold rings. She was the sister of James Feild the lathrender, and John left his property in the hands of James and of his father, William Feild, a husbandman at Childwick. So the Branch family was by that time quite prosperous. Another family of carpenters, the Hawgoods, owned their own house in Fishpool Street, but it was only rated at one hearth, and, in general, carpenters and joiners are more likely to be renting premises than owning them. At least two of these properties belonged to James Feild, and it is noteworthy that no less than seven of the ten joiners seem to have lived in the St Peter's Street area, at the south end of which was the Woodyard.

In spite of not being particularly wealthy, the carpenters and joiners were respected members of the community, as, for instance, Joseph Carter II and John Barnes, who were used as appraisers fourteen and nine times respectively. By the nature of their trade they figured in local life: Richard Fearnesly built the engine house in 1675, put up the freedom posts in 1681 and built a new pound in 1683; Joseph Carter II made a frame for the town clock in 1684 and John Hawgood put up the gibbet to hang Thomas Nashe in 1696.[18] But none played any part in civic life, with the possible exception of John Wilkinson who was an assistant from 1686 till 1708, and the identification is not certain.

WHEELWRIGHTS AND COOPERS

The leading family of wheelwrights looks to be the Longes of St Michael's and inventories have survived for both John and Thomas, probably brothers, but in neither case is there any detail of stock, tools, etc. John's inventory in 1679 speaks only of "his goodes without Doores" which make up £156 in a total of £186, and Thomas's in 1685 of "Timber and all other things belonging to his weelering trade" which account for £58 out of £163 (he has "hopfull Debts in Bonds and booke" of £70). John's house was rated at six hearths in 1663, while Thomas's has a hall, a parlour, a kitchen and two chambers. Their wills are not much more revealing: John has a large family, to whom he leaves a total of £140, and Thomas owns two or more cottages in St Michaels Street, so they are clearly men of substance, and Thomas's son, Thomas, was a churchwarden at St Michael's in 1707. Thomas Grigge is likewise prosperous, living in a house in Holywell Street in 1663 rated at four hearths and married to the daughter of William Hensman the lathrender, who lives next door.

The Stevens family, who owned the Chequer/Exchequer in what is now Chequer Street, combined innholding with both wheelwrighting and coopering, and in the process became very wealthy. William I's inventory in 1671 amounted to only £92, consisting entirely of the furnishings of the inn together with a sum of £25 for "weelers and coopers 1200 felos and 50 Axtrees 15 paire of shaftes and 1000 of hoopes". He owned also a meadow known as Wall Close (because it adjoined the brick wall belonging to Mr Robotham in Cock Lane) but, by 1678, the value of his son William's inventory was £749. William had inherited the inn but he lived in only part of it: the inn is described in his will as in the occupation of William Stevens and Robert Bryer, and his inventory is only for a hall, parlour, two chambers and a garret. Robert Bryer's name (s.v. Breers) is in the 1663 Court Leet list as an innkeeper, so it seems likely that he ran the inn while William concentrated on his other business. His stock-in-trade amounted to the huge total of £274, including £182 "in Copers stufe and Ruffe Timber and a leaden Trought", £60 "in Coach

Stuffe" and £25 in "shuinge Fellys" besides "4 loade of Ashin tops" and "106 Fellyes" in a garret. So he seems, like his father, to have done work other than coopering. Since his desperate debts (£254) were almost as great, he was presumably short of capital and conducting his trade on credit, although why he should have needed so large a stock is not clear. This may be a case where a probate account would reveal Stevens' own large debts. It is interesting that he also owned some premises in London, in Goswell Street in the parish of St Giles Cripplegate, which he asked his wife Dorothy to dispose of. So perhaps part of his wealth (and of his bad debts?) came from trading in London.

But the cooper whose name occurs most frequently in the records is Thomas Flindell, who with the grocer Thomas Heyward did the appraising for so many inventories of nonconformists. His father was a shoemaker who served as Warden of the Shoemakers in 1663. Thomas, however, served his apprenticeship as a cooper with William Stevens and in 1663 was occupying a property rated at three hearths in Middle Yard and had a Poor Rate assessment of 18s. But by the time he died in 1688 he owned not only this (which seems likely to be the house near the Malt Market included in his will) but also a house "formerly knowne by the name of the Castle"[19] which had a tenement and barns attached to it, and a house and land at "Wollam greene".[20] Flindell was obviously a wealthy man and, as appraising cannot have been so very profitable, most of his wealth must have come from coopering.

BLACKSMITHS, LOCKSMITHS AND FARRIERS

As with the carpenters and joiners, the blacksmiths and locksmiths are dominated by one or two families. The really remarkable man here is Richard Daniel of St Michael's, whose inventory total of £772 would put him among the merchant class and is largely made up of a sum of £618 "upon bills & bonds and upon surrender and upon deeds" and £115 in desperate debts. His real wealth might have been revealed by his will, as was the case with Robert Skeale.[21] On the other hand this large amount due to him may reflect his method of trading; a probate account might reveal his own large debts and this is the more likely because his house consists only of hall, chamber and kitchen; either that or he had retired. The inventory of Joseph Hanill in 1697 is much more interesting. Besides a hall, two chambers and a kitchen, his house has a brew-house, a drink-house and a shop, the last of which contains an anvil, a pair of bellows, ten hammers, a vice, a "beak horne"[22], a "box mole", scales and weights and other tools, with "three hundred of Iorn worked and unworked", some coals and two grindstones, valued in all at £8. As usual, there is a considerable sum for debts (£61 out of a total of £101). Likewise with John Hare, also of St Michael's (£50 out of £90), where no details of tools or stock are given beyond a total for them of £15. The will of his widow Jane makes it clear that he owned a house in St Michael's Street.

Other blacksmiths too owned their own houses; and William Element owned five tenements, three of them occupied by widows, as well as some copyhold land at Smallford. Besides bequeathing £80 to his family, he reckoned that the land should produce a further £20 each for his four daughters in due course, and he speaks in his will of securities, bonds and bills, which he leaves to his widow. He was clearly a man of substance.

The Element family is a clan of its own. As well as two Williams, father and son, who class themselves as blacksmiths, there is a Samuel, a Mathew, a Mathias, two Martins and a Walter, all of whom seem to be locksmiths, though one or two of them do other work in metal. The only inventory available is for Martin I, and if he is representative of the family of locksmiths, then they were not very prosperous. Although the house has a hall and three chambers, they are sparsely furnished, a number of the items being "old". Martin's shop contains a pair of bellows, an anvil, two vices, a "beackon" and other "od toules", valued in all at £1 10s. The younger Martin, it may be remembered, shared with a shoemaker a house in Holywell Street belonging to William Hensman the lathrender, and Mathias also lived in a house in Holywell Street which in 1648 belonged to Richard Ruth, perhaps the same house. Walter lived in rented property in Cook Row, owned by John New. Samuel, on the other hand, owned a house in St Peter's ward rated at two hearths in 1663. All of them worked at various times at St Albans School, and the family also turns up in the Corporation records – Martin I looked after the clock in the Clock Tower and rang the bell, while Walter was paid for supplying a hand for a direction post.

Just as the blacksmith group shades off into the locksmiths, so too do the farriers. The main family here is the Martins. Richard and Susan Martin were tenants of the house in Cook Row belonging to St Albans School from 1650-69, and, after Richard's death in 1669, Susan remained tenant until her own death in 1672, when she was succeeded by her younger son, William, until 1680. This is probably the house rated at three hearths in Middle ward in 1663, with a poor rate assessment of 4s. The only item of interest in Susan's inventory, which unfortunately is incomplete, is that she sub-let a room to another farrier, John Elisha, who subsequently moved on to the White Horse further down the street, where "John Elisha's room" is included in Walter Cowley's inventory. John Elisha did some work at St Albans School (presumably not shoeing horses), between 1684 and 1688.

BRAZIERS, PLUMBERS AND GLAZIERS

The inventory of John Sparling, the first of the two braziers, includes in a total of £189 a sum of £89 for brass, copper, iron, tin, beams, scales and weights, and of £49 for pewter, so presumably he worked in all these metals. There is no information on the size of his house, but he is probably the John Sparling whose son graduated from Magdalen Hall, Oxford in 1687. The other brazier, John Guise, occupied a property next to the Swan in Holywell Street in 1673, but whether he owned it is not clear.[23]

The only plumber for whom an inventory exists, John Carter, has a stock and materials which, in a total of £171, includes "Lead & Sodor pipe moulds and a melten pott", valued, with his clothes, at £36, and also "2 hundred of squeare and quary glase and glasing Lead" which, with "Cockes, bases & feralls" came to £4 11s; and presumably other plumbers kept a similar stock – whenever roof repairs are done at St Albans School (the present Lady Chapel) the plumber, usually either George Barnes or Belknap Theobalds, is paid for "lead and soder", and the glazier, usually either one of the Campions or one of the Kents, is paid for glass and leading. The lead costs 20s a hundred(-weight) and the solder 10d a pound. Quarries (small panes) of glass were 1d each and sheet glass 6d a foot.

It seems likely that besides plumbing George Barnes kept the Cock Inn, owned by the Robothams. Certainly a George Barnes, plumber, occupied a tenement near the Cock in 1680[24] and his name appears as an innkeeper in the 1663 Court Leet list. Probably his Hearth Tax rating of four hearths in 1663 is for the inn itself. He also makes something of a living acting as a surety for numerous marriage licences, sometimes described as plumber and sometimes as innholder. The Theobalds were also people of some standing. Although Belknap's father, Gregory, appears in the 1650 quit-rent list as occupying a rented house, which is rated at only one hearth in 1663, Belknap himself held a mortgage for £21 on a house in St Peters Street in 1670, was churchwarden of St Peter's in 1679 and before his death in 1690 was leasing[25] Lamb Close[26] which belonged to the church. He, like his fellow-plumber George Barnes, appears as a surety on a number of marriage licences. The only other plumber, William Butler, makes but a fleeting appearance: he obtained his freedom by purchase in 1682, became an Assistant, but in 1686 is recorded as having left the borough.

The glaziers John and James Campion regularly worked at St Albans School in the years between 1649 and 1665 repairing the many quarries (169 on one occasion) broken by the boys or otherwise, and James did repairs for the Corporation in the 1650s. Thereafter their place was taken by Anthony and Walter Kent who in 1686/7 had to supply no less than 532 quarries. They also worked for the Corporation in the 1680s and 1690s. Nothing more is known of the family except that James Campion was paid by the Corporation "for taking down the King's arms in the glass window of the Town Hall & setting up other glass in the place of it" in 1649, and that Anthony Kent, like Walter Element the locksmith, lived in tenements in Cook Row owned by John New. However, there is one will extant for a glazier, Samuel Heyward of St Michael's. He owns a house, divided into three, in part of which he lives himself with his wife, Hester, but he does not seem to have had much more in the way of assets than some unspecified shop goods and moneys.

BRICKLAYERS AND PAINTERS

Bricklaying, a not particularly prosperous trade, was centred on two families. George and John Agglington worked at St Albans School at various times and their names appear also in the Mayor's accounts. A third member of the family, James, lived in one of the tenements belonging to William Element the blacksmith. Of the Bradwyns, Robert lived in Fishpool Street in rented property and had a nil assessment for Poor Rate, while Thomas lived in a house in Holywell ward rated at two hearths with a Poor Rate assessment of 4s. A rather better-off bricklayer was William Harvey of St Stephen's, where he probably made his bricks, whose inventory totalled £40 (1670). But his money may have come from investment rather than bricklaying, for his will assigns £32 to "the lease" which appears to refer to the five market stalls sublet to butchers.[27]

Although the inventory of Robert Babb the painter in 1685 amounts to only £9 10s he owns the house in which he lives in Holywell Street, rated at two hearths in 1663, and another in Spicer Street. His name appears in the churchwardens' accounts as having painted the King's arms and the commandments at the Restoration, and he figures also in the mayor's accounts as having painted the freedom posts in 1681/2. His son, Thomas, followed his father's trade and left an inventory of £15 in 1690, including the bond for £12 which is mentioned in his father's will as owing to him.

Another family of painters, the Hicksons, is known only through the freedom list and their work at St Albans School. A painter-stainer of London, John Zacchaeus Cole, is worthy of mention as having married a member of the Rechford family, who were ministers of St Peter's, in 1686. He may possibly have been related to the Cole family who provided two rectors at the Abbey. John came into ownership of the Saracen's Head in Bowgate, and by 1719 was living in St Albans.

GARDENERS

So far as can be seen, almost no yeomen or husbandmen lived within the borough[28] although agriculture seems to have been practised on a small scale, because in 1702 the mayor's court ordered that only corn grown in the borough should be exempt from market tolls. But there is a small group of people who call themselves gardeners, meaning market gardeners. Two of these, Henry Tull and Henry Townsend, occupy premises in Fishpool Street. In the years 1676–8 Townsend paid a rent of 1d a year to the Corporation for the diversion of the watercourse in Fishpool Street into "pittocks". He died in the following year and Tull continues to pay the same rent till 1690, so he presumably took over Townsend's land.[29]

The other possible gardener of whom anything is known is a widow, Joan Fitch, who also appears as an alehouse keeper in the 1663 Court Leet list. In the 1650 quit-rent list she is described as owning a tenement in Middle ward and also, if Joanna Fitch is the same person, as occupying a rented farm in St Peter's ward. In the 1663 Hearth Tax list she pays on five hearths in Middle ward, and this fits well with her house in her inventory in 1684 but the inventory contains also a shop with a stock of rye, oats and peas, and fifty acres of wheat, barley and peas on the ground. As she pays on land in St Peter's parish in the Poor Rate assessment, it looks as if she occupied a farm just outside the borough and sold the produce in the town, so perhaps she is better described as a farmer than as a gardener.

LABOURERS

As might be expected, tie labourers whose names are known show no sign of any substantial wealth. The one exception is, John Long, who is able in his will to leave £60 to his son and whose inventory for a house with a hall and two chambers totals £88, of which £55 is in good debts. Moreover, one or two labourers outside the borough seem to own their own house thus labouring was not necessarily a last resort for those on the verge of poverty.

THE LEISURE TRADES - BOOKS AND TOBACCO

A small number of merchants and craftsmen cater for the leisure trades. Among these are the paper-maker John Philby, and the tobacco-pipe-maker, William Tryant. The first mention of Philby, who seems likely to have been the owner of the paper mill at Sopwell, is when he bought six houses in Sopwell Lane from Robert Sadleir in 1669.[30] These duly appear in his will in 1705, together with one other, included in which is his own house, and they are bequeathed to various members of his family. Besides the houses he owned also the White Lion and the Ship in Sopwell Lane. It would be interesting to know what happened to the paper that Philby made; the only signs of any local use are in the persons of a stationer, Jonas Heyward of St Stephen's, whose name turns up in 1684 as surety on a marriage licence, a book-binder, Anthony Boys, who is given permission to trade for a year in 1692 and is made free in 1695, with permission to buy the books of a Mrs Charnock[31] at valuation[32], and two booksellers: Richard Williams whose name is recorded in 1649–56[33], and is in St Michael's parish records as a stationer in the 1640s[34], and, at the other end of the period, John Hunt was the subject of an inscription in the Abbey, no longer extant: "Johannes Hunt, Bibliopola obiit 6 March 1722".[35] Whether these two represent a larger local trade remains uncertain.

William Tryant was not wealthy on anything like the same scale as John Philby: his poor rate assessment in 1663 was only 4s. Nevertheless, he was able to buy a house next to the Dolphin on Holywell Hill from Jeremy Fitch the baker for £148[36] and a list of Corporation leases in 1680 includes one for another house on Holywell Hill let to William Tryant, probably William II, who followed his father's trade.[37] William I died in that year. His inventory shows him to have had "money upon bond" to the value of £30 out of a total of £91 and it includes also £3 for " the Clay and the Tobacco Moulds and workeing geare" in the cellar.

The names of two other pipe-makers are known, one of whom, William Hunt, married Sara Tryant at the Abbey in 1682. According to the freedom lists, he ought to have been made free by purchase in 1686, but "gave up his bond". The other maker, Francis Maylin, turns up as a name on a marriage licence in 1673.

THE LIBERTY GAOLER

At the end of this long line of traders and artisans stands the figure of William Morris, the gaoler of the Liberty prison in the Abbey gatehouse. In some sense he may deserve to be classified, together with the exciseman, Ambrose Walker, among the professional men, as being the forerunner of the increasing number of government servants who in the course of the eighteenth century took their place alongside the older professions of law and medicine: but perhaps he is not badly placed next to the leisure trades, even if the leisure of his charges was an enforced one. Until 1651 only the lower part of the gatehouse was used as a prison, the upper floor being used for other official purposes. But in that year the local justices bought the upper part from the Crown and made it into a house of correction. In time the distinction between the two became blurred. As no separate house was built for the gaoler until the end of the nineteenth century, William Morris's inventory, which is for a parlour and kitchen, must be for the large room on the first floor of the gatehouse which has traditionally been known as the gaoler's room, together with the small room which opens out of it. Although the inventory amounts to only £10 6s 2d, it consists of a detailed list of possessions, including a clock and a looking glass (both comparatively rare items) and a "coffy pott tinn".

William was a man of some standing in the local community. He became an Assistant in 1676 and it is probably he rather than his son, William, who is Bailiff in 1676, 1684 and 1693. His daughter, Sarah, married a member of the Kentish family and it is William's son-in-law, Ralph Kentish, victualler of London, who is the signatory of a sworn statement as to the genuineness of William's will made necessary by the failure of any of the witnesses to sign it. It includes "money Bonds Bills my salary at London that shalbe due to me at my decease & my Quartridge here". Appropriately enough, he died in the year 1700.

NOTES AND REFERENCES

1   HALS D1082, D1085
2   DeLaune 1681
3   In 1686 the corporation leased to George Feild five stalls on the east side of the Counterhouse and one butcher's stall in the Shambles opposite the house of Edward Kinder, butcher, 'which is nearest the Bull Ring'(HALS 37965). Feild also undertook to set up and maintain the new pillory (City 710).
4   City 701 (1656), 755 (1671), 703 (1676), 708 (1676), 742 (1697),706 (1699); HALS 7308 (1651), 37965 (1655), D/ECc T58 (1669)
5   Will of Jane Long, 1692
6   The agreement was between representatives of the parishes of the Abbey, St Peter's and St Michaels and one John Hockley of Ware, a flaxdresser. Hockley was to run the workhouse and supervise the inmates in dressing flax, etc. but unfortunately he absconded with the money and equipment (City 115).
7   HALS D/E Sa5 describes the access agreement.
8   HALS D/Z18 T1. He sold it in 1675 to William Tryant, pipe-maker.
9   Carrington" in the will; a form cited in EPNS Beds and Hunts, p.146.
10 Its position is established by deeds (HALS D/Z18 T2).
11 Beds CRO PR24/18/5
12 Will of John Clarke, 1689
13 Polkinhorne can hardly have manufactured gloves so far from running water; he was presumably a retailer (City 960).
14 Will of John Graye, 1693
15 Contract 1655, HALS I.F12; Hist MSS Comm p.78
16 Harris 1985, p.34
17 John Choppin's inventory lists his carpentry tools.
18 Thomas Nashe was hanged for murdering his mother.
19 The Castle may have been the former inn on the corner of Shropshire Lane or

the house so named in Edward Nicholas's will of 1673 which stood near the foot of Holywell Hill.

20 Probably Welham Green, North Mimms, but possibly Woolmer Green, Welwyn. 'Wollam' does not match the forms of either name in EPNS Herts.

21 Skeale, a bricklayer who lived at Smug Oak Green and is outside the scope of this study, has a similar inventory but bequeathed five houses and £340 in his will.

22 A bickern or beak-iron, described here alternatively as a beak horne or beackon is an anvil with a horn-shaped end to it.

23 Will of William Jones(1673)

24 Will of Thomas Middleton (1680)

25 Will of James Middleton (1670/71) and HALS D/P93 6/11

26 Lamb Close was in the Gombards area, west of St Peter's Street.

27 A lease of the stalls in 1686 to George Field refers to them as "formerly in the tenure of William Harvey, dec'd" (City 710).

28 An interesting case, however, is that of John Woolman who lived in a substantial house in Holywell Street and described himself in his will as yeoman. He had been a servant of the Sympsons at the Bull but, according to a law-suit over the terms of his will (Woolman v Markham (1681) PRO C8 278/39) he had amassed a personal estate of '£1500 and upwards'. If the conjecture that the ostler ran a sep-arate business (above, Ch.7) is correct, Woolman may have combined that occupa-tion – which, at the Bull, would have been considerable – with farming.

29 Mayor's accounts pp.188-190, 191-8

30 These stood east of the Chequer/Crane along the south side of Sopwell Lane (HALS D/ELs T135). The present No.26 Sopwell Lane seems likely to be the one surviving house referred to in a note dated 1820 on the deed.

31 The Mrs Charnock concerned is likely to be the widow of John Charnock the scrivener.

32 Corporation Draft Minute Book 290

33 Plomer 1907

34 Everett 1935, p.67

35 Clutterbuck 1815-27, Vol.1, p.60

36 HALS D/ESa5. It was presumably this house for which Tryant was presented at the court leet in 1663 as having a stall outside.

37 City 960

TEN FAMILIES

THE TEN FAMILY histories which follow represent various aspects of seventeenth century St Albans.

The Coxe family is one of those, like the Jennings, the Robothams and the Sadleirs, which gained status through service to the Tudor court and bought or married into an estate on the outskirts of the town.[1] The Arrises came to prominence in a similar way but at a later date. Theirs was also a professional family, as was that of Joshua Lomax, one of several men of ability who came to St Albans from other parts of England and made their mark there. The Cowleys and the News are among the outstanding mercantile families which formed the ruling class in the town and attained gentry status by the holding of civic office. Below them the non-gentrified trading class is represented by the Kinders and the artisans by the Carters; and although this book is concerned mainly with the town and its inhabitants, it would be wrong to overlook the prosperous yeoman class living near the town, represented here by the Aylewards. Finally, the Marshalls are a maverick family which made its way up the social and economic scale, as many others did, and in their case finally overreached themselves.

THE COXES

The manor of Be(a)monds or Beaumonts, the seat of the Coxe family, was granted to John, the great grandfather of Alban Coxe I, at the Dissolution.[2] Sometime in the early seventeenth century Sir Richard Coxe, master of the household under Elizabeth, James I and Charles I and father of Alban, added to it the adjacent manor of Butterwick.[3]

The first Alban was born about the beginning of the century and died in 1665. Although he accepted office in 1636 under Charles I as custodian of the King's Stable, he was an active Parliamentarian in the Civil War and as a member of several local committees and the commander of the volunteer troop of horse that defended the county against Royalist incursions. He became a JP in 1649 and was appointed Governor of Guernsey although he seems to have spent only a short time there, as he was sent in May 1650 with troops raised in Hertfordshire to help Cromwell against the Scots. In 1650 he is described as in possession of the Abbey Gateway and several of the buildings still surviving at that time around the Great Court. He was one of the justices for the county and town in 1653 and MP for the borough in the Protectorate parliaments of 1654 and 1656, although challenged unsuccessfully on the second occasion by his defeated rival Richard Jennings, as having used force to prevent Jennings' supporters from voting. In 1655-6 he was Colonel of the new militia, but by the end of the decade he seems to have fallen from favour, being replaced in his command and failing to secure election to the Convention. After 1660 he fades from public life.[4]

Alban seems to have been an attractively moderate man. In 1661, at a time when accusations were being made against those who in the Commonwealth period had oppressed Royalist sympathisers, he was accused of having dealt "severely and unhandsomely" with ex-Cavaliers in the town and surrounding area. But a group of them, led by Thomas Coningsby, testified to their good treatment, saying that whereas in other places former Cavaliers had been "longe deteyned in a chargeable durance from their houses", they had not been "molested or disturbed", and that Coxe had on one occasion offered to resign his commission, having been informed against for saying "that a crown would become the head of a Steward (Stuart) better than a Cromwell", but had been persuaded to remain lest some more extreme person take his place.[5]

Alban's son Alban died young in 1656, and his second son, Thomas, who in 1666 had married Elizabeth, daughter of Thomas Cowley II, succeeded to Bemonds. Neither he nor his son, another Alban, who matriculated at Queens' College, Cambridge, in 1687, seem to have played any part in local life.

THE ARRIS FAMILY

Thomas Arris is an interesting representative of the seventeenth century medical profession, which was then still divided into its three branches of physicians, apothecaries and barber-surgeons. Arris's background was in the last of these; his grandfather was warden of the Company of Barber-Surgeons and his father became serjeant surgeon to Charles I.[6] But Thomas himself, born c.1622, graduated from St John's College, Cambridge, in 1643 and soon afterwards joined the élite of the profession as a fellow of the Royal College of Physicians. In 1651, when he was granted the Oxford degree of MD, the university authorities reported him "well affected to the present Government"; and in that year he was master of the Company of Barber-Surgeons.

It is not known when or why he came to St Albans. An earlier Arris, Henry, was a tallow chandler of London and sold the White Horse inn in Cook Row to Walter Cowley in 1629, so there may have been some family connection with the town.[7] But Thomas was from Essex, his father Edward, styled esquire, having bought the lordship of Great Munden (Herts.) in the 1620s and his wife, Olive, being from Stanway in the same county. It may have been when they married in 1650 that they came to St Albans. By 1657 Arris was living in a large house in Bowgate, rated at eleven hearths in 1663, and he also owned a considerable amount of land in St Peter's parish.[8] His mother Alice, described as of St Botolph's in Aldgate in her inventory, died in 1661 "at St Albans".

In 1660 Arris was appointed a JP for the county and liberty and in the following year embarked on a twenty-year political career as MP for the borough. He seems to have been a reasonably active member and in a speech in 1671 claimed to be the only physician in the House. This was during a debate on malicious maiming and wounding, when Arris made "an extravagant motion" for a bill to be brought in to punish any man that should speak a "reflective thing" upon the king, for which he had afterwards to apologise. However, his excessive show of loyalty may have been influential in his later being awarded two sinecures in Exeter, where he became comptroller of customs in 1678 and commissioner for oaths of allegiance and supremacy in 1679. He died in 1683 and was buried in St Peter's.

Thomas and Olive had four sons and four daughters. The eldest son, Thomas II, matriculated at Merton College, Oxford, in 1669 and in 1672 went on to Lincoln's Inn, so breaking the family medical tradition. He married Rebecca, the daughter of John and Rebecca Ellis of St Julian's, and his sister, Olive, married Lewys, the son of Lewys Mountgomery of St Stephen's. Both families had London connections like the Arris family, as also did two other families who were friends of the Arrises: the Rudstones, who were near neighbours in Bowgate, and Edward and Jane Nicholas. Both Mary Rudstone and Edward Nicholas (an apothecary) left rings to various members of the Arris family.

Thomas II was churchwarden of St Peter's in 1690. His younger brother Edward inherited the manor of Great Munden.[9] Another brother, Jasper, was apparently unmarried; in his will in 1685 (though the probate is not until 1696) he left all his estate to his mother, including some property in Giltspur Street in London left to him by his grandfather.

Socially, the Arrises must have been among the leading families in the town and professionally Thomas Arris no doubt regarded himself as much superior to the local apothecaries and barber-surgeons who bore most of the responsibility for day-to-day medical care and who became the forerunners of today's general practitioner.[10] It would be interesting to know what his relationship with them was.

JOSHUA LOMAX

"Stephen Ewer and Joshua Lomax, gentlemen, Attorneys at Law, dealt much in buying and selling of Lands, by which this Joshua Lomax obtained a fair Estate and was constituted Sheriff of this County in the year 1674".[11] So writes Chauncy, somewhat disparagingly. Joshua came from Bolton in Lancashire, where he attended Bolton School, and in his will of 1685 he gives detailed instructions for the support of a poor scholar from the school who may wish to go to university to study for the ministry of the word of God but whose relatives are not able to maintain him. In fact, the whole of the first half of Joshua's long will is taken up with charitable provisions, and first for the preaching of a sermon at the four churches in St Albans each on a different Sunday following his funeral, on "that choice text" Matthew 6,33, "seek ye first the Kingdom of God and his righteousness and all these things shall be added unto you"; in which the preacher is desired to avoid "any funeral Panegyric or Epaneticks of my life ... which the Auditors more breath after then sole Edification and tends not to the building them up in the faith". For this the preacher is to receive £5, and any householder who brings the members of his family to hear is to receive 12d. Moreover, a sermon on the same text is to be repeated at each of the four churches morning and afternoon on a set Sunday every succeeding year, and a shilling is to be given to each of twenty "poor housekeepers" who may attend morning and afternoon to hear it[12]; and Joshua particularly hopes that "some vile wretch who lives without God in the world for the lucre of 12d may come and bee converted". Similar provisions are made for an annual sermon at Harwood in Bolton parish.

Joshua was typical of his time in aspiring to the landed gentry and, in attempting to protect the estate he had built up, called in evidence the pronouncements of Solomon against children who sell a father's property. It was considerable: besides land and property in St Michael's, he owned the manor of Childwick (which he bought in the 1660s and where he built a country house that passed to his elder son Joshua II) and his manor of Westbrook Hay in Bovingdon (which went to his younger son, Thomas, who promptly built a "very fair Mansion House of Brick" there.)[13] Joshua's "buying and selling of Lands" explains his possessing other manors in Lincolnshire and Buckinghamshire, and land near Bolton was perhaps inherited. At least one manor, Punsborne[14], he seems to have given as a gift to a legal colleague.[15]

Most of his property he left to his wife, Anne, with instructions to sell what was necessary to provide for herself and their daughter, Elizabeth, including a marriage portion if she married according to her mother's wishes. If Anne died before administering the terms of the will, then the two sons were to take over the administration and provide £2,500 for their sister's portion and

£1,000 to be divided among Joshua's four grandchildren by their father, with respect to be had "to such of them as shall most sincerely serve God and obey their said father". Unfortunately, the situation which Joshua had foreseen seems to have come about, and the two sons, both of whom had been trained at the Inns of Court, went to law in 1691 to decide who should be responsible for the administration of the will.[16] The annual dinner which Joshua stipulated in his will should be celebrated by his family, at which they were to "rejoyce together" and "render praises to God with one accord for his mercies", and where his will would lie open all that day on a table in the dining-room for all to see, must often have been a frosty affair.

Clearly, Joshua had many of the characteristics of a Puritan, both good and bad. In the 'Evidence against the Phanatique Party' of 1661,[17] he is described as "allwayes accounted a Freind & assistant to ye Phanatique partie & when an unlawful assembly was in St Albans hee did in open Courte affirme itt to bee Lawfull and pleaded what hee coulde for ye meinteyninge of itt. And when a sermon was preached by Sir Harbottle Grimstons Chaplaine for the submission to and owninge of Government and Governors reported itt to bee a railinge sermon". He seems to have been an active dissenter but an occasional communicant, being presented for non-communion in 1683 but noted as having communicated in 1684. This made it possible for him to be sheriff in 1674. His sons went somewhat different ways. Thomas ceased any involvement with St Albans, took no prominent part in nonconformist life and may have abandoned it altogether. The changing times allowed the younger Joshua to be an open dissenter and he was one of the trustees of the Dagnall Lane chapel in 1698. He unsuccessfully contested the 1689 parliamentary election against George Churchill and Samuel Grimston but was returned to represent the borough in 1702.

Some parallel may be drawn between Thomas Arris and Joshua Lomax as representing the senior ranks of their professions. But there the resemblance ends. Lomax is much more of a self-made man than Arris, and one senses a certain ruthlessness about him which must have made him feared as well as respected.

THE GAPES

Like Joshua Lomax, John Gape II decided at a certain point in his life to move out of St Albans and purchase a property in the neighbouring countryside. In 1676 he bought Harpesfield Hall[18] from Robert Woolley, the descendant of a family of drapers which had itself moved out earlier in the century.[19]

The Gapes had made their money in tanning but John's father, John I, who died in 1675, was the last member of the family describing himself as a tanner.

10.1 Portrait of John Gape, d.1703.

The family appears in the heralds' visitation of 1634 but with only the briefest of entries, no pedigree further back than John II's grandfather, Ralph, and no coat of arms. However, by the 1680s they had remedied this last defect and their shield appears in the nave roof of the Abbey among those of the families that contributed to its repair at that time. John II himself was born in 1623, was educated at the grammar school, became an alderman in 1655 and mayor in 1658, 1668 and 1679 (Fig.10.1). But he was active also in a wider field. In 1658-9 and again from 1668-74 he was farmer of the county excise and at various times from 1660 onwards he was commissioner for assessment, first in the borough and then in the county also. He represented St Albans in the 1679 Parliament, defeating Samuel Grimston, the sitting member but he seems not to have made any great mark at Westminster and did not stand again.[20] In 1697 he became a county justice until his death in 1702.

The family house was in Fishpool Street (the present St Michael's Manor) where a number of tanners lived, and in 1646 John II married Anne Oxton, the daughter of a tanner and near neighbour, Thomas Oxton, who, like John, served as an alderman for more than forty years, and was four times mayor. To judge from his inventory, he was an active tanner until his death in 1677. John and Anne had six children: two sons, John and Thomas, and four daughters, Anne, Mary, Elizabeth and Abigail. John III, born in 1652, married Susan Cowley in 1679, was called to the bar at Lincoln's Inn in 1682, and followed his father by representing the borough in no less than six parliaments between 1701 and 1715. He was also sheriff in 1696. Of Thomas, nine years younger than his brother, little is known except that he seems to have fallen out with his father: in his will of 1701 John II cancels a previous indenture of 1685 and leaves Thomas only an annuity of £100 secured on lands in Cambridgeshire, the furnishings of a sleeping apartment and half his books. Of the daughters, Anne married into the prosperous Marston family and Mary married Robert Nicoll, gent, of Waterdell in St Stephen's parish, who had considerable land holding locally and in Cambridgeshire, Bedfordshire and Middlesex.

John II was a landed gentleman too. In his will he speaks of land in Cambridgeshire, including some at Caxton (where Robert Nicoll also had land) and by the time of his death he had added considerably to his holdings in Cambridgeshire and Lincolnshire. An indication of his local holdings is given in a lease to John III on his marriage in 1679,[21] which includes the Woolpack Inn, an alehouse in Sopwell Lane, four houses and nearly twenty acres of land.

John III and Susan had six sons of whom only one, William who became sheriff in 1738, outlived his father, who died in 1734. Thomas, however, educated at Trinity College, Cambridge and Lincoln's Inn, lived long enough to represent the borough in parliament in 1730. Three upwardly mobile generations saw the family move from tanning to the nobility when William's son Thomas married Jane, daughter of the 1st Viscount Grimston in 1743. It ought to be added, however, that there seems to been a more plebeian branch also, represented by Henry Gape, butcher, who c.1670 occupied a messuage in Market Place which he leased from the Corporation, and he probably owned the Three Tuns alehouse next door.[22]

THE COWLEYS

Two women of the Cowley (or Cooley) family have already appeared – Elizabeth, who married Thomas Coxe, and Susan, who married the younger John Gape; both were daughters of Thomas Cowley II. But the most remarkable female member of the family was undoubtedly Joan, who married Thomas Cowley I in 1613, and must have been over 90 when she made her will in 1688. She was able to include in it the names of nine grandchildren who had produced no less than twenty-six great-grandchildren with at least another seven still to come.

The eldest Thomas Cowley (I) was a mercer (though he is sometimes called a draper) and a wealthy and influential man, who was Mayor in 1633, 1650 and 1661. At the time of his death in 1673 he was living in a house in The Vintry next to the Corner Tavern. The house had a large extension at the rear (the "newe lodging or Long House" said to be lately built in an indenture of 1591[23]) the whole being rated in 1663 at eleven hearths. But he owned also a house in St Peter's Street, the Antelope inn in Church Street, some property and land in St Stephen's and land called Brick Mead near Bernards Heath. His inventory amounted to £1,206, including £1,000 owed to him in debts, and his house was notably well furnished, with plate valued at £24. He had been a stout Parliamentarian: in 1661 it was matter for complaint against him that he urged resistance to the king at the outbreak of the Civil War, offering his personal example, and was himself a member of the "Phanatique partie".[24]

Thomas and Joan's sons, Thomas II (the elder) and Abraham, diverged both in their religious leanings and in their careers. Abraham, who was in partnership with his father, seems to have been active in business to the end of his life – he left his shop fittings to Thomas Jones, probably the draper of that name – and died a wealthy man leaving an inventory valued at £1,741 and able to leave £600 to each of his three children. Probably he followed his father in being a dissenter of rigid principle, for he took no part in civic life; in 1683 he was presented for non-communion but claimed that he was not inhabitant at the time. Thomas II's life reflects more conformist sympathies, with acceptance of the prevailing orthodoxies as an alderman in 1657 giving way to those dominant in the years when he was mayor.[25] In his first mayoralty, in 1660, his opinions presumably reflected to some degree the national reaction against the Commonwealth, yet perhaps not very much for he was succeeded by his unbending father in the following year. By the time of his second mayoralty in 1672 he must have been an occasional communicant but, like his brother, he was presented for non-attendance in 1683. The contrast in nonconformist attitudes is reflected in the election of 1689: both brothers gave one vote to Grimston, but whereas Abraham gave his second to the dissenter Lomax, Thomas gave his to the anglican Churchill; and it is appropriate that in 1698 Thomas was a founding trustee of the meeting house of the most moderate of the nonconformist churches, the presbyterians.

Long before then the brothers drift apart, perhaps as much a matter of personal relations as of religion and politics, produced family repercussions. The effect must have been apparent fairly soon after the Restoration to judge from the statement in their father's will that he was making it (seven years before his death) "for the avoiding of all strife that may arrise betweene my wife and children". Nor can relations between them have been improved by the appointment of Abraham as joint executor with his mother of the will, and later as sole executor of her will.

Abraham inherited the Antelope. Before then he had lived in a house on or near the site of the present No. 6 Market Place, which he sold in 1672 to William Pembroke, an ironmonger and dissenter.[26] Among his friends were other prominent dissenters such as Katherine Hickman and Robert Pemberton as well as gentry like Robert Sadleir of Sopwell, Robert New of New Barnes and James Rudstone and Edward Nicholas. The last two were both friends of Thomas Arris, in whose circle people like Thomas Cowley II are likely to have moved. The gradual shift of opinion between the 1650s and the 1680s no doubt helped to limit social exclusiveness based on religious and political views.

Like the Gapes, the Cowleys had a less exalted branch of the family.[27] As already mentioned, Walter Cowley I bought the White Horse in Cook Row from Henry Arris in 1629. He was a baker, and served as assistant from 1631 until his death in 1664. His children, too, diverged in civic career and religion. His eldest son, Walter II, who inherited the inn and the bakery[28], was assistant for only seven years until his death in 1683; but his youngest brother, John, who was a mealman, more than compensated by a term of service stretching from 1677 until his death in 1713 at the age of eighty and is commemorated by a memorial in the Abbey.[29] It is interesting that none of them aspired to aldermanic rank. The two family traditions continued into the next generation. Thomas II's son, Thomas III, was mayor in 1688.[30] Walter II's son, Walter III, inherited the White Horse in 1673 and leased it to his brother, William, and two others. After being an assistant in 1676 William rose to be a citizen and salter of London, and in 1699, in view of the money expended by him on rebuilding and repairing the premises, Walter sold out to him.[31] In the main branch of the family Abraham's son, John (by his third marriage), likewise broke away from provincial life, being described as "of London, gent" when in 1708 he sold a house adjacent to The Antelope to a goldsmith of St Clement Danes.[32]

But Walter II's second son, Jeremy or Jeremiah, who lived in a house of five hearths in Fishpool Street in 1663 and had been constable of the ward in 1658, did not go that way, being apparently much of a mind with Thomas I in religion. He appears to be the Jeremy Cowley who is mentioned in connection with the Quaker meeting house in 1676 and it is entirely appropriate that in 1681 he was the overseer and appraiser for the will and inventory of Godfrey Scholfeild the fellmonger who had been a member of the Phanatique Party (and who also lived in Fishpool Street). In the will he is described as gentleman, and was still occupying a house in Fishpool Street in 1700.[33] Although none of the Cowleys achieved the professional or social position of the Lomaxes or the Arrises, this remarkable family played a greater part in the commercial, political and religious life of St Albans than either.

THE NEW FAMILY

If Joan Cowley impresses by the number of her descendants, Margaret New, who had no children of her own, is equally impressive in the multiplicity of her family connections. By birth Margaret was a Crosfeild, sister of the Gawyn Crosfeild who was an active Parliamentarian during the Civil War and mayor in 1634, 1645 and 1655; sister also of Edward Crosfeild, who married Mary Pollard of the prosperous brewing family which owned the Angel, the Christopher and the White Hart, and of the brewer Robert Crosfeild I, who married Mary, the sister of the Anne who was the wife of the elder John Gape. She was thus related to three powerful families in the town.

Her husband, Robert I, was the son of the William New, gent. and pewterer, who was mayor in 1630, 1641 and 1649, and who during his second mayoralty was arraigned at the bar of the House of Commons for giving preference to Royalist proclamations.[34] But as he was elected again in 1649 his parliamentarian sympathies can hardly be in doubt. It is not clear whether Robert was a pewterer, like his father, or a draper but probably the latter[35] In either case, he was a rich man, who owned a house at New Barnes (Fig.1.6) as well as a "mansion house" next to the Spread Eagle, which he also owned, and lands in Hertfordshire and Bedfordshire. His inventory of just over £2,000 in 1673 shows his New Barnes house as containing two parlours (including a "great parlour" with contents valued at £21), four chambers (including a "best chamber" with a French bedstead, down bed, silk quilt and wall hangings, valued in all at £59), plate valued at £20 and a brewhouse and mill valued at £94.

Robert's brother John I, usually called "the elder" to distinguish him from his half-brother, John II, the younger, does seem to have been a pewterer.[36] Like his father, he played an active part in civic life, and was mayor in 1659, 1670 and 1682. He owned considerable property in the town, some of it inherited from his father, to which he added the Bull at Leighton Buzzard. John I's inventory is curiously small, only £26, and it may well be that at the time of his death he was living at Leighton Buzzard and that the list of goods, with the unusual heading of "the goods and Chattles that have come to the Hands of Ann Haword" (his daughter) represents only the goods left behind in St Albans.

The marriage in 1657 of William's youngest son, John II (the child of his second marriage[37]) to Margaret Marston, formed a second link between the News and another powerful local family: her father, William Marston, was a draper, married to a Pollard, and mayor in 1651, 1662 and 1674. When John the younger died in 1671 he was described as ironmonger, "late of the parish of St Sepulchre's, London, but at St Albans", which probably means that he conducted the London end of the business whence came all the iron, while keeping his family in St Albans.

As if Margaret New's family relationships were not enough, her sister, Grace Crosfeild, married in 1651 Ralph Marston, probably a brother of William; and when he died in 1655, she married William Rugge, who was Mayor in 1671. Later in the century their daughter, Margaret Rugge, married another Ralph Marston, who was a son of William, and to whom the Christopher had been left by his grandfather, Ralph Pollard. The connection with the Gapes was further strengthened by the marriage of William Marston, another son of William, to Anne, the daughter of the elder John Gape and sister of the younger John.

By the 1673 will of Robert New I, part of his property went to his brother John the elder's son, John II, who was twice Mayor (1680, 1695) and (very confusingly) married a Crosfeild, Mary, in 1664.[38] The Spread Eagle fell to John's portion, and in 1705 it formed part of a property deal between another Robert (John II's son), by then a gentleman of Gray's Inn, and Edward Strong, citizen of London and Wren's master mason at St Paul's, who was his father-in-law.[39]

The New family represents above all others those characteristics of the civic families of the town, with their pattern of inter-marriages. Members of the family held the mayoralty six times between 1650 and 1700, and members of the Marston family five times. If the three mayoralties each of the Gapes and the Crosfeilds, the two of the Pollards and the one of William Rugge are added, the total of twenty represents a formidable hold on power by a town oligarchy rich in land and property.

THE KINDERS

Numerous though they were, and prosperous too, butchers seem not to have been considered eligible for the higher civic offices and consequently they remained ungentrified.[40] Otherwise the butchers were remarkable for the consistency with which family members took up the trade and practised it on the same premises – as, indeed, civic control of the trade compelled them to do – in succeeding generations.

The Kinders are typical in these respects but were unusual in the way the business was run. Like the Cowleys and the News, they also had a matriarchal figure. Susan Kinder, born Eames, had married Thomas Kinder in 1619, and they had five surviving children, four sons, Gilbert, Robert, Edward and Thomas, and a daughter, Elizabeth. But Thomas senior died in 1652, while Susan survived until 1678. In 1663 her name appears, like her husband's earlier, as an alehouse-owner but it is clear from a deed[41] of 1671 naming her as lessee of a stable and a slaughter yard that she also carried on the family butchering trade. From 1677 to 1684 her unmarried daughter, Elizabeth, paid both rents, though Edward appears as the occupier in a list of Corporation leases in 1680,[42] and in 1687 Robert pays the rent. By then Elizabeth and Edward – who must have been fairly prosperous to judge by a dispute over his will – had both died and Robert was ill, which explains why from 1688 twenty-two-year-old Gilbert II, the second son of Gilbert I, is the lessee; he was taking over what had been a joint enterprise conducted by two bachelor brothers and their spinster sister.

Gilbert I's absence from family affairs is because he married about the time of his father's death and set up for himself, with the expectation that his eldest son would succeed him but his second son was free to take over from his last surviving uncle. Gilbert I paid rent for a stall roomth in the Butchers' Shambles from 1654–79, and after his death in 1681 his widow, Margaret, continued to do so until 1684, when she was granted a new lease to set up "where she usually sets her stall" in front of the house occupied by widow Gilbert (another butcher's widow). From 1690 onwards the rent is paid by George Kinder, the eldest son of Gilbert I, who probably took over the business on the death of his mother.

Where did the family live? In 1676 the butcher, Thomas Watts, was granted a lease to set up a stall in the street of the borough in front of the house where Susan Kinder lived "where Thomas Kinder did for many years set up his stall".[43] This seems to be the house rated at four hearths in 1663. By 1697 the house was occupied by Susan's grandson, Gilbert II, and a deed of that year[44] makes it look as if it stood near the top end of Butchers' Shambles; and it may well be the house left by Thomas Cowley I to his widow Elizabeth and described in 1699 as standing on the corner of Flesh Shambles and Dagnall Lane and occupied by Gilbert Kinder. If so, it was obviously a rented house.[45]

But the family also owned a house. In 1663 Susan's son, Gilbert I, was assessed at four hearths for a house in Middle ward. This may have been the house in Dagnall Lane which is the subject of an agreement[46] in 1676 between Gilbert Kinder, butcher, and John Clarke, draper, by which Gilbert, "for the Naturell Love and Affeccon hee hath … for Margery Kinder his wife … and the better livelyhood … for Margery in case shee should overlive him" made over the house, recently purchased by him from Joshua Lomax, to her. The house is presumably the one on which Gilbert's 1681 inventory is based, and it was a substantial one, consisting of a hall, with a little room near it, three chambers, with a further little room, a kitchen, a buttery, a slaughter house and a stable. Gilbert owned 56 pieces of pewter, nineteen pieces of brass and one or two pieces of silver, and his inventory total of £135 and the owner-ship of the house, combined with the ownership of land in St Peter's parish, which appears in the Poor Rate returns, indicate that he was much the most prosperous of the Kinders. The family finally achieved gentility when Eliza-beth Coxe took as her second husband, Gilbert I's son Thomas, who there-upon abandoned butchering to take up residence at Bemonds.

Like the Lomaxes, the Kinders had trouble with a will. In 1688 Elizabeth Kinder, the daughter of Susan's son, Thomas, went to law[47] claiming that she was being deprived of £200 and some items of gold and silver left to her by her uncle Edward, who had died in the previous year. The survivor of the two executors named in the will, Joseph Marshall the coachman, claimed that as Susan had made her unmarried children Edward, Robert and Elizabeth, joint residuary legatees in her will and, as Edward and Elizabeth had since died, the remains of Susan's estate belonged to Robert, who was still living in the family house. Some plate, ready money and securities had been handed over to Mar-shall owing to Robert's illness but he was quite willing to return them at the request of the court. Whether Elizabeth got the two best silver cups and eight pieces of old gold which she claimed remains uncertain.

THE CARTERS

Just as butchering ran in families, so too did many of the artisan trades. The largest family grouping is undoubtedly the Elements in which two Williams, a Samuel, a Mathew, a Mathias, two Martins and a Walter were all in the metal trades, either blacksmiths or locksmiths, though little more is known about them. No other family can come near this, but many had two or more mem-bers in the same trade. The Carters to be described did not constitute a single family like the Kinders or Elements.

The Carters are interesting as covering two quite different trades, which is unusual. Inventories exist for a Joseph Carter I of St Michael's, who died in 1661, and for a John Carter I of the Abbey parish, who died in 1674, both of whom were carpenters, as was Joseph's son, Joseph II, but a John Carter II worked at St Albans School between 1684 and 1700 and for the Corporation between 1690 and 1700, and he was certainly a plumber.[48]

Joseph I does not seem to have been very prosperous. His inventory amounts to only £22 and he lived in a house with a hall, a chamber and a buttery, all adequately but sparsely furnished, and with nothing much else in the way of possessions. But he was more than a village carpenter, as his work at the fire-damaged Maynes Farm (above, p.187) shows. His part of the contract involved the laying of three floors, the making of roofs and window-frames for four new rooms, lintels, doors and three pairs of stairs, and the setting up of an end or bay 4.3m. (14 ft.) long to be joined to the barn next to the horse pond. He was to hew and saw all his own timber and was to be paid £20 for the job.[49]

Joseph's son, Joseph II, continued his father's work for the gentry. His name appears regularly in the Gorhambury steward's accounts in the 1680s, and in 1687 he makes a payment of £79 for "timber and spiers", presumably off the estate. Besides his work at Holywell House in the 1690s, he was regularly employed by the Marlboroughs in the repair of tenant farms on their San-dridge estate.[50] He also worked from time to time for the Corporation, for instance, taking the dimensions of the Abbey Church in 1679 so that they might be inserted in the brief being prepared at that time, or making a new frame for the town bell[51]. He also seems to have been much in demand as an appraiser for his name appears no less than fourteen times in the surviving inventories between 1671 and 1708.

John Carter I's inventory in 1674 included a notably well-furnished parlour together with £8 for linen, £12 for brass and £80 "for his stocke of Timber not cut out And bords redy sawed and lathes". He appears as working at St Albans School between 1659 and 1673 but is not otherwise traceable, family reconstitution having eliminated the eight occurrences of the same name in the parish registers.

That negative conclusion applies equally to John Carter II, the plumber, for whom two inventories exist. One of them is undated and describes him only as "John Carter late of the Towne of St Albans".[52] It covers under brief and general headings the contents of a parlour, a best chamber, a little room, a children's room, a garret and a kitchen, totalling £47, and five items for working materials. The whole is unusually untidy and ill-spelt, and the total contains only figures for shillings and pence, with the pounds figure missing, yet it has been signed by the two appraisers. The other inventory is notably well set out and the heading describes John Carter as "late of the town of St Albans … Plumber", contains a date almost pedantically fixed (Ano Dni Stilo Ang 1709)[53], and the names of the two appraisers, but it is unsigned and consists almost entirely of working tools and materials, with a strong resemblance to the other inventory but set out in much more detail.[54] At the end there is a brief mention of some domestic items in the wash-house, kitchen and parlour.

The total of this second inventory is £63 3s 1d, as against £104 6s 1d (if the correct pounds figure is supplied) for the other.

The conclusion is irresistible that the two inventories are for the same person and that the first represents some sort of rough copy which was then laid out in a more satisfactory form. But why were the domestic details not similarly laid out? And why do the appraisers sign the rough undated copy, with the total incomplete? It is just possible that there were two John Carters who were plumbers and died at about the same time and their goods were appraised by the same appraisers – but it seems unlikely. A father-son relationship between John Carter I and II is also improbable on present evidence and it may be that both are immigrants who were neither born nor married in St Albans. On the other hand, it is odd that apart from two apprenticeship references there is no information about a John Carter II who was a carpenter and no information about an earlier Carter who was a plumber.

The Carters as a whole are interesting for the light that they shed on both trades and, in the case of the Joseph Carters, on the extension of a carpenter's trade into a cross between those of an architect and a building contractor.

THE AYLEWARDS

Of the yeoman families farming in the immediate vicinity of the town the Aylewards were the most numerous; so numerous, in fact, that it is difficult to fit them into a satisfactory pattern. The difficulty stems in part from the way the family was established immediately prior to the Dissolution. Much of the manor of Cell Barnes was leased c.1531 by the nuns of Sopwell, who owned it, to John and Nicholas Ayleward.[55] Joint occupancy of a sizeable manor, particularly a former monastic manor, is a recognisable form of tenure[56] and one that led, in this instance, to the building of two houses some 75m. apart. The descent of the manor after 1531 has not been traced but by 1908 there were "two houses, Little Cellbarnes, a farmhouse and Great Cellbarnes, a square brick house".[57] The latter appears to be where two successive James Aylewards, who describe themselves as gentlemen in their wills in 1674 and 1688 respectively, lived. James I had two children: Anne (who married John Coxe, the son of Alban I) and James II, who inherited the house and part of the original manorial lands which by this time had been formally divided. The terms of James II's will, which included an annuity of £7 a year to his sister, Anne, from the nearby Winches Farm, indicate some sort of trouble: in leaving a shilling to his wife, Jane, he adds "whom not without much greife and sorrow I often call to mind", and he had only a single child, a daughter, also Jane, for whom the house and land were left in trust. Eventually, the estate reappears in 1732 in a will of Edmund Ayleward, who was an attorney and successor to

Thomas Richards II as common clerk of the borough. He had a reversion of Cellbarnes through a Mrs Welch, who was a grand-daughter of James Ayleward II.

The farm at Cellbarnes belonged to two successive Thomas Aylewards, yeomen. Although the elder Thomas describes himself in his will in 1670 as "of Breakspeares" he bequeaths to his son, Thomas, "all my messuage or tenement with appurtenances called … Cellbarnes", with the lands belonging to it, about 160 acres, provided that Thomas II pays £200 to each of his three sisters on their coming of age. The farm at Breakspeares, of about sixty acres, was left to Thomas I's second son, Daniel.

At the time when Thomas made his will, neither of his two sons was of age and this, combined perhaps with his retirement or ill-health, may explain why both farms were apparently being worked by a neighbour, Thomas Robines of New Barnes. Thomas Ayleward's arrangement for Cellbarnes did not work out as expected, however, and Thomas II, who is described as a tallow-chandler of St Martin-in-the-Fields, sold the farm in 1678 to his brother-in-law, Nathaniel Brooke, a London apothecary, and he in turn sold it to the Grimstons in 1681.[58]

The third section of the family includes William Ayleward of New House, yeoman. His house still stands, just south of Birklands on the west side of the London Road, and it was a centre for meetings of Dissenters. His wife was Martha Nicholls, and Martha's sister, Anne, had married a William Smith of Wooley in Kent. After her husband's death she came to live with the Aylewards, and in her will of 1688 she leaves everything to her sister except the contents of a leather trunk which is left to Martha's daughter, Hannah. Fortunately, Anne Smith's inventory has survived, and it is possible to identify the "one leather trunk & all yt is in it", valued at £4.

Further round to the south of St Albans lies Hedges Farm where another branch of the Ayleward family lived. A William Ayleward of Hedges pays rent for a corn shop in the borough in the 1650s and 1660s, and this seems likely to be the William, yeoman, who made his will in 1668. It is a curious will: in return for a sum of £100 to be paid to his executors, he left to his eldest son, James, "all that money which he was to pay me for the stock of Selbarnes which is three hundred pounds Also all the rent which is behind of twenty pounds a yeare which he was to pay me soo long as I lived Except the rent of the last two years which is behind". Other land is divided between two other sons, William and Thomas, who has a wife, Ann. Thomas seems likely to be the Thomas who appears in the Gorhambury steward's accounts[59] in the 1680s as farming at Hedges and who married Ann Rolfe from neighbouring St Julians.

Quite what the connection is between William and Cellbarnes is not clear, though it is possible that his son, James, was the elder of the two James

Aylewards, gentlemen. It may be that this is another complex family situation quite different from the conventional one of a farmer or a master craftsman at the head of a family. It appears that several Aylewards had some rights in the working of what may have been the family's chief property – its seat, to use a later term – and that in the eighteenth century such rights were extinguished in favour of one member.

In spite of all the uncertainties, the information available about the Aylewards shows them as farming a great swathe of land stretching from Winches, east of the town, through Cunningham Hill and Cellbarnes to Hedges, a combination rivalled only by the various Sleap(e) families round Smallford and Sleapshyde, or the branches of the Kentish family round Potters Crouch and Bedmond. Although none of these families seems to have played any part in the civic life of the borough they must have exercised a considerable influence on the agricultural aspect of its economy.

THE MARSHALLS

Most yeoman families living in the countryside seem content to have remained yeomen, with no aspiration to gentility. But for the small number describing themselves as yeomen who lived in the town the way was open to gentility via the holding of civic office, and the Marshall family is one which took it.

The family first appears in 1658 when John Marshall made his will and divided all his assets between his two sons, John and Joseph, with a life interest in the lease of his house for his widow Abigail. From her will in 1665 it is apparent that she had been married before and that she was the mother by that marriage of six Pricklove sons, one of whom, Stephen, is known as a coachman and another, Nicholas, as a shoemaker. In 1663 she is rated for Hearth Tax at three hearths in Middle Ward, and this is presumably the house in John's will. She makes no mention in her will of her two Marshall sons, who were probably sons of an earlier marriage of John's. In any case, they were well provided for in their father's will, and she was able to divide up her goods among her Pricklove grandchildren, which she does with admirable efficiency. There is a chest standing behind the kitchen, one in the garret and another "standinge at my bedsfeete", a little box standing "by my bedside", and another little coffer "in my Bedchamber", and all these and their contents are variously assigned. Finally, two other grandchildren receive "all the goods which were mine now in the wool-sacke Chamber over the gatehouse", which gives John Marshall both rural and trading connections.

Of John's son, John, nothing is known unless he is the John Marshall who served as constable in Fishpool Ward in 1656/7. But Joseph was ambitious. He first appears in a conveyance[60] of 1671 when he buys the Flower de Luce from

John Sympson II, and he is still described as a yeoman. He served as a constable in Middle ward in 1673/4, as bailiff in 1678/79 and from 1677 until his death in 1702 as an assistant. In that time he had become a coachman and in 1681 ran a service to the Cock in Aldersgate on Mondays, Wednesdays and Fridays and returning on Tuesdays, Thursdays and Saturdays.[61] In the following year, being then a widower of about fifty, he married Elizabeth Long of St Michael's, almost certainly the widow of Thomas Long the wheelwright, who had died at the end of 1679. It may be typical of a certain cavalier attitude on the part of Joseph that the surety for his marriage licence is John Doe, one of the standard names for 'warrant men'[62] in eighteenth century regiments.

As Elizabeth was forty-five by that time, Joseph's five children were clearly the product of an earlier marriage. His will of 1701 shows them to be widely scattered. Thomas, described as a butcher of London, is overseas, and can only claim his inheritance if he returns and resumes his trade. Robert is a sword cutler and William a gingerbread maker, both also of London. Rachel is married to Edward Hayward, a coachman of Dunstable, and her name reappears in a deed[63] of 1722 where she is described as a widow deceased, mother of William Howard, a coachman of York (a similar name change occurs also in St Albans). The deed concerns a property by that time known as the Crown in Fishpool Street left to her by her father, and these must be the premises in Fishpool Street mentioned in his will.[64] Joseph the younger, the eldest son, who had bought the Flower de Luce from his father in 1695 and the King's Head from John Gape in 1707[65], was left his father's "Four and Twenty Mans Gowns" and his Great Bible.

Although he served as an Assistant for twenty-five years, the elder Joseph did not proceed further in civic office. Joseph II, however, after serving only eight years as an assistant, became an alderman in 1704 and mayor in 1708. He died in 1715 at the age of 57. His father's stone, which typically, perhaps, was a re-used stone, still lies in the nave of the Abbey, though the inscription is almost illegible.

The end of the Marshall story is something of an anti-climax. Joseph II's son, John, was also a coachman and was mayor in 1723. But there is a record of a John Marshall, stage coachman, who went bankrupt in 1733,[66] and this may well be the same man. It is interesting that his ruin occurs when there is some evidence that the coaching trade in St Albans was beginning to decline.

NOTES AND REFERENCES

1 The Grimstons and the Jennings have not been chosen, as they are adequately dealt with in other publications.

2 VCH, Vol.2, p.416

3 Chauncy 1826, Vol.2, pp.305, 314

4 Much of the information in this paragraph has been supplied by Dr Alan Thomson.

5 Quoted, Clutterbuck 1815-27, Vol.1, p.113. An interesting series of letters addressed to him in the Civil War period exists at HALS 70538-77.

6 For much of this paragraph and the third see Henning 1983; also Chauncy 1826, Vol.2, p.73.

7 HALS D/E Ch T111

8 Based on Poor Rate assessments.

9 Chauncy 1826, Vol.2, p.73

10 Holmes 1982, pp.166ff

11 Chauncy 1826, Vol.2, p.251

12 The sermons continue to be preached on the specified Sundays at St Stephens and St Peters but not, since 1930, at the Abbey and St Michaels.

13 Chauncy 1826, Vol.2, p.476

14 "Punsborne" is probably Ponsbourne near Hatfield.

15 Chauncy 1826, Vol.2, p.15

16 Lomax v. Lomax, PRO C8/422/74

17 HALS 8B/67

18 The site lies under the 1930s de Haviland airfield.

19 VCH Families 1907, p.157

20 Henning, 1983

21 HALS 9250

22 City 739

23 Title deeds held by Barclays Bank, Peterborough.

24 HALS VIIIB/67; above, Ch.5

25 Thomas Cowley II, whose occupation is uncertain, lived in the Prior's house, which he had bought c.1653 and which was on or near the site of the present Deanery.

26 HALS D/E Cc T20

27 Although the relationship is not clear, Walter I may well have been a brother of Thomas I. One or other Thomas witnesses Walter I's will in 1664, and Thomas II appraises the inventory of Walter II in 1683.

28 The inclusion of a bakehouse with a bolting mill, meal, etc., in Walter II's inventory implies that the bakery was in the inn yard.

29 The inclusion of a bakehouse with a bolting mill, meal, etc., in Walter II's inventory implies that the bakery was in the inn yard.

30 An Almetius, son of Thomas of St Albans, gent, entered Merton College in 1677 but nothing more is known of him (Alumni Oxonienses).

31 HALS D/E Ch T111

32 HALS D/EB 1873 T15

33 HALS D/EB 1873 T13/9

34 Gibbs 1890, p.275

35 Robert New appears in the 1635 apprenticeship list as apprenticed to his father.
    On the other hand, a Robert New, draper, figures in a deed of 1658 (City Supp
    Doc I) as buying two houses in Market Place. Robert's wealth makes the trade of
    draper the more likely.

36 He is so described in a marriage licence for Isaac Halsey and Mary Gape in 1669.

37 To Ellen Choppin(g), who seems likely from her name to have been a relative of
    Joan Cowley née Choppin(g).

38 She was the daughter of Robert Crosfeild and therefore Margaret New's niece
    before becoming her niece-by-marriage.

39 City Supp. Doc. I

40 Edward Seabrook III had moved into tallow-chandling (see p.182).

41 City 755 (Court Leet 1663)

42 City 960

43 City 708

44 City 707

45 HALS 11756. It may also be the same as a property described in a lease (City 742)
    of 1697 as being in the occupation of Robert Kinder, brother of Gilbert II, situ-
    ated "over against" the Counterhouse. It had a yard attached to it, perhaps the old
    slaughter yard from the days of Susan Kinder. See also City 706.

46 HRO D/EB 898 T19

47 PRO C8 Mitford 402/33

48 Other references point to two possible Carters: a John who was a son of John I
    and a carpenter, and a plumber who was the father of John II. The parish regis-
    ters do not resolve the problem. See City 290, 291.

49 HALS I.F.12. He is referred to throughout as Joseph the elder.

50 Harris 1985, p.34

51 Mayor's accounts passim

52 HALS A25/4987

53 The abbreviations stand for 'Anno Domini Stilo Anglicano' (according to the Eng-
    lish style).

54 HALS A25/5028

55 VCH, Vol.2, p.414

56 Smith 1992, pp.106-11

57 VCH, Vol.2, p.414

58 HALS IVC 1-16

59 HALS XI 22

60 HALS D1083

61 DeLaune 1681

62 These were names of non-existent soldiers put on the muster roll to increase the
    total of allowances and connived at by the authorities.

63 HALS 78546

64 The recurrence of the name of Richard Keene as occupier confirms the identity.

65 HALS D1086 and D1090

66 Jones 1993, p.175

11

DAILY LIFE

A TYPICAL SEVENTEENTH CENTURY household or 'family', to use the contemporary term, had at its head a craftsman who was responsible for his wife, children, apprentices and servants and, to a lesser degree, for the journeymen he employed. One such was Walter Cowley II who combined the trade of baker with ownership of the White Horse inn in George Street, where he lived with his wife Mary, his mother (for three years) and no more than four of his seven children at any one time. But his family certainly included other people: perhaps one or two apprentices, probably a personal maid for Mary, a footboy for Walter and at least one maidservant. This is the kind of better-off household that occupied many of the houses in and around the market and in this instance some more people were employed in the bakery. The unknown number of people who worked in the inn and formed part of the innkeeper's family have been excluded because no inn rooms are listed in Cowley's inventory, so presumably their furnishing together with responsibility for the running of inn were wholly the innkeeper's. Such families formed the smallest unit of a highly patriarchal society whose records are dominated by the male activities occupying most of this book. Now something will be said about the very inadequately documented majority comprising women and children.

Children were born and died but otherwise hardly appear in the historical record. Many failed to survive the dangers at birth and the first year or two of life – the unhygienic conditions which exposed them to more or less serious digestive problems, diarrhoea and various 'fevers' – and even at the domestic fireside not a few, it seems, were burnt in the cradle.[1] Swathes for the swaddling that was customary in the first few months were to be had of Thomas Gill, haberdasher, who also stocked the leading strings, the equivalent of reins, needed to help an infant walk and keep it from what was seen as the animal-like activity of crawling.[2] Still, dangers notwithstanding, children must have been everywhere, as the age profiles (Fig.6.3) reveal. Many in poorer families were at risk in circumstances where a carer was not thought necessary or was absent or when vigilance was relaxed. Responsibility for looking after a very young child was often given to an older sibling. Sawpits, piles of building

materials and the other nuisances against which presentments were made in the
mayor's court all presented dangers to children, the more so since they would
mostly help with adult tasks from about the age of seven: fetching and carrying
water or fuel, turning a spit, making candles, working at long forgotten tasks in
the kitchen, like the "boy that scraped trenchers".[3] Moving around among
horses and waggons in inn yards and narrow streets carried its own risks and
the temptation to hang on to a moving cart was irresistible; old people can yet
remember being warned of the perils of the 'horse road'.

A special category of children comprises those babies brought from
London to be wet-nursed. St Albans parish registers contain few entries of
infant deaths at nurse and the town, despite being on a major road, was not a
major centre of the occupation.[4] St Peter's, probably the healthiest of the
three parishes, had most nurse children, but a wall tablet in the church is a
reminder of the fate of many of them, even those of well-to-do families:

> Two daughters of William Dobyns Esq. [of Lincoln's Inn] and Elizabeth his
> Wife (both of her Name) lye near this place in the same grave with their Brothers
> Abraham and Robert. The Eldest Daughter was born 26 of July 1682/3 and
> dyed 12th February Following, the Youngest was born 21st of October 1685 and
> dyed 10 of July 1686. All these four children (as also their Brothers William and
> Henry yet liveing) were Nursed at this Town of St Albans.

Occasionally the need for wet-nursing arose when the parish was compelled to
take responsibility for orphaned babies and infants, as in 1700 when money
was "layd out for Cocks children whilst they were at Nurse Brayes and her
looking to them"; the style given to Braye implies that she was a wet-nurse,
performing this task first while the mother was ill and then after her death.

Over the last twenty years the emotional relationship between parents and
children in the past has become matter of controversy. Were parents harsh for
religious reasons and hardened by child deaths into a comparative indifference,
or were they just like the stereotypical loving parents of today?[5] Abraham
Cowley, however concerned he may have been for his children's souls, showed
no sign of a puritanical attitude where their comfort was in question: the
"Childrens Chamber" had a feather bed, a bolster and pillow and a pair of
green laced curtains. They were the kind of well-cared-for children for whom
Thomas Gill stocked gloves and waistcoats, the latter being of flannel and the
equivalent of the modern vest.[6] Even so, Cowley, who had endured the death
of five of his six children before his first wife died, and whose second wife died
less than two years after giving birth to a daughter, must surely have married a
third time with a certain fatalism or at least religious resignation about the survival prospects of any offspring, yet, as it happened, all four outlived him. An
indication of parental love is often inferred from the desire to be buried close
to children, as John Selioke wished in his will of 1700 to lie "in a grave of my

late daughter Elizabeth Dec'd", although such sentiments could equally well be linked to a very literal belief in resurrection.[7]

EDUCATION

Thos Gill, haberdasher, sold books designed to help the more fortunate children read. His inventory (1678) includes horn books – shaped like table-tennis bats bearing the alphabet, numerals or the Lord's Prayer and protected by a thin film of horn; primers – little books to teach children to read and to pray; and "Chilldrens Guides" which provided instruction in good conduct or pointed the way to salvation.

Just how much education did children receive? Alice Veryard, who died a widow in 1701, had in her house a schoolroom equipped with a table, six forms, a leather chair and desk, and "In the Passage" (which evidently adjoined it) were two tables and *a small desk* for school use as required. She could probably have taken about twelve to twenty pupils according to demand, and the leather chair was either for her or possibly a master, the "Mr Smethe" whose room is listed after the passage and was no doubt on the other side of it. What Alice taught and the age of her pupils is obscure but, to judge by the few teaching materials in her inventory, she imparted a fairly elementary education. A higher level of schooling was provided by Mr Thomas Clarke who had in his "school & study" the scholars' forms, a settle, table and standish (for pens and writing materials), a chest for the boys' books, a desk, bookcase and "all other his mathematicall Instruments". It also had "The Partitions", suggesting that there was more than one class. The instruments can hardly have been for any other purpose than teaching land measurement and surveying, the kind of technical education required in the age when the great estates were building up.

The scholastic institution of highest prestige was the grammar school, founded to teach Latin to pupils proceeding to the professions via the universities and the Inns of Court and situated in what is now the Lady Chapel of the cathedral.[8] It had suffered a setback during the Civil War and Interregnum and the appointment of the learned rector Edward Carter as master benefited the library without increasing the very small number of pupils. That was a task for his successor, Dr James, who held the post from 1668 to 1695 and brought the number of new entrants to eleven or twelve each year, with a total size approaching sixty. Regrettably, the loss of all lists of pupils makes it impossible to trace their careers or to know if the teaching of Dr. James and Jones the usher, who was a Latin poet, albeit of no great merit, had any effect.[9]

One of the varied tasks the overseers of the Abbey parish undertook was to provide the children they maintained with some education. In 1658-60

Table 11.1 People signing or marking wills

	Signed Number	Percentage	Marked Number	Percentage	Total
St Albans 1650-1700					
Women	12	26	35	74	47
Men	63	52	59	48	122
St Stephens 1650-1700					
Women	3	23	10	77	13
Men	16	46	19	54	35

Thomas Beeton received £2 10s for his boy's schooling, perhaps at a school like Thomas Clarke's, where Turvervile's son was definitely sent for some time at a cost of 2s 6d to the overseers. At the most basic level, Pye's children were taught to read over twelve months by Widow White in what was probably a small dame school, and William Jones was given a three-penny primer and schooled by John Barnard for thirteen weeks. For this latter service Barnard received 2s 2d in 1657/8 and in 1665/6 the overseers paid him 1s 4d to school Clempson's two boys for a period of four weeks. St Michael's parish was less well provided, for in 1671 the archdeacon was told: "Schools – We have none except some poor women that teach only a few ABCdarians". The level of literacy resulting from these efforts can be judged by the proportion of testators who signed their names rather than made a mark.[10] In the three St Albans parishes about a quarter of the women and half of the men signed, and these proportions were only slightly lower in St Stephens where in 1676 the churchwardens reported "as for schoolmasters we have none" (Table 11.1).

DOMESTIC LIFE AND WORK

What was life like in houses that were both home and workplace? Probate inventories suggest that some rooms in comfortable, well-furnished houses were dual-purpose, both sitting room and bedroom regularly or at need, just as in inns. Ralph Gladman's parlour, for example, contained a curtained bedstead in addition to a table, three stools and two chairs, while William Ewer's chamber over the hall had two tables, three forms and two "joynt stooles", and his chamber over the kitchen a little table and a desk. Small children left hardly a trace of their existence in the form of furnishings; no cradle, cot or walking frame is mentioned, either because they were of too little value or had been passed on to another generation. There is only the "Childrens Roume" with "beden [bedding] and other things "to the value of £1 10s in John Carter's inventory of 1674 to add to Abraham Cowley's well-furnished "Childrens Chamber" already mentioned.

Nor are women's lives much more observable in our documents. Little can be learnt about them, even those women who carried on their husband's business after his death, except through the inventories of widows and spinsters, although their domestic activities can have differed little except in the extent to which they looked after others. A spinning wheel, for work specific to women, appears rarely: Ann Adams, widow, left in 1686 "2 wheeles & a Reele"; Mary Gladman, spinster, in 1674 "A wheele … A parcell of flax & yarne"; whereas Dorothy Lane, widow, in 1680 left linen and linen yarn without a wheel, unless it was one of the "other things" in her two rooms. The appearance in Thomas Robinson's inventory (1710), "left unadministred by Anne … the Relict & One of the Extors", of her "Old Spinning wheel" is due to her negligence (through depression, perhaps?); in normal circumstances the appraisers ignored the widow's possessions. A surprising occupation, given her background, is that of Anne, eldest daughter of Thomas Cowley I, mercer and mayor, who died with £519 of "debts sperat" and worth £624 in all; she is described as seamstress, " a needlewoman whose occupation is plain sewing …".[11] One widow, Mary Scott (1679) brewed beer; "In the molte howses" were "the Ceston An a molte mill An all other lumber and fire wood". Straw plaiting, a domestic industry beginning to be important in the late seventeenth century,[12] is not mentioned in the surviving inventories of men or women probably because it was an occupation for 'the poorer sort' who are under-represented in that kind of document. Lace, though, then as always, was in demand and Mary Wood earned a modest living with her "Bobin pillow to make Lace on two Images" – patterns, presumably.[13]

Women's mundane everyday tasks, cooking excepted, left few traces apart from the smoothing irons belonging to Ann Phillis Miles (1701) and the widow Frances Billington (1671). The latter had a pincushion, listed with oddments worth only 1s. all told, whereas the grouping of Mary Gladman's thimble and two bodkins with two gold rings and money in her purse implies that they had some intrinsic value. These provide the only evidence of sewing and needlework; no doubt appraisers often lumped such insignificant items as thimbles and widow Billington's pincushion in with "other lumber".

None of the domestic occupations pursued by women required formal training and it appears that the apprenticeship customary for boys was sought for girls only when they were thought suitable for a trade. On occasion churchwardens paid for girls to be apprenticed, as when "Wethered's girl" was apprenticed to a Mr Hitchcock in 1670 and Elizabeth Cooper to Martha Kemp in 1700 for £4 5s, while at the other end of the social scale Abraham Cowley in 1693 left £10 to his niece Mary Kentish "to be bound as an apprentice"; but in no case is the trade known. It may well have been "huswifry".[14]

WHERE DID WIDOWS AND SPINSTERS LIVE?

Anne Lomax, who lived in style at Childwickbury, the country seat outside the town built by her gentleman husband, is hardly relevant to the St Albans story, despite her strong family connections with the town. At the opposite extreme is Mary Long, spinster (1685), whose inventory suggests she occupied only one room with goods and ready money valued at £14 15s, yet her lack of cooking equipment and good debts of £190 make it likely that she boarded in a relative's house. The same imbalance between goods and money at loan and the same lack of cooking utensils appear in the inventories of Sarah Turner, spinster (1693) and the widow Mary Watts (1697), who had less owing to them but were still well-off. Poorest among these single-room women is Elizabeth Rugsby, spinster (1669), whose only goods were her wearing apparel worth a mere 5s; it is inconceivable that she lived entirely alone, awaiting payment of "debts owing upon" a small legacy bequeathed her by Henry Rugsby. Mary Cowley, alone of the women apparently living in one room and not cooking for themselves, is one of the few whose place of residence can be conjectured. She was the widow of Walter I who died in 1665 owning the White Horse and probably went on living there after her son, Walter II, took over and until her own death in 1668. Possibly the widowed Ann Gladman did the same after her husband Rafe, a baker, died in 1670, passing her last four years with her son Henry, innholder of the George, while Anne Cowley the seamstress may well have lived with her younger brother, Thomas II, who was mayor in 1688. And clearly Elizabeth Bocket (1693), despite having a bedstead, furniture and cooking utensils "in the Parler" was in a similar situation in an unknown location but retaining a greater degree of independence; had she been lodging with a stranger the words "the Parler" would hardly have been appropriate. A lower standard of living is apparent with Susan Martin (1672) who had only "the chamber over the shoppe" and "In John Elisha's Roome, one old standing bedstedd & a Cord one curtaine and two Rodds" valued at 7s.6d. Now John Elisha's room also figures in the inventory (1683) of Walter Cowley II, baker and innholder of the White Horse with the same contents, so Susan may simply have rented a chamber in the inn, the bed being kept in lieu of the last payment.

Some of these women may have been in the same situation as Ann Smith who, in 1688, is described as "widdo late of woolley [Woolwich?] in the County of Kent & since boarder with Wm. Ayleward of newhouse in the parish of St Peters outside the borough". The word 'boarder' presumably has its customary sense of a person paying for food as well as lodging, despite the two spits she possessed which might suggest otherwise; but in the absence of utensils Ann Smith cannot have done any serious cooking. Men might be boarders too, like Richard Holland, gent., who in his one room had an unusual number of books, a desk and a cupboard with three bottles in it, but nothing to cook with or to eat off.

Where the rest of the women on their own lived is not known but we can say something about the nature of their accommodation. Among those who occupied a small house is Mary Scott, whose premises for brewing required one; she had a hall, "sellar" – not necessarily underground – and "the Chambers", the whole amounting to a two-room ground plan with a central chimney-stack. Similarly, Jane Long's inventory (1693) mentions her kitchen, best and "other chamber" but the further item, "her stok of trading goods", implies she had a shop too, making the requisite four rooms. Frequently, a widow occupied part of the house from which her husband had conducted his business, as, for example, Frances Deacon, who occupied three living rooms – hall (which was also the kitchen), the chamber over it and the chamber over the shop – but whose inventory (1684) does not include the shop, which was presumably leased. Elizabeth Bradbury (1667) had no room called a hall, the only ground-floor room being the kitchen. The chamber over it was a bedroom, the little chamber, which had a fireplace, was furnished like a parlour – round table, two wrought chairs – but also had a bed, and the light chamber, with "five Joyn stooles ... & ix Middlen Chaires and one great Chaire" looks, functionally, like a hall without a fireplace. Someone else occupied the rooms beneath the little and light chambers. And in 1691 the well-to-do Mrs Lydia Hope found her requirements met by a hall (with cooking equipment), wainscot chamber, also with fireplace, and a little chamber with furnishings worth £8; also gold and silver items valued at £29 9s 6d and good debts amounting to £119.

Some women had only an upstairs and a downstairs room. Alice Mott (1690), for example, whose inventory opens: "In the Shopp; The Goods there" £24 2s and continues with household goods (unspecified), ready money and wearing apparel amounting to £21 10s, probably had a second room, perhaps over the shop. Ann Adams' two were called by the appraisers "The First Roome under stairs next the streete", which had a hearth equipped for cooking and the utensils for it, and "The First Chamber upstairs"; they obviously formed a self-contained part of a larger building. Other habitations named in less specific terms may have been similar. Mary Turner and Joan Woodward, for example, both widows, had a hall and chamber over, although Turner was not poor with £55 in debts owing good and bad, whereas Woodward was worth only £6 14s and had cooking utensils. Nor, perhaps, was Joan Rugsby (1673) poor; her inventory lists only her wearing apparel worth 5s but was appraised by two people styling themselves gent. and the way her two rooms are distinguished as "Below stairs" and "above stairs" suggests she was living in

a sizeable house, not simply in a ground-floor room with chamber above. Poorest of all the women who had two rooms were the widow Hurst (1698), with a
chamber and lower room and goods worth £2 1s 6d, and Mary Field (1667)
whose barely furnished hall contained only one little table, a chest, one cupboard "with other lumber", valued at 7s 6d, and cooking utensils worth 7s; and
she had a chamber.

Purpose-built hall-and-chamber houses of the kind implied by some of
these inventories hardly exist in St Albans except for some medieval craftsmen's shops in George Street,[15] so most of the widows and spinsters must have
had rooms cut off from a larger building by partitioning or simply by locking a
door and removing the key. The gabled wing of a medieval house on Lower
Dagnall Street illustrates the process: the open hall has long been separated
from it and demolished, leaving a two-room house that would have been large
enough for one of the more comfortably-off widows. Somewhat smaller
medieval houses were split up to create little houses[16] like those occupied by
the widow Hurst or Mary Field.

SERVANTS

Domestic servants figure little in the documents at our disposal and during the
seventeenth century and long afterwards they were part of the background,
noticed no more than an article of furniture until needed. From Gregory
King's estimates, inaccurate though they may be, we know that servants
abounded but can only guess their numbers in St Albans. Alice Veryard, to
take one obvious example, needed several servants to assist with her fourteen-
room house and school – a personal maid, a cook, two housemaids and probably a handyman seem about the minimum, with perhaps a waiting-woman too
– and her household included the "Mr Smethe" whose room is listed and who
may have had his own servant. Another household with several maidservants
was that of Abraham Cowley, whose inventory includes, in the "Maides
Chamber" two feather beds, one flock bed and one pallet bed for perhaps as
many as seven people. Katherine Hickman may have needed fewer people for
her nine rooms which included a "Maids Chamber" with one curtained bedstead (for at least two maids). At that social level the mention in James Rudston's inventory of "the Man's Chamber" and in Abraham Cowley's of "the
Boys chamber" are reminders that all gentlemen and merchants are likely to
have had a personal servant: their numbers and the numbers of footboys who
accompanied their masters and did every kind of errand (as Pepys' footboy
did) are beyond guessing. Many women, though, must have had a living-in
maidservant; Lydia Hope, for example, had in the Wainscott chamber her own
curtained bedstead and also a pallet bed for her maidservant – a use that

accounts for the many pallet or truckle beds in houses and inns alike. Servants
had of necessity to be within call of their masters or mistresses; only Elizabeth
Gould and Ann Adams had in the hall, at the fireside, the "pare of belles" that
were the only other form of summons, albeit a rather ineffectual one.[17]

LEISURE AND ENTERTAINMENT

No personal documents such as letters or a diary remain to show how people
spent their leisure and indeed only the landed gentry needed to find ways of
passing the time. Among them Edward Crosby, notorious for killing a nonconformist preacher in 1662, is the most interesting figure.[18] Crosby maintained a
huntsman, who is mentioned in his will, and his hounds were no doubt followed by members of other landed families in the district, making him a pre-
cursor of one of the oldest organised hunts, the Puckeridge, founded in the
early eighteenth century.[19] With hunting goes shooting, and both may have
afforded recreation for Thomas Birchmore of St Michaels, who is described
alternatively as husbandman or yeoman. He kept his fowling-piece, as is clear
from its place in the inventory, above the fireplace, and he had horses if he
wished to follow the hunt. Both men may have enjoyed the occasional horse
racing on the course, about which hardly anything is known except its bare
existence, that was maintained by the Grimstons at Gorhambury.

For those lower down the social scale recreation was sought as occasion
offered. [20] The working day was not bound by a strict routine, and professional
men and tradesmen particularly, but to some degree people of all occupations,
enjoyed the freedom to break off work to talk, drink or take whatever amusement was available.[21] Their pastimes are mostly associated with inns. Churchmen and puritans alike enjoyed bowls and, unlike cockfighting or stage-plays,
the game was not forbidden by Commonwealth legislation. It was played at a
green behind the Fleur-de-Lys and perhaps other inns, but some greens were
apparently not so connected, such as one between Lower Dagnall Street and
George Street and "a parcel of ground now used for a bowling green in Cooke
Row" mentioned in the will of John New I. The game of shovelboard, in
which a coin is propelled by a blow of the hand along a smooth table top to
compartments at one end, was played in the larger inns such as the Bull and
White Hart, where a room was devoted principally to this long piece of furniture. Both bowls and shovelboard were for a minority of the male inhabitants,
since the cost of the woods and maintenance of the green must have made the
former expensive and the shilling coin that seems to have been ventured in the
latter was beyond the reach of many. One kind of amusement that was probably patronised by all and sundry whenever it was to be had was the travelling
theatre, whose existence is implied by an order of the mayor's court in 1708

that "John Hayward, carpenter, have leave to set up a stage on the waste ground near the house of Mr John Toombes, the ancient and usual place for such purposes".[22]

For a majority of men the simpler pleasures of drinking and smoking at an inn or alehouse were the usual pastime. Drinking was no doubt carried, in St Albans as elsewhere, to excess; drunkenness was a normal feature of social life.[23] Close links between inn or alehouse keepers and pipe-makers are exemplified by William Tryant, who was the principal creditor mentioned in an innkeeper's probate inventory, and by George Wilsher, pipe-maker, who lived at the Three Horseshoes alehouse in Fishpool Street. A rarer pleasure was that of attendance at the mayor's annual feast on 21 September, to which a surprising number of people were invited. An order made in the mayor's court in 1700 laid down that invitations should not exceed 200,[24] a figure made credible by the purchase in 1698/9 of six spits for the Counterhouse. If, therefore, the number of adult men has been correctly estimated at about 600 quite a high proportion of them enjoyed mayoral hospitality. Other official feasts were more exclusive, these being the annual venison dinner provided for the mayor and burgesses by the Steward and the Sessions dinners when the mayor and assorted burgesses attended the justices. The regular dinners when the mayor sat as clerk of the market were the more modest entertainment appropriate to a routine business occasion but they, like the grander occasions and also the two companies' corporate eating and drinking, provided a sociable reinforcement of the burgesses' common interests.

The enjoyment of music as revealed by the possession of musical instruments appears to have been confined to the gentry, although there are reasons for thinking this not an entirely true picture. Anne Lomax's bass violl reflects the family music-making which was the most typical amusement of cultivated persons at that period, one that was shared by two gentlemen, Ralph Gladman who in 1670 had "One pair of Virginalls" in his hall, and Edmund Smith (1686) who had "One pair of Harpsicalls" in the chamber over the parlour. Professional musicians were rare, only Jeremiah Hopkins in 1684 being so described, whereas the similar-sized town of Uttoxeter had a piper, a drummer and a fiddler in the 1690s.[25] Public performance of music is mentioned only at the proclamation of James II when the mayor paid pipers, drummers and fiddlers, many of whom, presumably, were part-timers; and the fiddlers must have been required from time to time by the persons whom the sole recorded dancing master had taught.

Gentlemen and professional men whose houses stood in a large plot could enjoy the more contemplative pleasure of a garden. On the southern fringe of the town Richard Jennings at Holywell House had in the garden house one little table, three chairs and a stool (1668), while at the opposite end in St

Peter's Street William Ellis's "Outer Studdye" – a loggia, perhaps, containing only a frame table and a form – hints at a taste for reading in the open air.

BOOKS AND READING

Not surprisingly, the first signs of a book-buying public in St Albans occur in the time of intense political and religious argument after the Civil War when many of the issues must have been of keen interest to dissenters finding their way amid conflicting sectarian views. Here in the late 1640s John Geree, briefly minister of the Abbey church, engaged in some of the contemporary controversies, publishing a defence of child baptism and dating another work, *The Character of an old English Puritane, or Non-Conformist*, "From my Study in St Albans". A single bookseller is known at this period, Richard Williams, active 1649-56, whose name appears on two pamphlets of 1649, one being *Bloudy Fight in Hertfordshire*.[26] In these years Abraham Cowley, born in 1621 and one of the richest and most notable dissenters, was forming his opinions, and no doubt he and like-minded people were ready buyers of such material. His possession, at the time of his death in 1693, of twelve folios and twenty-two quartos shows that he was a serious reader of more than controversial literature, without taking account of the hundred lesser volumes. The value of £2 assigned to the whole suggests an unfamiliarity with books on the part of the appraisers.

Abraham Cowley's collection suggests that for the wealthier inhabitants book-buying was becoming usual. A few devoted a room wholly or largely to books: thus William Ellis's study in 1672 contained "One parcell of Books" and James Rudston's two years later had books valued at £6. Titles are hardly ever specified apart from the Bible. Robert Long's "one great bibel" implies a size appropriate to the "Iron standere to lay a book on" that was owned by John Malcott (who had two bibles), while Thos Marston in 1690 left "2 bybles one pracktis of pyetie". Only in the inventory of Richard Holland gent., who appears to have lived in one room, is there interesting detail: he had a bible, "a folio book of ancient and modern times and about 50 thin books in 4to and 8vo and" – a noteworthy entry – "some other written books". The practice of circulating and copying books in manuscript is attested by John Aubrey and in the lives of many contemporary scholars; one wonders what Holland's particular interest was that could not be satisfied by printed works, and one ceases to wonder, bearing in mind what St Albans society was then like, at the frequency with which such books were lost or destroyed by executors and legatees.[27] In our period, though, unquestionably the best library was that of Edward Carter, the rector, whose collection was sufficiently important to attract the attention of Dr Godolphin, a bibliophile friend of John Evelyn's who came with him to inspect it – valued at £300 – after its owner's death in 1688. Another library of some size is implied by the condition imposed in 1692 on Anthony Boys, that he buy the books of the late John Charnock, scrivener, from his widow at valuation before gaining freedom to trade in the borough. A collection large enough to attract the attention of the corporation is unlikely to have been exclusively professional in character.

Few women left books of their own other than a bible. An inventory of Anne Lomax's goods taken in connection with a Chancery suit in 1690 includes a book stand in the little parlour but ignores the books, which may have been in the three boxes and shelves in the study. These, though, may have been acquired by her late husband Joshua. Alice Veryard's inventory includes "Twenty old books" in one of two closets that appear to have opened off the little parlour, a location suggesting they were not for the school she ran; their valuation at five shillings is the commonest one for women's books and not a reliable indication of literary worth. It is regrettable that the appraisers of Katherine Hickman's inventory in 1682 did not specify more closely the "Goods in the Closett viz ye Bookes…£3", which implies a special book closet and is much the highest valuation of its kind for a woman. The second most valuable collection, at £1 10s, belonged to Anne Cowley, one of the wealthiest women of the period, and Lydia Hope's and Anne Gladman's, at fifteen and ten shillings respectively, must have comprised a fair number of volumes. All are likely to have comprised books of lasting worth and usefulness, of the kind implied by a distinction in Mary Wood's inventory: "A parcel of Bookes bound & paper Bookes".

Some member or members of the Lomax family evidently shared the wide-ranging curiosity characteristic of many professional men of the period. Anne is the only known possessor of a map – presumably hanging on the wall – and "two Globes", no doubt terrestrial and celestial, all of which mark an interest not otherwise apparent in this small town.

CHANGES IN FURNITURE AND MANNERS

The Restoration saw the enthronement of a well-travelled monarch who had seen the latest fashions in architecture, furnishings, dress and manners at several foreign courts. John Evelyn blamed Charles II for the introduction of the corner fireplaces he disliked while at about the same time the vertical sliding sash window, which was in use in France in the 1630s, makes its first appearance at Whitehall palace.[28] The influence of continental taste in furniture, ornaments and the like in a small English town is harder to assess, largely because little attention has been paid to the speed with which new fashions penetrated down the social scale.

One change is apparent in the different ways the room called the hall is furnished, between the old style before the Civil War, when it was the principal room, and the new post-Restoration style in which it becomes in effect a reception room. Only Robert Graves, it seems, kept "2 old Sords and bandelears" in his hall, and this as late as 1677, but William Ellis's hall with its table and frame with 9 stools and chairs, all no doubt of oak, had an old-fashioned air in 1672. For someone of gentry status that is surprising: not so for the yeoman Thomas Birchmore whose hall was dominated by "one long table". By then, perhaps, the rich townsman Abraham Cowley had ordered his hall as it was inventoried in 1693, with a table, six cane chairs, six "Turkeyworkt" (embroidered) chairs and a Turkey worked carpet that may have been, since it is listed quite separately from the table, a floor carpet. It was a completely different life-style. This kind of change was uneven; no room in Cowley's well-appointed house is called a dining room or even the alternative eating parlour, whereas by 1691 Anthony Wilson had a dining room furnished with two tables, ten chairs and six cushions, the hall, reduced to two tables, four chairs, a settle and a clock, being no longer a general eating place.

Furniture, though not often clearly identified by type or style, shows similar changes of taste. Tables are increasingly described as round or – apparently the height of modernity for this town – oval, which probably means with folding ends. In 1677 James Dell, yeoman of St Michaels, had a round table in the hall as well as a "drawing table and frame", but the eighteen Turkey work chairs in the parlour went with an oval one; and Alice Veryard had an oval table in the great and little parlours. Chairs changed too, and once again Abraham Cowley is in the vanguard with seven "Dutch chairs" in the "Best Chamber"; these are the recently introduced Roundabout chairs with circular seats and they are followed successively, in terms of fashion, by the considerably commoner cane chairs that came in after the Great Fire of London in 1665 and by Turkey work chairs which were superseding the older style of leather chair listed in a number of inventories.[29] Pictures are rare: Ralph Gladman, baker and gent, had a collection of eight in the chamber over the hall, Richard Holland had two in his only room. Very probably they were the portraits that were so favoured in England at that time. In the largest house for which we have an inventory, Holywell House, Richard Jennings relegated four pictures to the garret next to the stairs; the only other one mentioned he could not move, being a picture chimney-piece in the dining parlour, that is, a painted panel in a bolection-moulded frame above the fireplace and shelf. Advanced taste had reached St Albans quite quickly in this instance. In another well-appointed house, Alice Veryard's, the only pictures were four "In the Work house" with carpenter's tools, and "some" in the store room with old bedclothes, candles and other lumber. Apparently the visual arts did not excite much interest at any social level.

Accompanying the improvements in the fittings and furniture of houses went a refinement of manners that is reflected principally in tableware. In 1650 wood was still, as it had been time out of mind, the predominant material for the majority of the townspeople. It is difficult to judge how quickly it was superseded by other materials because wooden vessels, being of less intrinsic value, may well have been consigned by appraisers to "other old lumber" when they compiled an inventory. But in 1686 Ann Adams of St Peter's Street had eighteen trenchers and eight wooden dishes as well as six porringers, six platters, two "platts" and four "sacers" (for condiments or sauces) of pewter, all of which were serving dishes. Contemporary custom is revealed by her one tumbler, one tankard and one quart pot, all of pewter, that were the only drinking vessels Ann possessed; they circulated among the diners, who ate from an individual trencher or wooden dish, using their own knives. A few years later trenchers were absent from Jane Long's table, replaced by twenty dishes and ten porringers of pewter – but still only two pots and a silver tankard. And in 1692 Thomas Clarke, schoolmaster, appears to have abandoned trenchers for his pupils use, for otherwise "The pewter in full weighing ¾cwt.8li. [that is 92lb. or 42 kg.]" would hardly have been necessary.

Trenchers appear to go with personal knives. How quickly the latter went out of use at table once pewter plates became common is not observable from inventories, in which knives and forks are rarely mentioned. Mary Wood's possessions[30] included five old knives, three old forks and five pounds of (pewter) "plates old" in a small total of £6 5s, with many things being described as old or ragged. Yet she had comparatively uncommon items such as "6 or 7 botles 2 Drinking Glasses and other Glasses" which suggest she led a comparatively sophisticated style of life for this small town, and this in turn may imply that knives and forks were not yet usual. Glassware is the most rarely mentioned kind of table furniture. A gentry inventory like Ralph Gladman's (1670) lists none; he and his guests drank from the six silver wine cups, a silver tankard, a silver gilt wine cup and no doubt some items from the eighty-two pieces of small pewter; they ate off thirty-three pewter platters. Fine glass vessels liable to breakage afforded a more transitory display of conspicuous consumption than the silverware that could be banked in case of need.

NOTES AND REFERENCES

1 Hanawalt 1977–78, p.12; Hanawalt 1986, p.175
2 Illick 1974, pp.318, 320; Dick 1987, p.84
3 Hutchinson 1904, p.135
4 Fildes 1988, p.146
5 Stone 1977 brought the question, already posed by Aries, to the forefront and set the agenda for a generation.

6   Pepys 10, *Companion*, p.99
7   Cf. Thomas Ford (d.1635) who wished to be buried "with my fourteen teeth which are in a paper in a little red bag which I usually carry with me"; Prest 1986, p.362.
8   Illustrated, VCH Vol.2, opposite p.490
9   This paragraph is based on Kilvington 1986, pp.26–8
10 Spufford 1979, pp.201–3
11 OED
12 VCH Vol.2, p.482
13 Not given precisely this sense in OED
14 Information from Professor Nigel Goose
15 17th century survivals usually have an attic room as well.
16 Nos.72–76 St Peter's Street, facing the church green.
17 Pepys, 10, *Companion*, p.195
18 Even for an ex-Cavalier officer this was extreme behaviour, found only in such dissolute figures as Charles Saville, Lord Buckhurst; Pepys 1970–83, 22 Feb. 1662, 1 July 1663
19 Carr 1986, pp.81-2
20 As is apparent from Pepys' diary even in the later, more assiduous years.
21 Thompson 1991, pp.352–403
22 Gibbs 1890, p.104
23 Gough [1701] records many men and a few women who declined in fortune and status through drunkenness. At a high social level, Henry Martin and Richard Corbet, Bishop of Norwich, are examples of socially acceptable heavy drinking; Aubrey 1949, pp.215, 288
24 Gibbs 1890, p.97
25 McInnes 1987, p.122
26 Plomer 1907
27 Aubrey 1949, pp.129–30, 139
28 Baggs 1997, pp.168–71
29 Gloag 1969 for Caning, Dutch chairs, Roundabout chairs
30 Her inventory is undated.

12

CONCLUSIONS

For two hundred years after the dissolution of the monasteries St Albans seems to have been regarded as something out of the ordinary run of small towns, as the remarks of William Smith and Daniel Defoe (but not Celia Fiennes) suggest. That there was some truth in this is apparent from the long-standing and still continuing division of Hertfordshire east and west, two parts looking respectively to Hertford and St Albans. Hertford as the county town benefited from the assize and quarter sessions, with consequent opportunities for traders and innkeepers, but the road north led only to Cambridge, Ely and Lynn. The principal advantage enjoyed by St Albans was that it lay at the junction of the route to the whole of north-west England with an easy east-west route and thus had proved a suitable location for an important Roman town. Here occurred the execution of someone who came to be venerated as a martyr, a crucial historical accident that led in the early Middle Ages to the foundation of an abbey and later a market. From then on its location on a well-made major road provided the developing town with a service function in a growing economy almost irrespective of what its inhabitants might do in the short term. Under the heavy-handed control of the abbots the monastic town appears to have flourished to the extent that it is credited with a population of 2,500 in 1377 rising to 3,770 in the 1520s[1] and, however approximate these figures necessarily are, the taxation they are based on points to growing wealth.

Some decline following the dissolution of the abbey in 1539 was inevitable and is common to many similar towns. How severe the setback was for St Albans has not been calculated but thereafter the town's prosperity, over and above its market function, depended on the capacity of its inhabitants to respond to the opportunities offered by changes in the volume and speed of traffic on the Chester road. Within a generation the building of a town hall and the building or rebuilding of inns show that economic growth had resumed. The impression given by the only measure available, the admittedly imperfect one of architecture, is that the town continued to prosper into the early seventeenth century, perhaps up to the second setback, the outbreak of the Civil War. For St Albans, though, the war proved less disastrous than for many other towns despite the hardships caused by the quartering of large numbers of soldiers on the inhabitants, so that before the Restoration signs of rebuilding and improvement are appearing and they continue after it, even allowing for the imprecise dating of buildings.

Nevertheless, after a hundred years of apparent prosperity that were interrupted only briefly in the 1640s, the population of the borough in 1675 was, even on the most optimistic estimate, no more than 3,500, much the same as it had been in the 1520s. Confirmation of this is provided by property development. Late medieval building extended to the limits of the main streets: to St Peter's church, along Holywell Hill to beyond Sopwell Lane, far down Sopwell Lane itself, and along Fishpool Street to St Michael's. By 1700 the situation had not changed, with no evidence of new building either beyond those limits or along the minor roads and lanes; whatever increase occurred after 1650 was a more intensive development of already built-up areas.

Inns provide evidence of improvement or enlargement, as several mentions in probate inventories of "the new lodgings" and two surviving detached ranges of lodgings show. This is a matter of wider concern than St Albans and one that has scarcely been noticed by architectural historians. Why additional accommodation should have been provided in a building quite separate from the main body of an inn, with the consequent loss of control of movement, is not obvious; there must have been some compensating advantage. Since the accommodation itself does not seem to have been better than that in the inn proper such ranges may perhaps have been used by wealthier travellers desiring privacy, the kind of person who would buy all the seats in a coach.[2]

A second form of development, encroachment on the market place, also has implications beyond St Albans. The new building there (Fig.2.7) has to be seen against the invariable preference of owners, on grounds of cost, for alteration and remodelling rather complete rebuilding, however attractive that idea may have been.[3] Consequently, it is so usual to find older timber framing behind seventeenth century brick fronts that where none exists it is reasonable to suppose that the building either had no predecessor or one so inferior that it could not be adapted to a new purpose. That consideration has a bearing on the long process of encroachment on what began as a large open market place. The generally accepted view was expressed by William Page: "By the process of leasing the sites of the market stalls, permanent structures began, in the fourteenth century, to take the place of the temporary stalls".[4] Yet there is not much sign of permanent building before the sixteenth century and encroachment, some of it on sites that can never have been occupied before, went on until the end of the seventeenth century. On present showing permanent encroachment, although it undoubtedly began in the early fifteenth century, acquired momentum in the sixteenth, and if this is true it implies that the town recovered from the dissolution fairly quickly.

Coinciding with the infilling of the market place was a change in the nature of the buildings, from those put up in the fifteenth or sixteenth century that were simply commercial premises, for example No. 2 Market Street, to those that combined house and workplace, until gradually all buildings incorporated living accommodation. Thus by 1700 the triangular south part of the market place, formerly open, had become four streets lined with buildings, some of them bigger and taller than anything seen fifty years earlier. Many more people now lived in this comparatively small area and, if the population did not increase markedly, most presumably came from elsewhere in the town. Accompanying the growth in numbers was a growth in comfort but also an increased risk of illness in a crowded and insanitary environment. Nothing was done to improve the gutters that were the only means of removing wastes from all the encroaching buildings, nor were the principal streets paved – perhaps for lack of suitable stone – so that in a wet winter the various market places must have been a muddy mess – which is just the impression given by a Varley drawing (Fig.2.8).

Although the total population remained fairly stable there is evidence of some immigration which is almost certainly understated in the records. The explanation must be that London was drawing people away from St Albans as from most other places and that here the inward and outward flows were evenly balanced. Much has been said in previous chapters about London trade connections and the strong evidence of people working there and living in St Albans at weekends, as some professional men must have done, or of people who were brought up in St Albans moving to live permanently in London and retiring years later to their native town.

Trading connections with the City were indeed crucial to the town's economy.[5] Some merchants will have been like those Edward Chamberlayne had in mind when speaking (in relation to the Great Fire) of "The dead time of the week, being Saturday night, when Traders were retired to their Countrey-Houses".[6] Others will have divided the responsibilities so that either father or son stayed in London and the other in St Albans and, although no specific instance of this has come to notice, its likelihood can be inferred from the comparable operation of the Hickmans' ironmongery business, in which father ran the St Albans end and son the Hemel Hempstead end.[7] One or other of these ways of conducting trade must account for a considerable number of people who left little record of a connection with St Albans beyond being buried there, as, for example, John New III who is described as "late of ... St Sepulchre's, London, but at St Albans" and whose goods are listed in two parts, the first implicitly in London, the second in St Albans. In fact, the economy of the town was quite largely dependent on the capital, with much of what was grown in the catchment area finding its way there, whether through the market or private dealing, and in this respect St Albans was no different from any other town within a similar radius of London.

Study of probate inventories suggests that St Albans was a reasonably prosperous town but the small sample of the population that they represent and the scarcity of studies of comparable towns makes it hard to know whether it fared better or worse than other places. Certainly there is little evidence of an urban renaissance.[8] Few new houses were entirely of brick, not many older houses were refronted with it, and generally timber-framing continued in use. Even so, St Albans can show nothing comparable to a three-storey pargetted range of shops of c.1660 in Hertford and a smaller range nearby[9] that testify to someone's faith in the town's future. They, though, have no successors, and overall Hertford gives the appearance of gradual modest improvement, as does Hitchin, so that in Hertfordshire St Albans may not have been exceptional.

A prosperous town might be expected to draw in people to meet an increased demand for labour, of which there is little evidence in corporation or parish records. Insofar as the town prospered, it did so through innkeeping, which has left more evidence of economic growth than any other trade. With it flourished transport and associated occupations, all of which no doubt stimulated trade generally. Many towns on the Great Roads benefited from the growing number of coach and carrier services but St Albans, standing at the junction of five roads, had an unusually fortunate location. Even so, its inns may have begun a relative decline not long after 1700 and perhaps most thoroughfare towns experienced comparable changes due to the increasing speed of transport but on different time scales. All the town's inns were timber-framed and all but two or three were built before 1650; only one, the not very important anonymous establishment in Holywell Hill, was new-built in brick and not one was refronted in the half-century of this study. There is nothing comparable to the impressive stone-built inn the Saracen's Head at Towcester, for example, and the absence of any striking refronting in brick after the early years of the eighteenth century confirms decline by then.

To what extent the town benefited from the presence of a great church is difficult to assess; it was, after all, expensive to maintain. Although the abbey church can never have drawn large numbers of visitors it seems that a steady stream of people came to St Albans to see it and that some people passing through may have stopped in the town rather than in a smaller place nearby because it provided an interesting overnight stay.[10] Its prestige and nearness to London probably induced both John Geree and Edward Carter to come to St Albans, to the benefit of the social and cultural life of a town drained in those respects by its proximity to the capital; and in Carter's time, when Dr James was master of St Albans school and had the learned Jones the Usher as his assistant,[11] serious readers like Abraham Cowley and Richard Holland may well have enjoyed a social life somewhat different from that of the ordinary market town.

As remarkable as any economic or social development was the political change that began at the Restoration with the presentation of a loyal address by the recorder William Foxwist, a notable dissenter and parliamentarian, "and some of the burgesses of that towne, accknowledging their loyalety and manifested theire joy for his Majesty's restoration to his crowne and dignity".[12] Charles II may well have felt a certain scepticism about the burgesses' sincerity and in the event it took a quarter of a century before they and their successors persuaded or forced the townsmen to give full support to the royalist regime. The following pages attempt to explain a national political shift in local terms without direct evidence. An inevitably speculative account thus goes beyond earlier cautious inferences and if it thereby becomes controversial, so much the better.[13]

The gradual process of accommodation can be observed in the political and religious sympathies of the mayors. In the 1660s they were drawn from the same body of parliamentarians and dissenters who had held office during the Commonwealth decade, although their views may by then have been modified or discreetly concealed. Certainly any political discord arising from the Restoration appears to have been overcome comparatively easily in St Albans. Only the murder of John Townsend, a dissenter unafraid to protest against high-handed action by a former royalist officer, hints at otherwise unexpressed discontents. Yet not many years later the mayoralty of William Marston I, the last person whose sympathies had once lain with religious and political dissent to hold the office (in 1674), heralded a complete reversal of fortune and ushered in an unbroken succession of known or presumptive Tories lasting to the end of the century.

It may be significant that three years later, in the mayoralty of the strongly Tory Thomas Eccleston, the many vacancies that had occurred among the assistants over a period of twenty years began to be filled. Five of those who became assistants in 1677 subsequently served as mayor and one of the assistants chosen in the following year, John Selioke, innholder of the Red Lion, was to be the most fervent Tory of them all. Since the failure to fill vacancies among the assistants over so long a period conferred no obvious material benefit on the decreasing numbers of those still in office or on the aldermen a political explanation may be conjectured: that the former Commonwealth men felt their predominance threatened by a younger generation that had never been touched by the ideals they themselves had grown up with and took the only action they could to keep its representatives at bay.

That explanation agrees with the record of post-Restoration mayors. Those who held office or were made aldermen under the Commonwealth can be regarded as retaining some measure of opposition to the restored monarchy and church to the end, however diluted, unless there is reason to think otherwise (Appendix I). Those whose support for James II was expressed or can be inferred by association were certainly Tories and others are likely to have been so because they were chosen assistants or aldermen at a time of Tory domination.

Thomas Cowley II is interesting in this connection. In 1660 his political opinions can hardly have diverged very far from those of his predecessors. What they were at the time of his second mayoralty in 1672 is impossible to judge. In 1687, some months after the first Declaration of Indulgence, Cowley was second choice as mayor to Edward Seabrooke and the automatic choice for 1688. By then he must have had Tory sympathies strong enough to satisfy the intruded Tory dignitaries who would hardly have countenanced him other-wise. But he remained a dissenter, being presented for non-attendance in 1683 and a trustee of the Presbyterian chapel in 1689; evidently he was one of those dissenters who accepted James II's policies of religious toleration at face value and supported him accordingly. Thomas Hayward and John Doggett are likely to have been of the same mind and later, in the time of William and Mary, John Tisdall's split vote continued the tradition of Tory dissent.

Thomas Eccleston, mayor in what seems to have been the pivotal year 1677, appears to have been highly influential in determining the future political complexion of the corporation. At the time of his election the only assistants were three elderly survivors from Commonwealth days, so giving him the chance to appoint like-minded men. It is not surprising, therefore, that in his time several assistants or aldermen were chosen who duly became high Tory mayors. How strong Eccleston's Toryism was appears in his appointment as deputy in 1685 by someone as close to the king as Henry Guy who was the nominal mayor, and it may not be a coincidence that during his first term of office there had been talk of Charles II's visiting St Albans.[14] Indeed, his first mayoralty seems to have been a real turning point, after which the ageing aldermen of the post-Restoration years, who had no obvious successors, had no hope of maintaining their weakened position. It seems, though, that the assistants elected in 1677 were not all of the same mind as Eccleston, for in March 1685 two of them, John Tisdall and Christopher Loft, were removed, allegedly for 'neglect of duty';[15] yet Tisdall's subsequent election as alderman in 1689 and mayor in 1693 suggests that the real reason for his removal had been political. Since he and Loft are unlikely to have been Whigs and have no connection with dissent they presumably lost their places for opposing the arbi-trary proceedings of the then mayor, John Selioke.

Eccleston seems to have changed the political composition of the corpora-tion very effectively even though others may have secured the beginnings of Tory power. Selioke is the second most important of the Tory mayors. His opinions have been discussed earlier and he was undoubtedly instrumental in securing the return of two MPs favourable to James II in the election of 1685, using bribery at the instigation of Henry Guy. Moreover, one of the threats of which he was accused at that time, that he would have dragoons quartered upon the town's innkeepers and alehouse keepers at a ruinous rate, was a very real one, for in the accounts for his year of office are two payments, unfortunately not dated, for carrying away the dragoons' baggage when they went out of town and another "to the Quartermaster when my Lord Ferrers' regiment lay in town to remove 2 companies to Redbourn and Hemel Hempstead". None of these payments can be linked directly to the election but his opponents knew it would have been perfectly easy for Selioke, instead of encouraging a quartermaster to take his dragoons away, to see that he billeted them selectively.[16]

But what did the townsmen think? Whatever the dominant opinion in the corporation may have been it is noteworthy that the freemen elected two MPs of contrasting opinion in each of the four parliaments of Charles II, right up to 1681. In the late 1670s they remained more evenly divided than the corporation, to the extent that the Whigs among them succeeded in electing Sir Samuel Grimston who, though he is not known positively to have been an exclusionist, nevertheless somehow gave deep and lasting offence to James II. How far this popular sentiment was able to influence the election of assistants or aldermen cannot be known: probably little, and the casting out of Tisdall and Loft may not reflect a principled stand on their part so much as a position like that of some Anglican and royalist opponents of Charles I prior to the Civil War who were opposed only to specific measures about which they felt strongly.

How closely religious opinion matched the political swing is hard to judge. Tolerance between people of markedly divergent opinions in the interests of parish administration appears to have continued through the 1660s until, first, it was strained by the enforcement of the penal laws in 1677 and then further eroded successively by the exclusion crisis of 1681 and the attempt on the king's life in the Rye House plot two years later. Most must have shared the hope "that there may not be any *lingring war* again in *England*, which is the greatest misery and calamity that can ever happen to a Nation";[17] and Rye House was uncomfortably close to home. It seems likely that the events culminating in the plot weakened political resistance to Eccleston and his Tory colleagues. What local shifts of opinion occurred subsequently as a result of James II's policies are not known but following the Toleration Act of 1689 there appears a hardening of the division between established and dissenting congregations that is symbolised by the building of the Presbyterian chapel.

Although the shift of opinion in religion and politics corresponds broadly to a change in the national mood, that hardly explains the extent of the shift represented by the mayors of St Albans, from Thomas Cowley I in 1661 to John Selioke in 1684. It is, of course, possible that strong personalities and strongly-held opinions sufficed to carry the day but a more historical explanation may tentatively be offered. It lies in the relation between St Albans and London, which went beyond the many economic ties with the City to what is more important in this context, the links, fewer but influential, with highly conservative professional bodies such as the College of Physicians and the Inns of Court and, through MPs, with parliamentary opinion. Already in 1671 Thomas Arris, MP and one of "The Principal Physitians, who now practise in London",[18] had introduced a motion intended to prevent criticism of the king that was too extreme even for the Cavalier Parliament. Among Arris's friends and relations by marriage[19] only Edward Nicholas, an apothecary and almost certainly a Tory, entered local politics briefly in 1673, but many professional men with gentry and London connections no doubt held similar views. They prevailed in 1685 but after the turbulence of James II's reign a fear of civil disorder probably induced general acquiescence in the more moderate Tories who held the mayoralty to the end of the century.

All in all St Albans may have been regarded as somewhat exceptional among the towns in the Chilterns and south Midlands, having something of the standing and a little of the society of a small cathedral town but a centre of nonconformity too, as well as being a busy, bustling place. In economic terms the town can probably stand for many places that enjoyed a modest growth in the fifty years covered by this study, and in the end what may set its history apart is the remarkable swing in political power accompanied by the decline in influence of its once powerful nonconformist element.

NOTES AND REFERENCES

1   Dyer 1991, p.72. The statement that the town's population was declining (p.55) is contradicted by the table at p.72.
2   As Marmaduke Rawdon did in 1655 when travelling from Exeter to London; Crofts1967, p.126
3   John Evelyn, who did not build himself, was apt to lament such economies practised by others.
4   Page 1920, p.18
5   Chapter 7, pp.137–145
6   Chamberlayne 1672, pt.ii, p.204
7   Chapter 7, p.146
8   Borsay 1989
9   Smith 1992, p.159-60
10 Taylor 1637; Fiennes 1947
11 Kilvington 1986, pp.25-8

12   Rugg 1661, p.99

13   Above, chapter 3

14   "Spent ... when the Company met together to consult what should be done when
     the King intended to come to this Burrough"; mayor's accounts, 1677/8. Professor
     Ronald Hutton pointed out in a letter that the intention may be explained by
     Charles II's liking to visit different parts of his kingdom; but the coincidence with
     Eccleston's mayoralty is striking.

15   Gibbs 1890, p.85

16   Selioke's high-handed proceedings and his arbitary reduction in the number of
     voters from about 600 to 100 are made clear in Hennings 1983, pp.271-2.

17   Chamberlayne 1672, pt.ii, p.163

18   Chamberlayne 1672, pt.ii, p.270

19   See Chapter 10 for the Arris family

APPENDIX I

MAYORS AND THEIR KNOWN OR
INFERRED POLITICAL STANDPOINT

Bold = Parliamentarian/dissenting leanings

Italic = Tory leanings

Remainder uncertain at that date

* = alderman (previously principal burgess) under 1664 charter

\+ = alderman named in James II's charter

Year	Mayor	Assistant	Alderman	Alderman replaced	Comment
1645/6	**Gawin Crosfeild**	1625	1631		
1646/7	**William Humphrey**		1623		
1647/8	**Ralph Pollard I**		1624		
1648/9	**John Sympson**		1645		
1649/50	**William New**	1619	1627		
1650/1	**Thomas Cowley I**	1626	1632		
1651/2	**William Marston I**	1629	1648	Richard Ruth (dec'd)	
1652/3	**Ralph Gladman**	1622	1649	**Dr John King** (retired)	
1653/4	**Robert Ivory**		1627		
1654/5	***Edward Eames**	1624	1629		
1655/6	***Gawin Crosfield**				
1656/7	***Thomas Oxton**		1632		
1657/8	**William Humphrey**				
1658/9	***John Gape I**		1655	**Ralph Pollard I** (dec'd)	
1659/60	***John New I**	1634	1655	**John Sympson** (dec'd)	
1660/1	*Thomas Cowley II		1655	**William New** (dec'd)	
1661/2	***Thomas Cowley I**		1657		
1662/3	***William Marston I**				
1663/4	***Robert New**	1645	1659	**William Humphrey** (dec'd)	
1664/5	**Robert Ivory**		1657		
1665/6	* Ralph Pollard II		1662	Ralph Gladman	
1666/7	***William Rance**		1664	Cromwellian captain	
1667/8	**Thomas Oxton**		1659		
1668/9	**John Gape I**				Quaker sympathies
1669/70	William Oxton		1666	Gawin Crosfeild	
1670/1	**John New I**				
1671/2	William Rugg		1666	Edward Eames (dec'd)	
1672/3	*+Thomas Cowley II*				

Year	Mayor	Assistant	Alderman	Alderman replaced	Comment
1673/4	Thomas Hayward		1668	Thomas Rotherham (dec'd)	Ousted 1684
1674/5	**William Marston I**				
1675/6	John Doggett		1669	**Robert Ivory** (dec'd)	
1676/7	+Ralph Pollard II				
1677/8	+*Thomas Eccleston*		1673	**Thomas Cowley I** (dec'd)	
1678/9	+*William Marston II*		1673	Edward Nicholas (dec'd)	
1679/80	+*John Gape I*				
1680/1	+*John New II*		1675	**Wm. Rance** (dismissed)	MP, defeated Grimston
1681/2	+*Stephen Adams*		1677	**William Marston I** (dec'd)	
1682/3	+*John New II*				Ousted 1684
1683/4	*Thomas Crosfeild*	1673	1677	**Thomas Oxton** (dec'd)	Ousted 1684
1684/5	+*John Selioke*	1677	1681	**William Oxton** (resigned)	Retained as mayor 1685
1685/6	*Thomas Eccleston (Deputy)*				Henry Guy, mayor
1686/7	*John Selioke (Deputy)*				Sir Francis Leigh, mayor
1687/8	+*Edward Seabrooke*		1683	William Rugg (resigned)	
1688/9	*Thomas Cowley II*				Voted for Churchill 1689
1689/90	*Thomas Hayward*				
1690/1	*Edward Horsell*		1688/9		
1691/2	*Henry Dobyns*	1677	1688/9		
1692/3	*Samuel Loft*	1677	1689	Ralph Pollard II	
1693/4	*John Tisdall*	1677	1689	'Mr Browne'(unknown)	Dismissed 1685
1695/6	*John New II*				
1696/7	*Nicholas Sparling*	1684	1692/3	?Thomas Hayward	
1697/8	*Stephen Adams*				
1698/9	*John Sparling*	1686	1694/5	?Thomas Cowley II	
1699/1700	*Thomas Crosfeild*			Thomas Eccleston	Re-elected alderman 1687

BIBLIOGRAPHY

PRINTED SOURCES

Place of publication is London unless otherwise stated.

Alldridge, N. Hearth and home: a three-dimensional reconstruction *in*: Alldridge, N
(ed.) *The Hearth Tax: Problems and Possibilities*, Hull, 1985, pp.85–106

Alvey, N. Estimating population growth in St Albans: 17th to 19th centuries, *The Local
Historian*, Vol.30, No.3, August 2000, pp.150–59.

Annual Abstract of Statistics 1998. Office for National Statistics (Statistics 1998)

Anon *Law Unknown or Judgement Unjust*, n.p., 1662. A copy in the Lewis Evans Collection, City Library.

Anon *The First Book of Kensworth 1675*. A copy in the City Library.

Arkell, T. Multiplying factors for estimating population totals from the Hearth Tax,
Local Population Studies, No.xxviii, 1982, 51–57.

Aubrey, John. *Brief Lives and other selected writings*, ed. A.Powell, 1949

Baggs, A.P. The First Sash Window?, *Georgian Group Journal*, Vol.7, 1997, pp.168–70

Bate, F. *The Declaration of Indulgence 1672: A Study in the Rise of Organised Dissent*, 2nd edn
1968, original edn. 1908.

Berry, B.M and Schofield, R.S. Age at baptism in pre-industrial England, *Population
Studies*, Vol.25, 1971, pp.453–63

Borsay, P. *The English Urban Renaissance: Culture and Society in the Provincial Town
1660–1700*, Oxford, 1989.

Braithwaite, W C. *The Beginnings of Quakerism*, 1912.

Brigg, W., ed. *Hertfordshire Genealogy and Antiquary*, 3 vols, 1895–8.

Brown, W.N., The receipt of poor relief and family situation: Aldenham, Hertfordshire, 1630–90 *in*: Smith 1984, pp.405–22

Browne, Sir Thomas. Letter to a Friend, *in*: *Sir Thomas Browne, The Religio Medici and
Other Writings* [1690] (Everyman edn, 1906)

Bunyan, John. *Grace Abounding and The Life and Death of Mr Badman* [1680] (Everyman
edn.,1928)

Cambridge Agrarian History, Vols 4, 5i

Campbell, B.M., Galloway, J.A., Keene, D., and Murphy,M., *A Medieval Capital and its
Grain Supply: Agrarian Production and Distribution in the London* Region *c.1300*, Hist.
Geog. Research Series 30, 1993.

Carr, R. *English Foxhunting*, revised edn, 1986

Chauncy, Sir Henry. *The Historical Antiquities of Hertfordshire*, [1700], 2 vols, 1826

Clark, P. and Hosking, J. *Population estimates of English Small Towns 1550–1851*, 2nd edn,
Leicester, 1993, Centre for Urban Studies

Clutterbuck, R., *History and Antiquities of the County of Hertford*, 3 vols, 1815–27

Cousins, R., *Lincolnshire Buildings in the Mud-and-Stud Tradition*, Sleaford 2000

Crofts, J. *Packhorse, Waggon and Post*, 1967

Defoe, Daniel *A Tour through the Whole Island of Great Britain*, 2 vols, [1724–26]. ed. G.D.H.Cole,1927

DeLaune, Thomas. *The Present State of London*, 1681

DeLaune, Thomas. *Angliae Metropolis*, 1690

Dictionary of National Biography (DNB)

Dodds, G., *The Church Bells of Hertfordshire*, Welwyn Garden City 1994

Dyer, A. *Decline and Growth in English Towns*, 1991

Ekwall, E. *Street- names of the City of London*, Oxford, 1954

The History of Thomas Ellwood written by his own hand [1714], Morley's Universal Library edition, 1889

English Place-Name Society (EPNS)

EPNS Beds and Hunts Mawer, A. and Stenton, F.M. *Bedfordshire and Huntingdonshire*, Cambridge, English Place-Name Society, 1927

EPNS Herts Gover, J.E.B., Mawer, A. and Stenton, F.M. *Hertfordshire*, Cambridge, English Place-Name Society, 1938

Evelyn, John, *The Diary of John Evelyn*, E. S. de Beer (ed.), 6 vols, Oxford, 1955

Everett, J. *A Fair Field*, privately printed, 1983

Featherstone, A. *The Mills of Redbourn*, privately printed, 1993

Fiennes, Celia *The Journeys of Celia Fiennes*, A. Powell (ed.), 1949

Fildes, V. The English wet-nurse and her role in infant care, *Medical History*, vol. 32, 1988, pp. 142–73

Firth, C.H., and Tait, R.S. (eds), *Acts and Ordinances of the Interregnum 1642–60*, 3 vols, 1911

Freeman, M. and D. Lane, 'Excavations in Holywell Hill 1970', *Herfordshire Archaeology*, vol. 6, 1978, pp.101–10.

Furnivall, F.J.(ed.)., *Harrison's Description of England*, 3 vols, 1877

Gardiner, S.R. *History of the Commonwealth and Protectorate 1649–60*, 3 vols, 1894–1903

Genstat 5 *Genstat 5 Reference Manual*, Oxford, 1988

Gerhold, D. The growth of the London carrying trade, 1681–1838, *Economic History Review*, 2s.,vol.41, 1988, pp.392–410

Gerhold, D. *Road Transport before the Railways*, Cambridge, 1993

Gibbs, A.E. *Historical Records of St Albans*, St Albans, 1890

Glass, D.V., Two papers on Gregory King *in:* Glass and Eversley 1965, pp. 167–200

Glass, D.V. and Eversley, D.E.C. *Population in History: Essays in Historical Demography*, 1965

Godber, Joyce. *Friends in Bedfordshire and West Hertfordshire*, privately printed, 1975

Gough, R. *History of Myddle* [1701], ed. D.Hey, Harmondsworth 1981

Gretton, R.H. *The Burford Records*, Oxford, 1920

Grof, L *Children of Straw*, Buckingham, 1988

Gwilt, J. *Encyclopaedia of Architecture*, ed.Wyatt Papworth, 1888

Haines 1987 Haines, E. The Kensworth Baptist Congregation, 1675, *Hertfordshire's Past*, No.22, 1987, pp.8–11

Hanawalt, B. Child-rearing among the lower classes of late medieval England, *Journal of Interdisciplinary History*, Vol.8, 1977, pp.1–22

Hardy, W.J. ed., *Herts County Records: Sessions Rolls*, Vol.1, 1905

Harris, F. Holywell House, St Albans: an early work by William Talman?, *Architectural History*, Vol.28,1985, pp.32–9

Hatfield WEA, *Hatfield and its People*, Hatfield, 1959–64

Hebditch, F. *J.H.Buckingham: a Window on Victorian St Albans*, St Albans, 1988

Henderson, B.L.K. The Commonwealth Charters, *Transactions of the Royal Historical Society*, 3rd Series, Vol.6, 1912, 129–62

Henning, B.D. ed., *The History of Parliament : the House of Commons 1660–1690*, Vol.1, 1983

Henry, L. *Techniques d'analyse en demographie historique*, Paris, 1980

Hertfordshire Archaeology 1, 1968– (*Herts Arch*)

Hey, D. G. *An English Rural Community: Myddle under the Tudors and Stuarts*, Leicester 1974

Historical Manuscripts Commission (Hist. MSS. Comm),
Portland MSS
Verulam MSS

Holmes, G. *Augustan England*, 1982

Hoskins, W.G. Harvest Fluctuations and English Economic History 1620–1759, *Agricultural History Review*, Vol.16, 1968, pp.15–32

Houghton, John. *Collections for the Improvement of Husbandry and Trade* (weekly), 1692–1703

Houlbrooke, R.A., *The English Family 1450–1700*, 1984

Howe, Pat. *The survival of protestant non-conformity in St. Albans during the years of persecution 1660–1689* (unpubl. dissertation, The Polytechnic of North London), 1988

Howe, Pat, Identifying nonconformity in late-seventeenth century St Albans. *Local Population Studies*, No.68, Spring 2002, pp.9–24.

Hutchinson, Lucy. *Memoirs of Colonel Hutchinson* (first publ.1848), 1904

Illick, J.E., Child-rearing in seventeenth century England and America, *in* de Mause 1976, pp.303–50

Innocent 1916 Innocent, C.F. *The History of English Building Construction*, Cambridge; repr. Shaftesbury 1999

Jones, A. *Hertfordshire 1731–1800 as recorded in the Gentleman's Magazine*, Hatfield, 1993

Jones, E.L. The reduction of fire damage in southern England 1650–1850, *Post-Medieval Archaeology*, vol.2, 1968, pp.140–9

Kilvington, F.I. *A Short History of St Albans School*, 2nd edn., privately printed, 1986

King, N. *The Grimstons of Gorhambury*, 1983

Laslett, P. *The World We Have Lost: further explored*, 3rd edn., 1983

Laslett, P. and Wall, R. (ed.), Household and Family *in: Past Time: Comparative Studies in the Size and Structure of the Domestic Group over the last Three Centuries*, Cambridge, 1972

Laslett, P. *Family Life and Illicit Love in Earlier Generations*, Cambridge 1977

Luttrell, N. *Brief Historical Relation of State affairs 1678–1714*, 6 vols, 1857

Macfarlane, A. *Marriage and Love in England 1300–1840*, Oxford 1986

McInnes, A. 'The golden age of Uttoxeter' *in:* Morgan, P. (ed.), *Staffordshire Studies: Essays presented to Denis Stuart*, Keele 1987, pp.113–28

McInnes, A. The emergence of a leisure town: Shrewsbury 1660–1760, *Past and Present*, No.120, 1988, pp.53–88

Marcombe, D. *English Small Town Life: Retford 1520–1642*, Nottingham 1993

Matthews, A. G. *Calamy Revised*, 1934

de Mause, L., *The History of Childhood*, 1976

Mercer, E. *English Vernacular Houses*, 1975

Miller, John. The Crown and the Borough Charters in the reign of Charles II, *English Historical Review*, Vol.100, 1985, pp.52–84

Moran, M. Re-erecting houses in Shropshire in the late 17th century, *Archaeological Journal*, Vol.146, 1989, pp.538–53

Mullins, S. *St Albans in Old Photographs*, Stroud 1994

Munby, Lionel. *Hertfordshire population statistics*, Hitchin 1964

New Shorter Oxford English Dictionary, 2 vols, 1993 (New ShOED)

Oxford English Dictionary, 11 vols, 1884–1930 (OED)

Page, W. *St Albans* The Story of the English Towns series, 1920

Pantin, W.A. Medieval inns *in:* Jope, E.M. ed., *Studies in Building History*, 1961, pp.166–91

Parker, J.H. *A Glossary ... of Gothic Architecture*, 5th edn.,1850

Parker, Meryl (ed.), *All my Wordly Goods*, Bricket Wood 1991

Parker, Vanessa *The Making of Kings Lynn*, Chichester 1971

Pepys, Samuel *Samuel Pepys, Diary*, ed. Latham, R. and Matthews, W., 11 vols, 1970–83

Phelps Brown and Hopkins 1956 Phelps Brown, E.H. and Hopkins, S.V. Seven centuries of the prices of consumables, compared with builders' wage-rates, *Economica*, new series, vol.22, 1956, pp.296–314.

Phillips, C.B. Town and Country: economic change in Kendal *in:* Clark, Peter (ed.), *The Transformation of the English Provincial Town*, 1984, pp.99–132

Plomer, H.R. *Dictionary of Booksellers and Printers at work in England, Scotland and Ireland 1541–67*, 1907

Prest, W.R. *The Rise of the Barristers*, Oxford 1986

Ratkowsky, D.A. *Nonlinear Regression Modelling*, New York 1983

Reay, B. (ed.) *Popular Culture in Seventeenth Century England*, 1985

Records of the Committee for the Advance of Money

Reynolds, Susan. *An Introduction to the History of Medieval Towns*, Oxford 1977

Richardson, J. *The Local Historian's Encyclopaedia*, New Barnet 1986

Roberts, E. *The Hill of the Martyr*, Dunstable 1993

Rose, J. *Historic Sandridge Revisited*, Sandridge, 1999

Royal Commission on the Ancient Monuments of Scotland, *The City of Edinburgh*, Edinburgh 1951 (RCAM)

Royal Commission on the Historical Monuments of England, *Hertfordshire*, 1912 (RCHME)

Rugg, T. *The Diurnall of Thomas Rugg 1659–61*, ed. William L.Sachse, Royal Historical Society, Camden Third Series, vol. 91, 1961

Ruston, A.R. *Old Presbyterian Meeting House, St Albans*, privately printed, 1979

St Albans and Hertfordshire Architectural and Archaeological Society Transactions, 1883–1961 (St Albans Trans)

Schofield, R. English marriage patterns revisited, *Journal of Family History*, Vol.10, 1985, pp.2–20

Slack, P. *The Impact of Plague in Tudor and Stuart England*, Oxford, 1990

Slater, T.R. Benedictine town planning in medieval England: evidence from St Albans *in:* Slater, T.R. and Rosser, Gervase (eds), *The Church in the Medieval Town*, 1998, pp.155–76

Smith, A.H. *Elements of English Place-Names*, 2 vols, 1956

Smith, J.T. A clay fireback at Hitchin, Herts, *Post-Medieval Archaeology*, Vol.12, 1978, pp.123–4

Smith, J.T. Short-lived and mobile houses in late seventeenth-century England, *Vernacular Architecture*, Vol.16, 1985, pp.33–4

Smith, J.T. *English Houses 1200–1800*, 1992

Smith, J.T. *Hertfordshire Houses; selective inventory* 1993

Smith, J.T. A builder's estimate of 1720 and its implications, *Herts Arch* 1994–6, 129–34.

Smith, R.M. (ed.) *Land, Kinship and Life-cycle*, Cambridge, 1984

Smith, William *The Particular Description of England, with Portratures of certaine of the cheifest Cities and Townes*, [1588], ed. Wheatlye, H.B. and Ashbee, E.W. London, 1879

Snedecor, G.W. and W.G Cochran, *Statistical Methods*, edn 7, Iowa, 1980

Spufford, Margaret. *Contrasting Communities: English Villages in the 16th and 17th Centuries*, Cambridge, 1979

Spufford, Margaret (ed.). *The World of Rural Dissenters 1520–1725*, Cambridge, 1995

Steele, R. *A bibliography of Royal Proclamations of the Tudor and Stuart Sovereigns, 1485–1714*, 2 vols, 1910

Stone, L. *The Family, Sex and Marriage in England, 1500–1800*, 1977

Tate, W.E. *The Parish Chest*, 3rd edn. 1969, repr.1983

Taylor, J. *The carriers cosmographie*, 1637

Thompson, E.P. *Customs in Common*, 1991, pp.352–403

Tittler, Robert. *Architecture and Power: The Town Hall and the English Urban Community c.1500–1640*, Oxford 1991

Toms, E. *The Story of St Albans*, St Albans 1962

Turner, H. (ed.). *Diaries of Oliver Heywood*, 1882

Turner, G.Lyon (ed.). *Original Records of Early Nonconformity under Persecution and Indulgence*, Vol.1, 1911

Urwick, W. *Nonconformity in Hertfordshire*, 1884

Victoria County History of Hertfordshire, 4 vols, 1902–14 (VCH).

VCH Fam *Hertfordshire Families*, 1907

VCH Gloucs *Victoria History of Gloucestershire*, vol.8, 1968

Wales, T. Poverty, poor relief and the life-cycle: some evidence from seventeenth-century Norfolk *in:* Smith 1984, pp.351–404

Walker 1912 Walker, T.A. *Admissions to Peterhouse*, Cambridge

Weaver, O.J. and Poole, D. The Crown and Anchor Inn: an interim report *in: Transactions of the St Albans Architectural and Archaeological Society*, 1961, pp.44–9

Wilson 1600 Wilson, Thomas. *The State of England Anno Dom 1500* [1600], ed. F.J Fisher 1936.

Wilton, C. *A Plan of the Town of St Albans, made by Benjamin Hare in 1634* [?StAA&A Trans/separate pubn]

Winter, H.. *Last of Old St Albans*, St Albans, 1897–8

Wrightson, K. *English Society 1580–1680*, 1982

Wrigley, E.A. and Schofield, R.S. *The population history of England 1541–1871: a reconstruction*, Cambridge, 1989

Wrigley et al. 1997 Wrigley, E.A., Davies, R.S., Oeppen, J.E. and Schofield, R.S. *English Population History from family reconstitution 1580–1837*, Cambridge

MANUSCRIPT SOURCES

The principal source, the one on which chapter 3 is wholly based, is the mayors' accounts. These were examined for the years 1650–1700 by Betty Masters who divided the material into several categories:

Officers

National events

Suppliers of goods and/or workmanship

Suppliers of entertainments, wine, beer etc.; Inns or taverns

Thomas Eccleston

Mayors' inventories

Clockhouse deeds

Miscellaneous expenses

Rents and encroachment rents: miscellaneous properties

Butchers' shambles: stalls and stall roomths

Cornshops in the Market House

Encroachments: of a house upon the waste near the Leather Market; house adjoining the well house in St Peter's Street; of Thomas Watt's house upon the Hay Market; of rails before a house in St Peter's Street; ground in the street whereon Dr Arris's rails stand; of rails before Robert Crosfield's house in St Peter's Street; of ground in Spicer Street whereon rails stand, latera brick wall; ground in St Peter's Street whereon a porch and pales stand; a little piece of ground enclosed within Thomas Hayward's house near the Bull Ring; house (later two houses) in Sopwell Lane; of Robert Gregory's house upon Roomeland; a house in Fishpool Street; a house near the Woodyard; a house upon the waste (later, the street by the Pillory); a house on Holywell Hill Miscellaneous expenses

For chapters 4 and 5, churchwardens' accounts.

For chapters 7–10, probate inventories were used extensively. All those of the period 1650–1700 and a few others were transcribed, as were some in the PRO. Photocopies of all of them, arranged alphabetically, have been deposited with HALS.

Wills were also examined at PRO.

Hearth Tax – transcripts.

A photocopy of a chapter on corporation property and expenditure, much fuller than that which now appears, has been deposited at HALS.

INDEX

HERTFORDSHIRE PUBLICATIONS

Hertfordshire Publications began 40 years ago and was re-launched as an imprint of the University of Hertfordshire Press in February 2001. It is published by the Press on behalf of the Hertfordshire Association for Local History (HALH) whose membership includes both individuals and local history societies in Hertfordshire. Members receive a discount on the retail price of books published in the series.

Hertfordshire Bellfounders
Joyce Dodds
ISBN 0 9542189 1 4 paperback, 352 pages, £19.95
Bells cast in Hertfordshire are to be found not only in that County but in a large area of East and South-East England and the Midlands. Eight have migrated to Honolulu and one to Chicago. This thoroughly-researched book deals with the men who cast them and the near exhaustive catalogue of their work should appeal to all archeologically-minded bell ringers as well as to local historians and the parishioners of the churches where these bells are hung.

Tracing your Family History in Hertfordshire
Hertfordshire Archives and Local Studies (HALS)
ISBN 0 9542189 2 2 paperback, 152 pages, £9.99
This practical and comprehensive guide provides an introduction to everything family historians need to know in order to trace their ancestors in Hertfordshire. Every aspect of our ancestors' lives has been considered, from their birth and baptism to their death and burial. Examples of source material, together with photographs and drawings, illustrate the text. All major sources are covered irrespective of location and web addresses allow preliminary searching to be done online.
"This book will be of enormous help to all those who attempt to trace their ancestors in the county".
Anthony Camp, President of the Hertfordshire Family History Society and Former Director, Society of Genealogists

Cinemas of Hertfordshire
Allen Eyles with Keith Skone
ISBN 0 9542189 0 6 paperback, 172 pp. £9.99.
Almost all of these buildings in Hertfordshire have disappeared or been altered out of all recognition but this book recalls and describes each of them and also records the triumphant arrival of the county's newer multiplex cinemas. This is a book that will intrigue and entertain film buffs, local historians, and anyone who has ever had a liking for "going to the pictures". It contains some 149 black and white photographs and includes every cinema in Hertfordshire since the first opened its doors in 1908, arranged by town for ease of reference.

The Common People are not for nothing: conflict in religion and politics in Hertfordshire, 1575 to 1780
Lionel M. Munby
ISBN 0 901354 80 5 paperback, 178 pages, £9.95
The theme of this book is the reverse side of traditional history, a turning upside

down of what has been a conventional viewpoint. The existence of a continuing undercurrent of social opposition to the established society and the way this found religious forms of expression are the underlying themes linking the separate chapters. The studies are all local to Hertfordshire but provide a rich source of new material and insights for the study of local history in all parts of the country.

Hertfordshire Brasses

Mary Rensten

ISBN 0 901354 20 1 paperback, 103 pages, £5.95

This popular guide to the figure brasses in the churches of Hertfordshire, with 76 illustrations and a detailed index of names and places, is the first complete guide to the brasses of Hertfordshire to be published since1903. Includes a short introduction to brass rubbing, a glossary and guide to further reading.

So that was Hertfordshire: Travellers' jottings 1322 to 1887

Malcolm Tomkins

ISBN 0 901354 87 2 paperback, 91 pages, £6.95

Hertfordshire history seen through the books, diaries, journals and letters of those who visited the county or merely passed through it. The 'innocent eye' of the visitor, from foreign kings and princes to humble travellers on foot, provides a colourful, informative and occasionally funny insight into Hertfordshire people, agriculture and industry. Arranged chronologically with an index of travellers, places and houses.

Garden Cities and New Towns

ISBN 0 901354 58 9 hardback, 115 pages, £14.95

As well as describing the growth of the two original Garden Cities in Hertfordshire, Letchworth and Welwyn Garden City, and four of the post-war New Towns, from original concept to the present day, this book looks at their influence on the new towns which followed.

Hertfordshire Inns and Public Houses, an historical gazetteer

Graham Jollife and Arthur Jones

ISBN 0 901354 58 9 paperback, 177 pages, £12.95

An attractive new edition of Branch Johnson's pioneering work, *Hertfordshire Inns*, first published in 1962 in two volumes. Mostly consisting of 'pubs' predating 1900, it is arranged alphabetically by parish and gives former names and a brief history of each house. Extensively illustrated.

Hertfordshire 1731 to 1800 as recorded in *The Gentleman's Magazine*

Edited by Arthur Jones

ISBN 0 901354 73 2 hardback, 266 pages, £18

This book containing all Hertfordshire material of any importance published in *The Gentleman's Magazine* from 1731 to 1800 is a rich resource for research: history, news items of every kind, reports of robberies, court proceedings, executions, fires and, of course, the obituaries for which *G.M.* was particularly famous. Arranged chronologically with a detailed index of names and places and with supplementary listings for births, marriages, bankruptcies and deaths.

Hertfordshire in History
Edited by Dr Doris Jones-Baker
ISBN 0 9542189 4 9 paperback, 311 pages, £18
An important collection of eighteen papers from the thirteenth to the latter part of the twentieth century compiled in honour of Lionel Munby, one of Hertfordshire's leading historians, reprinted as a paperback edition.

The following title has been accepted for publication

Behind the Plough: the agricultural society of nineteenth century Hertfordshire
Nigel Agar
ISBN 0 9542189 5 7 paperback. To be published: March 2004
'Behind the Plough' is the story of Hertfordshire in the nineteenth century. It was to be the last century when the life of this county was based upon agriculture. Innovative and dynamic, farmers carried out in Hertfordshire some of the first experiments that laid the foundations of modern agriculture.

UNIVERSITY OF HERTFORDSHIRE PRESS
The University of Hertfordshire Press also publishes the following academic books on regional and local history under its own imprint

Population, economy and family structure in Hertfordshire in 1851
Volume 1: The Berkhamsted region; *Nigel Goose*
ISBN 0900458-73-9, 416 pages, paperback, £14.95
Volume 2: St Albans and its region; *Nigel Goose*
ISBN 0 900458 83 6, paperback, 704 pages £19.95
ISBN 0 900458 84 4, hardback, 704 pages £35

Studies in Regional and Local History
Volume 1: A Hertfordshire demesne of Westminster Abbey: profits, productivity and weather; *Dr Derek Vincent Stern; edited and with an introduction by Christopher Thornton.*
ISBN 0 900458 92 5, 320 pp, hardback, £29.99
Volume 2: From Hellgill to Bridge End: aspects of economic and social change in the Upper Eden Valley circa 1840–1895; *Margaret Shepherd.*
ISBN 1-902806-27-1, hardback, £35.

The University of Hertfordshire Press
University of Hertfordshire, College Lane, Hatfield, Hertfordshire AL10 9AD, UK
Tel: 01707 284681 Fax: 01707-284666 Internet: UHPress@herts.ac.uk

A printed catalogue is available on request but for the latest information see the catalogue on the web at: http://www.herts.ac.uk/ UHPress/